"Chef Tell made cooking on TV the new frontier. He did it with humor, a thick German accent, and was rather bossy. 'Let me show you how to cook this,' he would say. He showed, we learned, we laughed."

—Jan Yanehiro,
First Co-Host, *Evening Magazine,* **San Francisco**

"WOW! is a great start for Ronald Joseph Kule's *Chef Tell: The Biography of America's Pioneer TV Showman Chef.* This is a wonderful account of one man's voyage and how in so many ways every reader will connect with something. It is engaging, and takes you through all the emotions of life, leaving you to decide what is next for you; and how will you make the most of your today."

—Tracy Repchuk,
Bestselling Author, International Speaker and Motivator

"The story you have written is fantastic! I knew Chef Tell as a talented Master Chef and works as his pastry chef for more than 10 years. This book puts his story together very well."

—Suladda May,
Restaurateur of Thai Orchid, Grand Cayman Island

Before Wolfgang, Emeril, Paul, Jacques, Bobby, Mario,
Cat & Rachel, there was . . .

CHEF TELL

CHEF TELL

The Biography of America's Pioneer TV Showman Chef

Ronald Joseph Kule

FOREWORDS BY

TV hosts Regis Philbin and Chef Walter Staib

Skyhorse Publishing

Skyhorse Publishing books may be purchased in bulk at special discounts for sales promotion, corporate gifts, fund-raising, or educational purposes. Special editions can also be created to specifications. For details, contact the Special Sales Department, Skyhorse Publishing, 307 West 36th Street, 11th Floor, New York, NY 10018 or info@skyhorsepublishing.com.

Skyhorse® and Skyhorse Publishing® are registered trademarks of Skyhorse Publishing, Inc. ®, a Delaware corporation.

www.skyhorsepublishing.com

10 9 8 7 6 5 4 3 2 1

Library of Congress Cataloging-in-Publication Data is available on file.

ISBN: 978-1-62636-004-4

Printed in the United States of America

DEDICATION

To his millions of fans—home cooks, professional chefs, and gourmands who know, appreciate, and love food—this story and Chef Tell's NEW included recipes are for YOU.

To Elaine Tait, former food writer extraordinaire for the *Philadelphia Inquirer*, who was among the first to recognize Tell Erhardt's influential place in the heritage of Philadelphia's—later America's—culinary renaissance . . . Thanks for the inspiration, Elaine . . . wherever you are!

CONTENTS

ACKNOWLEDGMENTS

People from all walks of life helped bring this work to the world. Tell's son, Torsten Erhardt, provided insight, photos, and research documentation. Bunny Erhardt, Tell's widow, added vital connections and support.

Busy professional chefs—notably Georges Perrier, Susanna Foo, Freddie Duerr, Nunzio Patruno, Vasile Bageag, Lesley B. Fay, Chris Soule, Paul Drew, Suladda May, William B. Reagor; Walter Staib and his assistant Molly Yun, Steve Marks, and Iron Chef Cat Cora—graciously shared their time and offered important suggestions. Thank you, all.

TV host Regis Philbin and his wife, Joy; executive in charge of production for *LIVE! with Kelly and Michael*, Art Moore; Tell's producer, Victoria Lang, and her husband, Tony Baarda; Susan Winston, widow of Richard Winston, nephew and executive V.P. of Harry Winston, Inc.; attorney Nina Reznick; producer Bob Croesus; Helen and the late Russell Baum; Theresa and Don Pfeil; Alicia and Dan DeGowin; Christine Hess; Francesca Kennedy; Barbra Murphy; Faye Litzenberger; Theresa Badmann; Ian "Boxie" Boxall, and Naul Bodden—offered anecdotes and made me cry, laugh, and marvel about Chef Tell's antics. Thank you, thank you, and thank you.

Carolyn Eischens of Nordic Ware; Alex Bartlett of the Germantown Historical Society; Pam Sedor and Ann Etris of the Radnor Memorial Library; "Crazy TV Lenny" Mattioli; Herbert Engelbert, sommelier of the International Wine & Food Society of Philadelphia; The *Chaine des Rôtisseurs* of Philadelphia; Philabundance of Philadelphia; *Wine*

Spectator magazine; Jill Walker, CEO of Total Tape Services, and my representatives Derek Britt and Courtney Williams of Derek Britt Entertainment—all assisted selflessly and with generosity. My hat is off to you.

Megan Oldfield, my personal editor, held me to a high standard. Early-draft readers Diane Austin and Linda Batdorf kept me on point in the story's early stages. Well done!

J. David Miller, AAA 2012 Football Coach of the Year, best friend, co-author of *Pressure Makes Diamonds a Timeless Tale of America's Greatest Pastime*, mentored my writing flawlessly. Thank you, David. The temperature is always nine.

My sister, Theresa Pfeil, a generous being with an open heart, understood the importance of this work and always had my back. None of us will ever be the same because of you, Tee.

My wife, Sherry Kule, put up with my long hours away and endless drafts read aloud to her. She encouraged and shared my journey from its beginning. *Somos siempre, Enamorada.*

To Jeremiah and Justin, my son and grandson, More than you know, you increase a father's love just by being a part of my life.

FOREWORD

by

REGIS PHILBIN

"I think there's a little bit of sizzling here. Honestly, I can feel it.
The ions are flying back and forth."

—Regis Philbin

I said that while doing a TV show with my friend, the late Chef Tell. That's what I think about when I think of him. His legacy encompasses not only good food and fun, but also his guts and determination to overcome many obstacles and succeed in his line of work. Details about America's leading pioneer of the phenomenon of TV showman chefs are revealed in these pages and are well worth reading.

In some ways we were different, but we ended up good friends. I grew up in the Bronx, a borough of New York City named after Jonas Bronck, an early immigrant from Denmark. When I was born, tenement buildings and single homes in the Bronx mixed as well as the Irish, German, Italian, and Jewish cultures that inhabited the area; just as African-American and Hispanic-Americans do now—we all got along.

Chef Tell, on the other hand, was born in Stuttgart, Germany. Their high-rise buildings for the most part were rubble in the aftermath of World War II. The Germans got by on their meager gardens and with C.A.R.E. Packages sent overseas through Philadelphia, which made it all the more interesting that Tell, one of my favorite guest chefs on my TV show, would end up, of all places, living in Philadelphia, a hop away from my native New York City.

As a young man, I could revisit the Bronx and the neighborhood to which my parents moved on Long Island pretty much any time I wanted. Right across the street from where Edward and Mary Hinz raised six children stood my parents' house in Mineola on 12th Avenue. I lived there after my two years of U.S. Navy service, following my graduation from the University of Notre Dame. As a page for NBC, I commuted to Manhattan every day, like many fellow New Yorkers.

Tell left home as a teenager, worked as a cooking apprentice and, after he came to America, he lived far away from his roots. Although his father lived into the 1980s, he lost his mother at an early age. My parents were with me well into my adult life.

Through television our diverse lives crossed paths.

Before Tell and I became celebrities, we started our careers from scratch. We shared an irreverent sense of humor—something we needed to help us get through those lean years. I suppose you could say that we were similar in that respect.

People call me "the hardest-working man in show business," but Chef Tell was one of the hardest-working chefs I've known. He started locally and, like me, went national. His audience, I've heard, was actually eight times larger than that of Julia Child.

I like to eat good food; I'll even go out of my way for it. Aside from the food I could get out of Chef Tell's appearances on my show, I had to fly all the way to his Grand Cayman Island restaurant to get one of his meals—not that I minded too much, let me tell you, because Chef Tell cooked good food. His Lobster Chef Tell's Way was *incredible!*

He aired his cooking shows as syndicated TV segments, and, of course, I worked my daily time slot. More than that, though, we had a lot of fun doing television shows together. It was uncanny how we started from the cue cards, somehow left them way behind—with Chef Tell you never knew where he was going to go—and always came back to the cards to wrap up the show. None of our crew knew what he was going to say; for the most part we worked unscripted. We had a give and take like that, which I liked. The one thing you could count on, though, was Tell's food was always fresh, always prepared well. When it came to that, he was a very special person and chef. He really knew his art.

And his desserts were *out of this world!*

Outside of our work, we became good friends, naturally. My wife, Joy, and I visited Tell and his wife, Bunny, on Grand Cayman Island. The restaurant he operated, The Grand Old House, will always be a place of fond memories for us. The meals were delicious, and Tell's waitstaff offered great service.

We were fortunate to know Tell and Bunny off-camera, away from the kitchen. Let me tell you, the Philbins enjoyed good times and a few wonderful dinners with the Erhardts at their home at Rum Point.

We came to understand what a love Tell had for our country. He was born a German, but he became a naturalized American citizen. As deeply as his work ethic in food, Tell studied the history of our nation's struggles leading up to the Revolutionary War. He was well versed in our forefathers' activities. He loved America, which leads me to the words of His Eminence, the late Cardinal John R. Krol of Philadelphia, "I am conscious of our beloved country, the bold idealism that inspired it; the courage that gave it birth. May God grant that our prayers, the moral integrity of our lives, the clarity of our teaching, and the sincerity of our patriotism, help increase the spiritual resources without which no nation can survive."

Tell spent much of his career in and around Philadelphia, the bedrock of our nation's revolutionary times. Precisely because of the historical significance, he chose to operate restaurants there and started on television there. After he departed the Cayman Islands, he returned to his beloved City of Brotherly Love.

What you saw on-camera was what you got off-camera with Chef Tell. His charisma was a combination of professional perfection, respectfulness and "a lotta, lotta fun."

I am more than happy to tell you here that his fascinating life's story, really a timeless recipe of life lessons, is written within the pages of this book. I enjoyed my time with Chef Tell immensely. It's a shame he is not with us now. But his memory lives on with this book, which I'm sure you will enjoy reading.

Chef Tell—my friend—was a winner.

Regis Philbin

FOREWORD

by
CHEF WALTER STAIB

"I knew early on that somehow my life would revolve
around food."
—Chef Walter Staib

In more than forty years of cooking in and designing kitchens internationally, I have probably seen the inside of more of them than
anything else in my life. My family required my services in their
commercial kitchen when I was four years of age, for I am a fourth-
generation chef. By the time of my first formal apprenticeship at four-
teen, I already possessed ten years of cooking experience at the Gasthaus
zum Buckenberg, my Aunt Ruth's and Uncle Walter's establishment.

Chef Tell and I grew up in southwestern Germany—he from
Stuttgart, I from Pforzheim. We experienced the same military-style
cooking training. We learned the hard way: he boiled (burned, really)
potatoes without being told to use water, and I hung spaghetti pasta, one
by one to dry on a rope, until we realized the joke was on us. We got even
when we got smarter.

We first met at a National Restaurant Association convention in
Chicago. We laughed about the good old days of "character building"—
cleaning and harvesting restaurant gardens, which we did on our "days
off." We agreed, though, that the training helped our careers and our

outlooks on living. Later, when we met in Philadelphia through the Chaine des Rôtisseurs, we became fast friends until Tell passed away.

Our motto was, "Never experiment with new recipes or cuisines when entertaining friends!" As you can see, we laughed a lot!

Seriously, though, sharing a laugh rather than fighting with Tell was smart, because he was prodigious with his knives. He wielded his blades with such machine-like precision and speed that he could dress out, and fully butcher, an entire wild boar in minutes. You didn't want to be standing close to him when he did it!

I remember when we ran into each other at Philadelphia's Reading Terminal Market and talked with our favorite butcher Siegfried, who made the best sausage. We ended up staying for hours, eating what must have been five pounds of sausage and washing it down with a few beers—that's a story for another day.

The thing about my friend Tell—he was willing to learn something new. He would say, "Yes!" far sooner than ever saying, "No." That trait led him to become the first TV chef in America with a solid audience of forty million people in the 1970s. His recipe books sold in the hundreds of thousands, but he didn't care about the good money as much as he cared about cooking well and teaching others what he learned.

Tell and I—I miss my friend—were "old school." We gave back what we knew. We were grateful for the opportunities we received. We opened doors for others and we pushed for formal trade recognition for training cooks and chefs in America, since in our earliest days there was none.

Tell and I often talked about how much of our roots influenced this industry and country. We noted how many great chefs, techniques, and ingredients came from the Black Forest that are still around today.

Today, I am an ambassador to the Culinary Institute of America. I know Tell would have been proud of me and of our professional heritage when our home country, Germany, awarded me the Ritterkreuz des Order of Merit (Knight's Cross of the Order of Merit). He would have loved the big party when I was knighted.

Filming my appearance on *Iron Chef America* (2010–2011 Season 9, Episode 19: Chef Walter Staib versus Chef Bobby Flay), I thought of Tell and my predecessors, who made reality-cooking television possible. These giants paved the way for future cooks, including myself, to appear on the Food Network, PBS, and other TV channels. I can share my passion for cooking with millions of viewers at home because of them.

My children used to watch Chef Tell almost every day on the 6 o'clock news in Philadelphia. He was such a natural, such a charismatic figure. As a result, we ate a lot of carrots sautéed with parsley, which was the Chef Tell plate my children liked and requested most. And my wife did the cooking at home.

Tell knew a lot more than the average chef. We shared so many stories and bits of information, not only about foods and cooking, but also our interest in America and its history. We shared an affinity for the Caribbean islands and for Caribbean cuisine. A selfless friend, he was proud for me when I was the first chef inducted into the Caribbean Culinary Hall of Fame.

The culinary atmosphere in Tell's time, unlike the competitiveness that exists today, was one of great cooperation among chefs. That ambience was created among his peers and his audiences by Tell, who made cooking fun.

One could easily say that Chef Tell set the pace and was the role model for both German and American youths who wanted to become chefs. He had a passion for his work, was organized and skillful, and he obviously loved it. This story marks many transitions of our industry and of his life and recognizes the roles of others in both.

The day Tell passed away was a hard day for Germany—hard for me personally. We were filming episodes of my Emmy-nominated show, *World Cuisine of the Black Forest,* when we heard the news that our friend was gone. The whole region was devastated.

That's why I'm thrilled about this book, which shares the story of Tell's life. I'm excited that you will get to know the man that I knew and loved. Not a perfect man, but sincere, he worked hard at every endeavor he tried. He had ups and downs—like we all do. He had to learn hard lessons—like we all do. He had to face the economics of living—like we all do. But he left us a legacy, commemorated now in these pages. And he left us his recipes, some of which are here, which we can cook forever.

Chef Tell's life fascinated me. If his story, here and there, changes lives for the better, he will be happy. I know he changed mine.

PREFACE

Top professional chefs around the globe still love Chef Tell. They miss him. Millions of Baby Boomers followed him on TV, bought his recipe books, aprons, and steak knives, ate his food and laughed at his jokes. They never knew the hard knocks this inimitable, friendly TV chef endured and overcame to become their legendary pioneer TV chef. Today, they still remember him and wonder what happened to him.

That said, this book, dear reader, was almost never written. Chef Tell had a polarizing, mercurial effect upon people who came into contact with him or his story. You loved him, hated him, or wondered whether you should love or hate him, but you couldn't ignore him.

The people contacted in the course of research and writing this book fit into any of those categories, at times, including myself, his closest family, friends, and associates. Still, no matter where the highs and lows of the data or other people's opinions took me on different days, good and bad, I—like others in their experiences—couldn't shake or ignore one, simple overriding factor: Tell Erhardt connected and made me feel special. He opened his true heart to me for one, early-morning breakfast at his home, which he cooked and ate with me. That feeling and the words that we shared that day never faded. Knowing Tell even briefly pushed me to persist and to finish this legacy undertaking, which, hopefully and with all humility, will honor his time among us and the influence he continues to have upon his successors.

"The book did much more than I ever anticipated: it brought to life the reasons—common recognition and appreciation of excellence and achievement—that were why my husband and I became friends with Tell. Reading the draft I realized that [later] so much negativity from others had distorted my memory.
"This work also confirmed the love that existed between us and Tell. So many memories were dusty from lack of use but reading the book removed the passage of time. I know that I was smiling—grinning really—and thinking, WOW, Tell, that was you! You really accomplished all that! Suffice it to say, I cried at the end."
—Susan Winston,
jewels broker and widow of the late
Richard Winston of Winston Jewels, Inc.

"In a nutshell, the way that you have presented this gentleman to me, who had been a total unknown, never-heard-of stranger until your book, made me feel not only like I knew him, but that I shadowed him through his life. I can only say I wish I were there. The book is thoroughly enjoyable—you introduced me to a stranger I came to love."
—Diane Austin,
professional photographer, counselor, and mother

* * *

A chef's life is about restaurants, but also theater. Restaurants *are* theater. Entertainment venues, they live or die by the marquee value of their chefs and the quality of their staged output.

Chef Tell's story required eighteen months of continual research, many pages of writing, and numerous drafts. This feast of his lifetime—the result of scores of decisions and more than one hundred thousand words—will be devoured in mere hours. Like a playwright's dialogue at curtain's rising or a chef's plated presentation placed before a discerning palate, this story goes "live" the moment you hit page one.

Stage plays, restaurants, and books are matters of execution and timing, but they can be timeless, too. Chef Tell's life—his colleagues would agree—was a managed, complicated, and temporary affair. However, his impact continues: Chef Tell changed two industries and the lives of millions of home cooks as he pioneered a journey no other chef had ever taken.

This is an account of an extraordinary man—the most-watched television and live-showman chef in history up to his time. This account aims to suspend your disbelief and transport you into a world where surprises, delicious and horrific, are emotional and intellectual tugs-of-war. Chef Tell's difficulties, low points, and eventual glorious successes are life lessons that may uplift lives and bring hope.

The view from "behind the line" reveals how long and hard Chef Tell worked, why so many loved him, and why he remains so missed by those who met or knew him. If this work entertains, shocks, and upsets you; if it makes you think, makes you hungry, and then makes you understand how this one man impacted his and your world, call it a successful mission.

Chef Tell lived and died by his marquee personality and his skills as a master chef. In his words, his lifelong pursuit of excellence proposes a moral for us all: Life is simple. People make the difference.

The short chapters pay homage to the master chef, who preferred to sample many small dishes rather than select a large entrée from the menu whenever he dined out. Likewise, each chapter offers the reader's mental palate portions that are digestible, before moving to the next course. There is even a factually correct *entremets* in the middle.

The added glossary of culinary terms will help readers new to the culinary arts to enter the chef's milieu without trepidation.

An added, seven-course meal of *new* Chef Tell recipes is Chef Tell's posthumous gift to his many loyal and hungry fans, so, as Tell would put it, "Go ahead. Play with your food!"

INTRODUCTION

*"Rezepte sind nur Rezepte . . . im Rahmen des Zumutbaren Sie sie
ändern können."*
("Recipes are only prescriptions . . . within reason you
can change them.")

—Chef Tell

Chef Tell's recipe for making a star-bound chef/restaurateur went like this:

First, rise with the morning twilight. Visit the fish, meat, and produce markets daily to ensure your menu and daily ingredients are as fresh as possible. Chastise your vendors, if needed, for quality slippage in your last order, yet make them feel like they are part of your success.

Second, walk several miles daily within the same four walls. Regularly add water, salt, chicken stock, and splashes of wine to foods and to yourself. Even though you know it will take a toll on your body, taste everything you cook.

Third, ensure that your kitchen waitstaffs arrive on time, prepared and sober. Mix in your waitpersons, bartenders, hostesses, and accountants. Keep them honest with your cash register—every day.

Fourth, bring the first, second, and third steps to a boil by simmering under low heat in the first few hours of the day. Gradually turn up the heat.

Fifth, repeat the routine 312* days a year, year after year, despite how you feel, as long as you make your patrons happy. (*Six days a week.)

For super-star ranking add one more requisite: Culinary genius—the capacity to take consumable ingredients and envision them into remarkable, repurposed foods, flavors, and presentations; the capacity to be *avant-garde,* innovative, iconoclastic, and visionary and, in Chef Tell's case, funny.

Chef Tell followed the basic rules of cooking but he blazed new trails his way.

* * *

The night Friedemann Paul Erhardt (later known worldwide as Chef Tell) was born, bombs dropped and hunger was a constant. When suicide took his mother, and his brother was separated from him, he became a cook's *commis* (apprentice) at thirteen and a half. For the rest of his life, he was forced to work his way out of one predicament into the next, and then out of the next into another, as he blazed a trail on which other chefs would walk.

No chef-by-the-numbers road map existed in his era. Up until the age of the TV celebrity chef, master chefs, for the most part, stayed hermetically inside of their kitchens. When Erhardt ventured outside, he dared to tread where few chefs had gone before—soon joining the ranks of such American chefs as James Beard and Julia Child.

"Chefs weren't really respected other than being in the kitchen. You rarely saw them in the dining room interacting with people," said TV personality Chef Emeril Lagasse. Chef Tell changed that.

"Tell was a role model here and in Germany—always ahead of his time," recalled Chef Walter Staib.

Erhardt credited his television superstardom to his mother, Gisela (Gerber) Erhardt. Her lessons, born of postwar necessity and the lack of preschooling in those days, enabled him to reach a nationwide audience in America and then internationally. He entertained and taught TV viewers how to cook like his mother.

Erhardt soldiered his way to the top of his profession, becoming at twenty-seven the youngest master chef in German history. He championed foods and food-product innovations, which today are considered staples in any kitchen, commercial or private.

Though it was impossible to please all of the people all the time, he pursued culinary perfection as his lifelong quest. He never abandoned his dream, despite irrational fears of failure and the constant taunts of his ephemeral mistress, Success.

The lure of two worlds, the best and the worst, attracted Erhardt. The enticing sights, sounds, smells, and flavors; the excesses of fortune, fame, and connection excited his imagination. His world of cooking ran white-hot active—full of innovation, opportunity, and competitive challenge. A melting pot of fresh ingredients, newly acquired acquaintances, and creative culinary challenges made for a live-action reality show played out on themed stages. Cooking, for Erhardt, was nothing less than "Showtime, folks!"

He possessed talents to cook and teach on television that were extraordinary. Fires that burned others were mere sparks on the tail of the energy that propelled Erhardt's comet. He never stopped thinking about new ingredient combinations, improved ways to cook, and innovative cookware. Curious as a child, he sought and unearthed better ways to please more palates, which he then shared with America.

* * *

Friedemann Paul Erhardt was as vulnerable and imperfect as any of us. His extraordinary lifetime, for better or worse, ran a mercurial course. When he won, he broke off pieces of his good-fortune cookie and shared them with everyone he liked, even though some took advantage of him in return. When he lost, he lost big time, making mistakes and enemies under the powerful magnifying glass of the media.

When the spotlight passed, and bank accounts dissipated, Erhardt became his own worst enemy—a missile with nowhere to go but into the rebellious recesses of war-tortured memories and passionate regrets. At times, his life played like *Mission: Impossible* with a self-destruct button.

Misunderstanding this behavior, some people walked away from him with unexpressed hatreds, unable or unwilling to remember why they liked him in the first place. His true friends, on the other hand, understood him and took the bad with the good. Their integrity was intact. They "knew what they knew" about Erhardt—that he was, like them, a kind-hearted soul trying to make his way through a troubled world.

Amid the whirlwind of his celebrity lifestyle, Cupid guided Erhardt to "Bunny" Kule, who became his friend, fiancée, wife, and widow. Like a lighthouse keeper guides captains in danger of foundering, she watched him almost bash his keel upon the rock-laden shoals of broken fidelities. Yet, she stayed the course with him during his darkest passages when he floundered and nearly drowned.

In return, Erhardt loved her unceasingly, no matter how many times it looked otherwise. Through a quarter of a century plus one year, the constancy of their river's current flowed past deadfalls, hidden rocks, and waterfalls, over riffles and through deep pools.

* * *

Fernand Point, the "Godfather of Modern Cuisine," wrote, "As far as cuisine is concerned, one must read everything, see everything, hear everything, try everything, observe everything, in order to retain in the end, just a little bit."

Erhardt pursued "everything" from sunrise to bedtime for a lifetime.

Unfortunately, like a drug, what was available beyond the kitchen was addictive. So many sensations from temptation reached out to him. Opportunities to party too much, to eat, drink, and ingest other substances, would make him pay a high toll. A workaholic, "rock star" chef, Erhardt knew fame as his evanescent courtesan and he sensed that obesity, ill health, and infidelity lurked beyond its limelight and marked him as a target.

Still, he put himself again and again at center stage where the spotlight comforted like a warm hug. In the 1970s, '80s, and '90s, Chef Tell performed on television screens in more than two hundred cities with forty million people watching three times weekly. For most, he was only the man behind the apron, the moustache, and the smile, who told us— showed us—how to live and love through our taste buds. At home, still larger than life, he was a lovable, imperfect man.

Erhardt broke every mother's admonition (except his) to "stop playing with your food." Instead, he invited us to let go, to imagine new pleasures for our palates, with German, French, Austrian, American, and Caribbean food ingredients. "Recipes are only guidelines," he wrote, "not commandments. You can change them, within reason, if necessary."

Erhardt might have succeeded in any profession, but he had a passion to cook for people and to entertain them. Possessed with unusual charm and charisma, a *joie de vivre* that set him apart from the crowd, Erhardt mingled well with queens, kings, politicians, housewives, janitors, lawyers, musicians; men, women, and children, celebrated or uncelebrated.

"If you are not a generous person you cannot be in this field," wrote Point, who trained a generation of French master chefs that included Erhardt's contemporaries.

In a sense, Tell Erhardt's life defines our lives. How he conquered the long odds and devastating barriers that he faced helps us navigate our minefields. With him in mind, we realize anew that even the biggest of our dreams, if nurtured and continued, can and will some day come true.

If truth were told, in the culinary arts, as in the art of living, excellent, sustained achievement is accomplished only by superb execution of training basics and strict attention to detail in the face of harsh realities, plus imagination. Chef Tell Erhardt's life is the perfect template for us to examine that notion.

Skimping will not do where a five-star experience is desired. We must, therefore, start at the beginning: the night of his birth.

1

A SOUP BOWL OF CONFLICTS

"Sie brauchen nur ein wenig Salz und Pfeffer."
("You just need a little salt n' peppah.")

—Chef Tell

n November 5, 1943, the tree-lined ridges around Stuttgart, Germany, resembled the nearby Black Forest. They edged and defined the steep-valley makeup of the sweep of the city. Past nightfall, searchlights silhouetted the skyline, and air-raid sirens clarioned.

As they had done for three years, thousands of stoic men, frightened women, and bewildered children spilled out from their residences onto darkened, foggy streets and sought shelter inside large caves dug into the hillsides. There they waited for death or another peaceful respite. The safety of the dugouts assuaged little of their fear as earth-shaking, two-ton bombs exploded above and around them for hours.

A mother's hoarse screams of labor could not be heard over the constant din and the drone of 165 laded Allied bombers. The staccato pops of 49 heavy and light German anti-aircraft gunneries and the percussions of hundreds of detonations echoed loudly up and down the damaged hills and valleys and drowned her cries. Just as surely as Germans gasped their last breaths somewhere in that terrain, her newborn drew its first gulp of life-giving oxygen. It was a wonder that her baby boy survived the night.

Like clockwork, night after terrifying night, Stuttgart skies resounded with the recurrent screams of low-altitude bomber squadron payloads after their release. "Pink Pansy" flares lit up blackened ground sites and guided R.A.F. de Havilland "Mosquitoes" along marked pathways to their intended targets—Stuttgart's fighter-plane manufacturing factories. In time, new "Oboe" radar enabled the "Mossies" to operate without direct eyesight just as effectively as on clear nights, despite the fog and rain, and the bombing runs multiplied.

Between the air raid of October 8, when 342 Lancaster bombers of the Royal Air Force flew overhead, and the last large raid of 162 aircraft on November 26, more than 2,000 aircraft dropped over *3,000 tons* of bombs on Stuttgart.

The cacophony of the Allies' horrific lullaby pierced Friedemann Paul Erhardt's ears for the first fortnight of his life. He lived below the eerie glow of searchlights that dappled the smoky sky like Manet's brush strokes.

Decades later, the glow of restaurant gas burners on professional stoves would remind Erhardt of those early months, and of his mother's fears of the swastika and the Nazi party that reigned at the time of his birth.

Nazi leaders prided themselves on the willful creation and maintenance of Aryan-blood purity and committed upwards of forty million people to their deaths for the sake of their aim. Their idea of racial pureness emerged from laboratories and spliced genes slid under scientific microscopes by psychiatric eugenicists, which held the belief that Man was only flesh and bone. Earlier, German and Austrian philosophers speculated that human behavior was a product of the environment, not the other way around. They, too, denied Life's spirituality.

Oddly, the worst of the fascist Nazis abhorred both communist bolshevism and liberalism alike. They assigned "cause" for the existence of these curses to a quasi-race (as they saw it), the Jews. They also sought suppression of the Catholic Church, whose teachings influenced humanity toward spirituality. The Church's position that the soul is the ultimate arbiter of how cultures live, evolve, and move forward took hold and was embraced around the globe, but godless Nazi eugenicists abhorred its expansion and moved to strike a death blow.

Into this soup bowl of conflicting activities and notions, boiled over into a full-fledged world war, the youngest Erhardt arrived. He would grind out his meager childhood among the latest ruins of this centuries-old battle for minds, bodies, and souls. Survival would not come easily for his family or his nation as each struggled to rebuild itself and its identity.

Tell at age one

2

LIKE SON NOT LIKE FATHER

"Ich wusste, ich wollte nicht in das Zeitungsgeschäft gehen."
("I knew I didn't want to go into the newspaper business.")

—Chef Tell

Hitler considered Maximillian Erhardt's local newspaper, *Stuttgarter Nachrichten*, important enough to grant oversight of it to his Number Two henchman Heinrich Himmler, head of the Schutzstaffel—the feared "SS" secret service police formed in 1925 to provide for his personal protection. After Max was pressed into service along with the others at the paper, Himmler became their senior officer. Max's *schriftsetzer* (typesetter) position forced him to (at least appear to) step in line with Himmler. Though his personal, political, or cultural proclivities were not the same as those of the Nazi leadership, he dutifully published what was expected of him. More than 80 percent of national press "news" was Nazi-controlled anti-Semitism by the time he became a father in 1943.

The pragmatic Max was a handsome man of Aryan stock born into a family of lawyers and doctors on January 25, 1912. He married the upper-class Gisela Gerber, who, according to Max's statement to a

Max Erhardt 1943 ID book

Tell's mother

family member in later years, was one-sixteenth Jewish and a licensed, pediatric nurse—pediatrics was a marked profession, since more than a third of the fourteen-hundred-plus pediatric doctors were Jewish.

Gisela gave him his first son and would give him another five years after the war. War-torn Germany, however, offered no guarantee that his first boy would reach a ripe old age. In fact, as the fate of the Nazi regime soured, his odds of surviving at all ran long.

By 1944, the tattered remnants of the German army retreated in the face of the advancing rifles and artillery of Russian forces along the eastern front. The easterly push of the Allied command forces from the west, and the southern line crumbling in the face of American tank brigades from Italy, trapped the Erhardt family in the midst of a pincers movement late in the year. By early 1945 the threat had escalated. The apathetic mental states of local Nazi officers and complicit local officials included taking out anyone who even hinted betrayal before they committed their suicides.

During war operations, Allied bombers prevented Max from planning and developing a long-term future. Eventually, French troops liberated his city. Later, when the Americans arrived, he welcomed them and shared his fourth-floor flat with some of them. However, the Allies took precautionary measures because of his media position and

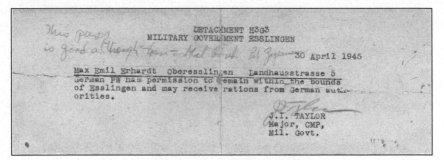

Max's 1945 pass for restricted movement and rations

extradited Max to a military intelligence camp in Texas for debriefing before repatriation without incident.

After the cessation of World War II hostilities, the number of SS members from southwestern Germany that were charged with war crimes ranked low on the list. Most Stuttgarters lived a postwar civilian life without restriction.

Max received an open pass dated April 30, 1945, for freedom of movement within Esslingen, a town outside of Center City by about eight miles. The pass, listing him as a homecomer, enabled his receipt of food rations. By August 23, 1946, he was free to move about within the greater district of Stuttgart. He took pride that he was able to help his family and keep his position at the newspaper, for in his mind he would one day transfer his domain to his eldest son in the tradition of his own father.

1946 pass for wider movement within Stuttgart

Papers show Max was not a P.O.W.

The years that followed were hardly the time for the heir to a newspaper position to contemplate a career in hairdressing or cooking, but Friedemann Paul Erhardt did just that. One of a postwar generation of Germans with youthful hopes, this young boy, surrounded by the remnants of war and the constant specter of starvation, set his sight on a different kind of future and harbored a dream that he would never relinquish.

3

STRUGGLING TO SURVIVE

"Altes Brot ist nicht hart, kein Brot, das ist hart."
("Old bread isn't hard . . . no bread, that is hard.")
—German proverb

In the early 1940s, Hitler offered no rationing plan for the German people. He opined that Germany's World War I loss came due to a severe rationing program, which demoralized its people. Nonetheless, when the war fortunes of his Nazi regime declined near the mid-1940s, he implemented rationing. Ethnic groups deemed more "pure" received higher daily caloric count allotments than others less fortunate, like the Poles or the lowly Jews. Food, though, was not the only problem that faced the populace at the time.

Max Erhardt did his part to provide warmth for his family during winter's coldest months. His miraculous deal for two hundred pounds of coal, when his boy was only four, helped his brood to survive the harshest hours of the hard winter of 1947–48. Milder winters followed, but Gisela's desire for cooked meals, though meager, drove her and her boy to filch wood wherever they could find suitable pieces to burn; having none would mean frigid nights and hungry stomachs. An enforced 2:00 p.m.

daily curfew limited their scavenger hunts to midday hours. Those found on the streets beyond the curfew risked death.

Actual conditions were much harder for the German survivors than the rest of the postwar world imagined. With food in short supply, most of the German population faced starvation. Lack of distribution and delivery means exacerbated the shortage problem. The whole German nation sorely needed a clean infrastructure of roads and an adequate supply of suitable vehicles, but not many other countries cared. Germany, after all, had instigated hostilities—wasn't she now deserving of her awful conditions?

Mother and son braved brutal weather and encountered other desperate housewives and their offspring as they stood in long lines and waited for their turn to pick from meager piles of greenish potatoes dumped on street corners by local farmers. Garden vegetables grown at home could be cobbled up with other indefinable scraps into potato-based soups.

Tell and his mother, 1947

Picking garden raspberries that belonged to someone else, however, was hazardous. "My mother and I had to go to a farmer to pick up some eggs. I was maybe five years old then, or four . . . a small kid. During the two-mile hike back home, we stopped to pick some wild raspberries. Suddenly we hear the sound of a shotgun blast and we stop picking. The farmer shot at us, because we were picking the berries," Tell related years later.

Real coffee—long supplanted by grain drinks—and fresh meats and rich dessert creams, cakes, and other delicacies were definitely off the menu. To make do, some young boys tended rabbit warrens for meals and for bartered exchanges. Erhardt didn't have that luxury. Instead, too many nights left him hungry and afraid in the dark. "Sometimes I only had a slice of bread in a day," he remembered.

From Friedemann Erhardt's constant hunger grew a desire to cook for others. From the age of six, this gastronomic purpose spilled out of the recesses of his creative mind filled with copious images of food, drink, and peoples' camaraderie. Perhaps unintended, his daydreams mocked *der Führer's* nostrum that one was merely a product of gene-pool struggles. Given the combination of a typesetter father with a pediatric-nurse mother, even the Third Reich's mathematics of superiority could not have added up to a cook or a chef.

Self-doubts, however, tugged at the young boy's mind: *Why are we hungry? What life is this? What's my place in this world? Where will I find love?*

Erhardt would struggle for a lifetime to answer such questions. He would search, like the rest of us, for an understanding of the origin of Life—what we like to think and maybe already know is our soul (our self).

As the years would add up, he would follow—pursue most vigorously—his appetite for physical, mental, and spiritual satiety through cooking, food, teaching, wine; all kinds of relationships, classical and country music, fast cars, motorcycles, fatherhood, and scuba diving. He would read historical biographies and history books; write recipe books; appear on television shows; make cooking and product demonstrations and do volunteer church work with children just to have a full cup of personal peace and understanding. Believe it or not, he would even cultivate herb gardens from childhood to grave—a necessary salve for his emotional wounds.

For now, though, Erhardt was simply a small German boy growing up under difficult circumstances.

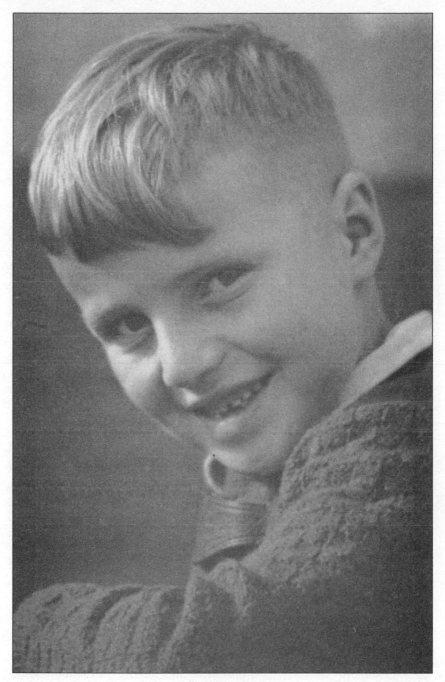

Tell at seven years

4

THE SEARCH FOR SELF BEGINS

"Ich wusste, auf sechs, was ich tun wollte. Ich wollte zu kochen."
("I knew at six what I wanted to do. I wanted to cook.")
—Chef Tell

His mother Gisela often cast the well-being of her family ahead of her own—she might have wished for him to become a doctor or other professional like herself. Instead, she pushed Friedemann toward the German cooking apprenticeship system whenever she could talk with her boy outside the influence of her husband. She feared his attempts to steer their son toward a newsprint career not suited to his sensibilities. *Have I not watched my husband work as a typesetter? To what end?* she thought as she inspected her surroundings. Her vision for her son was much larger than Max's.

Starving and tired, at times, she also spoke erratically and exhibited deranged behavior. More than once others misdiagnosed her symptoms of malnutrition and tiredness and committed her to "mental health" facilities. Given—or despite—this profound and ongoing situation, Gisela shared both her worries and her food knowledge with Friedemann at every opportunity, including one datum that she knew would serve him well for a lifetime: "Du wirst nie mehr hungern, wenn Sie einen Koch zu werden." ("You will never go hungry if you become a chef.")

From a mother who, despite her inconsistent behavior, saw real pitfalls around her son, those were wise words. She desperately wished for his escape to a clean start, if only to project upon him *her own desire* to stop the clattering, leftover images and emotional tugs of the past war, which she suffered in her mind. War had dealt Gisela a kind of post-partum that wouldn't go away as long as she remained in that environment.

For his part, the young Friedemann was impressed by his mother's skills. "I was always amazed what my mother could do. She made dishes out of nothing. That fascinated me. It was magic what she could do," he would tell a reporter much later.

Friedemann's final enticement to learn cooking appeared through an unforgettable advertisement that he found and read on a posterboard that announced available apprenticeships. The illustrated image of a chef selecting fruits aboard a cruise liner moored off the coast of an exotic island offered the promise of an abundant future. The colorful foods, tropical locale, and smiling face impressed the famished boy who, vowing that one day he would be that chef, tore the ad from the board and stashed it inside his pocket.

His road to that future would be a long and winding one.

5

AMERICA ON THE DOORSTEP

"Meine Mutter hat mich in der Küche beschäftigt."
("My mother employed me in the kitchen.")
—Chef Tell

America lifted its ban on assistance packages to Germany on June 5, 1946. By the following year, America arrived at the Erhardts' doorstep. C.A.R.E. (Cooperative for American Remittances to Europe, later known as the Cooperative for Assistance and Relief Everywhere), thanks to Arthur Ringland, Dr. Lincoln Clark, a consortium of twenty-two American charities, and the generosity of thousands of American individuals and families including President Harry Truman, would be a life-saving label on cartons that Friedemann would never forget.

The Erhardts were eligible to participate in C.A.R.E. because Max allowed their flat to be occupied by American officers. More than one hundred million such packages arrived at other doorsteps over the course of the next few years, most shipped from the port city of Philadelphia. C.A.R.E. Packages consisted of "10-in-1" food parcels—food for one person for ten days. They had been designed for an invasion of Japan that never materialized. They became a reliable means of food relief to European survivors facing starvation in the war's aftermath.

A typical C.A.R.E. carton—1.2 cubic feet, weighing 29.5 pounds—contained a pound of beef in broth along with one pound of steak and kidneys; 8 ounces of liver loaf; 8 ounces of corned beef; 12 ounces of luncheon loaf (like Spam); 8 ounces of bacon; 2 pounds of margarine; one pound of lard; one pound of fruit preserves; one pound of honey; one pound of raisins; one pound of Hershey's chocolate; 2 pounds of sugar; 8 ounces of egg powder; 2 pounds of whole milk powder; and 2 pounds of coffee—about 17 to 22 pounds of foodstuffs in all. Not enough to supply the whole family with three squares every day for a month, but something to look forward to on days of little to nothing.

The first C.A.R.E. Package that Erhardt ever saw he found under the Christmas tree, wrapped in paper like a gift. Once the wrapping was off the carton, and Friedemann had cleaned off his face smeared with Hershey's chocolate for the first time, he sat and watched Gisela separate the different contents and repackage them for later use. The locally supplied chicken eggs paired well with the corned beef, bacon, or margarine. Fresh vegetables grown in the yard and gathered in the right seasons rounded out the basic rations. After years of drinking grain substitutes for coffee, a jolt of real java now and then brought heaven in a cup.

His mother's industriousness impressed the boy. He could see how she was determined to help her family survive. He was fascinated as she stretched—the key word being *stretched* here—their rations into novel combinations, which, judging by the uncooked morsels she handed him from time to time, tasted pretty good. At the dinner table, he tasted the pleasures of the same foodstuffs after his mother had cooked them with other ingredients brought to the house by relatives and friends who arrived for meals. He observed the renewed sense of vigor and conversation that her cooking brought to each dinner-table participant. For the sensitive boy, that effect became what he wanted most to emulate, "Out of nothing she cooked outstanding dishes."

Gisela, in turn, listened to Friedemann's comments, which revealed to her that he could discern sweet from sour and bitter from salt—the four basic palate tastes. Mother and child were blessed with accurate palates, although he had one obvious dislike, which she accommodated by doing twice the work for his benefit.

"My mother—she cooks everything twice; once for the family, once for me without onions, which I hated," said Friedemann years later.

On the other hand, those sweet Hershey's chocolate bits conferred to him remained his special treat for years to come. To watch her boy—later two boys—delight in eating the chocolate morsels buoyed Gisela's morale, if only briefly.

Little by little, with Gisela's ingenuity and the garden's produce, the family regained the sense that survival was a certainty, not just a possibility. Each C.A.R.E. package's arrival reinforced the feeling, although on lean days Gisela continued to put her family's needs ahead of her own.

Left to their own devices, children will do just about anything to help their parents. With plenty of time on his hands every day, Friedemann was free to conjure up any ideas along that line that he could imagine; or to play with Astro, his German shepherd dog. Mostly he followed his mother's examples. When not outside with her, he searched for wood and other odds and ends that he thought might lessen the household burden his parents carried. Planting, weeding, and harvesting in the garden was pleasurable and safe—a far cry from the one time he turned a corner late in the afternoon and heard the sudden clicks of rifles.

Tell at nine years

6

AN INSATIABLE HUNGER

"Ich habe viel gelernt frühen."
("I learned a lot early.")

—Chef Tell

Friedemann presented a vulnerable target, walking the broken, deserted pavement since daybreak, accompanied only by Astro. Looking for whatever fancied his imagination, he forgot about the 2:00 p.m. curfew. When he turned a corner, the sudden, loud command of an American unit sergeant's "Halt!" seared his ears. Six cocked M1903 Springfield rifles pointed straight at his chest.

Astro barked fiercely. Friedemann's tears flowed. The soldier that shouted the order repositioned his weapon, and the others stood down. One of them squatted and calmed the dog. The officer in charge bent down, wiped the tears off the youngster's face, and reassured him that he wasn't going to die that day.

Asked who he was, Friedemann was too scared to speak. The unit confiscated his stash of cigarettes and cash. Alerted to reports of someone selling contraband American cigarettes, they had found their culprit. The youngster sniffled and, drying his eyes, tried to explain to the military unit as they escorted him and Astro to a tent set up as a make-shift holding cell that he had been handed the smokes by another Army unit, which encouraged him to sell them.

"I was only trying to do what I could to help my family," he explained.

"Sit here, Sonny. And don't try moving away," said one of the soldiers.

Hungry and overwhelmed, sitting alone on a sack of potatoes, Friedemann heard and felt his mother's words roar back into his brain like cognac on fire: *You will never go hungry, if you become a chef.* He pulled the worn illustration out of his pocket, unfolded it carefully, and stared at the chef's happy image. He resolved to one day leave behind the ruins of his motherland.

A different soldier approached, and Friedemann folded the paper hastily. He stashed it back into his pocket. The soldier marched him to another tent where three Germans that he had seen before recognized him and walked over and consoled him. One told the soldier the boy's identity and where he lived. His familiar hand on the boy's shoulder stopped the lad's shaking. When another soldier walked up and offered him pieces of a Hershey's bar, Friedemann smiled and accepted them.

Friedemann's eyes teared up again the moment his mother walked into the tent accompanied by a soldier. He ran straight to her. Although unhappy that her boy had been selling cigarettes, she didn't let on and, instead, comforted him and thanked the sergeant.

One of the soldiers handed her a sack filled with cans of powdered milk and other foodstuffs that he'd filled from a carton imprinted, "Made in U.S.A." Seeing several of these cartons and the abundance of food that he and his mother were handed, Erhardt decided he would one day go to the United States of America.

Under the watchful eyes of two more soldiers, mother and child walked home. When Gisela tousled his hair playfully, Friedemann knew he would not face trouble at home that night. For the first time in several hours, he breathed easily.

The promise of America's bounty remained a dreamland inside of Friedemann's mind, but he also realized that today he'd found a sort of commissary for his family. Thereafter, he maneuvered his "arrest" on a fairly regular basis and orchestrated his friends' "incarcerations" for the bargain price of a few nibbles from their Hershey's chocolate bars.

C.A.R.E. Package ingredients, garden herbs, vegetables from shared backyard or window boxes, and henhouse eggs helped Stuttgarters like Friedemann survive, but the pang from another type of hunger deep inside the youngster would not go away—this one reached far beyond American generosity and German garden plots: he yearned for answers to his private questions.

How would he quench the insatiable desire of that hunger, living in a place that was mostly rubble?

7

REBOOTING THE FUTURE

"Es ist keine Prahlerei, wenn Sie Ihr Produkt mit herausragenden
Leistungen produzieren kann."
("It's not bragging, if you can produce your product
with excellence.")

—Chef Tell

S tuttgart's condition right after the war made it a hellish place
to live. Residents not only required water and food, but also
renewed shelter and a viable local economy. Stuttgarters didn't
have time to sit and reminisce about what might have been; their
town needed infrastructure, and the broken remains of 39,125 store-
fronts, tenements, churches and factories lay in their way.

People walked to makeshift work sites and labored hard every day
for hours. With few other meaningful work choices available, able-
bodied men and women cleared edifices, one stone and brick at a time.
They transported fifteen million cubic meters of rubble outside town.
One "Schuttberg" (mountain of debris) known as Birkenkopf ("Birch
Head")—a 511-meter (1,677 feet) mountain of stone and steel rubble—
was topped with a monument erected to stand as a reminder to future
generations of the tragedy that happened here.

Time ticked onward in the German heartland. Life played out its changes. White winter flakes melted into color-splashed gardens. Spring showers gave way to layered summer greens, which descended into autumn's leafy blankets—Mother Earth's renewed coverlets for winters to come. Year by year, the four seasons brought counterpoints to Stuttgart's hollowed, broken, brick-and-mortar relics. From the echoes of architectural masterpieces rose steel and glass structures that renewed hope for the populace the way sunshine draws back winter's chill and renews spring's flower buds. Living conditions evolved and improved, and major business concerns resumed peaceful operations.

The international icon Daimler-Benz called Stuttgart home. In the war, the company supplied the inline engines of sleek Me-109 Luftwaffe fighter planes that knocked off Allied bombers with aplomb. When the conflict was over, the "Cradle of the Automobile" turned once more to building precision-crafted consumer vehicles and employed thousands in the process.

The improved economy boded well for a growing boy who would one day cook for paying patrons.

8

THE GENESIS OF "CHEF TELL"

"Das tapfere Mann denkt an sich selbst die letzte . . ."
("The valiant man thinks of himself the last . . .")
—Friedrich Von Schiller's *Wilhelm Tell*

During the dark years, like any other cultured people, the Germans tried to make the best of their lives through divergent activities. Indoor events brought welcome relief from the stark realities outside. The country's unique and popular football championship—an annual English rugby-styled tournament with roots in amateur clubs of the eighteenth century, in which teams vied for the *Viktoria* trophy—had continued since 1903 up to its brief two-year (1943–1945) hiatus during the war. Now the games resumed, albeit as football (soccer).

By 1948, German athletics had rebuilt and fielded enough talent in various sports events for a national team to compete in the first Summer Olympics since the war break, but they would not be invited back to the Games until 1952.

On the other hand, the chain of theatrical performances of German operas and stage plays advanced unbroken. Parents encouraged even their very youngest children to perform in these popular productions.

In fact, an amateur role in a school play written by Friedrich Schiller in 1804, *Wilhelm Tell*, in which Friedemann performed the lead for a few years, brought him his nickname Tell and foreshadowed his later decision to create the TV persona of Chef Tell.

* * *

As the plot goes in the sixteenth-century legendary play, a tyrannical ruler named Gessler refuses to release Tell after his public act of brazen discourtesy toward the ruler, unless Tell could shoot an apple off the head of his son with an arrow. Shooting the apple and not the child would not only let his son live, but also permit Tell and his family to leave and go wherever they wished. After Tell shoots the apple in the public square, he further rebukes Gessler, who at once detains him. Tell escapes and lives to make good on his pledge to one day rid the population of their maniacal leader.

Because the story characterizes a larger-than-life figure possessed of joviality and insouciance combined with true agility, Tell was the perfect role for Erhardt, who possessed a wickedly ironic sense of humor and an innate ability to laugh at his early-day troubles (at least publicly). With these traits, he would later put off those around him who would dare to take him too seriously.

By 1956, despite the nightmarish remnants of starvation-caused deaths of friends and a dearth of options around him, Tell ripened into a thirteen-year-old teenager determined to be a chef. He finished his eighth and final year of mandatory German schooling and affirmed that he would not lay bricks or press Mergenthaler brass mats onto newsprint slugs for the rest of his life. Instead, he would seek warmth, camaraderie, and opportunity amid the earthy smells of wood- or coal-burning stoves. He would prep and cook German cuisine in regimented stainless steel kitchens. He would swap schoolbooks for recipes and take up the arduous task of becoming a professional chef.

A chef in Stuttgart at the Hotel Graf Zeppelin offered one apprenticeship, and he was chosen for it after he had applied for the position without his parents' knowledge or approval. He was not worried that his mother would find his choice unappealing. His father, however, had made it clear that any choice other than entering a program to learn the typesetting craft would be unacceptable to him.

The law required that a boy inform his parents and obtain their endorsement before he could enter a state-approved apprenticeship. Tell knew the announcement of his decision to take up the trade of cooking would not go well with his father. He knew his request for endorsement would be a struggle, but he never could have foreseen the resulting consequences or the circumstances in which his father would let him leave. He would discover soon enough that in addition to his suffering through his cooking apprenticeship, he would have to find solace and safety in the hard work. Despite the dangers within kitchen walls, in which he would find himself almost every waking hour of every day for the next several years, the alternative, he would remember again and again, looked far worse.

9

BITTER SALTS IN
THE WOUND

"Die Leute sagen, 'Du hast nie sagen, wie viel Salz zu verwenden.'
Es hängt davon ab, wie du dich fühlst."
("People say, 'You never say how much salt to use.' It depends on
how you feel.")

—Chef Tell

Most survivors in Stuttgart and the rest of Germany had inhaled, exhaled, and assumed a vibrant, peaceful ambience by 1956. A few, however, stripped of their innocence and haunted by traces of war etched onto their minds, would never return to normalcy, Gisela included.

Her top-floor flat—no more than a meager space of a couple of bedrooms, a small galley kitchen, and a 12x14 main sitting room with one wall of books—had somehow survived the mayhem of fifty-three Allied bombings, but Gisela's mental disposition in such a tiny space became murky. The depth of her suffering would never be fully measured, only approximated by the manner of her untimely death.

On the fateful day in May of 1956 that Tell announced his decision to forgo more formal schooling and to begin a cooking apprenticeship, his words produced an acrimonious argument between Gisela and Max, which Tell and Ulrich, his younger brother, witnessed first hand.

Max, a mild-mannered man normally, roared, "He can't do it. I won't permit it!"

"I don't see why not, if he knows what he wants!" Gisela argued.

Tell interjected, "Mother, Father, don't fight. Please don't fight."

They ignored him. They had been fighting over Tell for years, since she doted on her favorite son.

"A boy must have respect for his father's wishes. Cooking is not what I have planned for him! He should follow me—come to work at *Stuttgarter Nachrichten*. This is what he should do!"

"But he wants to cook! What good is a newspaper when you want to cook? Let him work—do an apprenticeship."

The six-foot-two, stately-built Max towered over the frail boy and his defiant wife and demanded, "I will not. He will do as I say! Come here, Friedemann. You must understand what is best."

Max advanced toward his boy but was shielded by his mother's body. Gisela, tears streaking her flushed cheeks, exploded at her husband in a hail of words and flailing fists. Pent-up rage and frustration boiled up and spilled out.

Acting on motherly instinct alone, Gisela beat her fists harmlessly against Max's chest until she had no more energy to continue. But she wasn't about to back down. The life left inside her breathed solely for the safe passage of her children to a better world, and no matter what she would have to do to guarantee that, she was bound to act in their best interests. She gathered her boys' clothing into a satchel, prodded the children to the door, and turned to leave.

"Then we can stay here no longer, Max. I will take my children to my sisters' place, and we will live there. Over my dead body will you ever hold my boy back from his dream!"

Max said nothing.

At the aunts' apartment, in front of her boys, Gisela requested, "Promise me that if anything happens to me, you must take care of them. You must promise me that."

The promise extracted, she returned alone to her flat.

Unnoticed, Tell slipped outside to return home and rejoin his mother. Running into the building and up the staircase, looking down as he stepped, he at last reached the top landing outside of their apartment. He looked up and found Gisela's body hanging in the hallway—a cord around her neck, a chair kicked over beneath her. Alone, he screamed. Doors opened and neighbors stepped onto the landing. As Tell slumped, one of the women caught him before he hit the floor. Under his mother's body, he cried until he fell asleep in her arms.

One of the men searched the Erhardt apartment for Max, but he could not be found—gone, perhaps to give himself a talking to or to cool off with a draft-filled stein. When he returned in the company of his sisters-in-law and Ulrich, he found the neighbors and the police and, of course, Tell on the floor, curled away from the unnerving sight above him, held by the arms of one of the women. He reacted swiftly.

Max shook the boy awake, "You dumb ass! What did you do?"

Confused and startled, Tell screamed and cried, once again seeing his dead mother's body behind his assailant.

"What did you do?" Max demanded as the others restrained him.

Tell went numb. The meaning of his father's words sank in: he was to blame for his mother's death. Unable to think or care, he ignored his father's accusation.

To make matters worse, his two aunts, who had stepped into the Erhardt apartment, came forward and complained aloud about Gisela's fitness as a mother. They nattered about her extracted promise for them to care for both boys and assumed that she knew she was going to kill herself. Furthering the indignity, they wore the dead woman's overcoat and jewelry and flaunted them in front of everyone.

Their act was salt in the wound of death.

* * *

Had the continual wrestling over Tell's future set Gisela in the direction of suicide? Or had something else set her off?

No doubt war weaved unwanted textures into every survivor's memories, but a ghetto of internal graffiti etched mixed messages onto Gisela's mental images. Maternal birthing moments of extreme joy contrasted with miscarriages, stillbirths, and broken infant body parts—a midwife's leftover mental riprap—made her mental state more vulnerable than most. Grief and unexpressed resentments lingered. Apathies and fears laced with numbness loitered, and threats of death, horrific sounds, unwanted feelings echoed without end among her thoughts.

Gisela's work as a registered nurse and midwife no doubt delivered to her a hopeful pride for her personal contributions during the war, but it came with a terrible price in her case. For one thing, Hitler had taken note personally and awarded her a medal for "outstanding excellence" for her work—a double-edged sword, which only served to heighten her fears, considering her partial ancestry.

Though the silence of peace surrounded her, Gisela yearned for the cacophony inside of her head to be still. Bearing up admirably under such pressures, the last straw in her hidden struggle may have been her argument with Max. She had stood beside her husband through the war, and for more than a decade after, but his rattling of her most-cherished underpinning, the hope that her oldest child would find something better for his life, broke her will and spun her into an apathy that ended with her death.

It is difficult to let go of the impulse to make sense of a suicide; *impossible* to write a logical conclusion to the illogic. Questions remain. Whatever bothered Gisela enough to end her life left with her. What drove her away that day will never be fully understood by those left behind.

In the face of this mayhem, Tell might have opted for a self-destructive path, but he did not. He did not deny or turn away from his God, nor turn to drink or drugs. Though perhaps tempted to cave in and obey his demanding father, he did not. Instead, as he lay on the cold floor and clung to the thinned thread of his own purpose, he chose to go to work. Having concluded that he would work harder than anyone else, he hoped one day to prove to everyone that his mother was right.

10

FALLOUT

"Ich musste sogar mein Hund, Astro, hinter sich zu lassen."
("I even had to leave my dog, Astro, behind.")
—Chef Tell

Tell kept his thoughts to himself as he watched the officials take Gisela's body away and his aunts leave with his brother. Earlier, on the way home to rejoin her, he had stopped in a strudel shop and cajoled the owner into a small gift for his mother. Now his feelings hardened like the stiffened apple treat wrapped in silk that he clutched.

Truth be told, Gisela's death may have been just sour icing on an ill-baked cake. Tell and Ulrich had been sent away twice before for weeks to an orphanage run by Christian nuns. The untold reason for the familial disruptions was Gisela's commitments to asylums, which family members who had witnessed what they called "nervous breakdowns," enforced. One incident—a shopping trip when Gisela absentmindedly left Tell on a bus, to be returned home only with the help of the driver— was pointed to as evidence of her "mental imbalance." Yet, lack of proper nutrition and rest never entered their minds as a possible cause of her "irrational" behavior.

Through all of the past histrionics and, now, Gisela's tragic death, Max continued to work long hours. With her gone, he asked one of his sisters-in-law to care for both of his sons. She accepted Ulrich but refused custody of Tell, which, of course, further un-tethered the two brothers. Like badly executed tattoos grown grotesque with age, the distorted scars of these events festered and would lead to a later estrangement that continued past the last of Tell's days.

* * *

Tell eventually stood up. Inside of the apartment, he took the rainy-day money, which Gisela had confided to him was located in a cupboard. He gathered his belongings, announced to Max that he was leaving, and departed. The next day, the culinary institution located in Stuttgart welcomed him to the first day of his apprenticeship.

Tell the teenage commis

Max had not resisted Tell's departure and he, too, went to work at the newspaper where he stayed on until his retirement in 1975. Along the way, he married a woman, Liesel, whom Tell would tolerate, but never grow to love. Life among the family members pretty much stayed that way until another tragedy brought Max and Tell back into communication.

Like it or not, Tell became his own man that sorrowful day. As quickly as the flip of a tossed coin, manhood had crashed its heady burden down hard upon his shoulders. He hoped it wouldn't soon kill him.

11

MIND-NUMBING
HARD WORK

"Il faut (d'abord) durer."
("First, one must endure.")
—Ernest Hemingway

Tell's first apprenticeship year cost 20 deutschmarks monthly and his mother's reserve money barely covered it. In the second year he would be paid 20 DM a month; in the third year that would double. Of course, room and board at the hotel where he worked was complimentary, but largely a formality considering, as Tell put it, "One worked eighteen hours a day, six days a week, and slept on Mondays—the one day off."

That is, when he got a day off.

"When the restaurant was closed, we seldom got the day off, because there was gardening to do—planting or harvesting. We were told 'it builds character,'" said Chef Walter Staib, who later endured the same apprenticeship program.

The German cooking apprenticeship was a part of an organized system established in Germany in the nineteenth century. Three years of on-the-job training sandwiched between formal trade school classes offered nothing more than an opportunity to each participant, who had to make the most of his chance. One either worked every day, less one day per week to attend trade school classes, or worked each day for three months and attended classes for a month. After completion of the three-year mandatory program, student-apprentices passed or failed a battery of written, oral, and practical exams for certification.

Most chefs of noted fame, before and during Tell's time, began their careers the same way. Upon completion of the three-year program, the German certificate declared one a graduate cook, not a chef.

* * *

To the adolescent boy, the commercial kitchen he worked in was a confusing, jumbled, dangerous place. Slightly more than a decade earlier, hundreds of steel bombs cascaded nightly like rain upon Stuttgart, and now a rain of stainless steel in the chef's milieu scared him.

Ladles, tongs, forks, spoons, and knives commingled with hefty mashers, mixing bowls, flexible whisks, and spatulas—each encrusted with leftover orts and scrapings—thrust at him. He, the lowly dishwasher, the *chef de plonge*, labored furiously to restore them to pristine condition.

Saucers, sauté, and roasting pans of aluminum, steel, pewter, and cast iron; broiling sheets and baking sheets; double-boilers; one ounce glasses to multi-gallon jars and pots—begged to be scrubbed as fast as kitchen chefs required them throughout the two nine-hour daily shifts he endured six days a week.

In scattered free seconds of relief, Tell glanced across the room and glimpsed the torrid action of chefs managing matches, burners, open flames, and coal stoves. He took in the sights, sounds, smells, and activity of heating and cooking myriad combinations of foods—day after day, night after night—to exacting German standards of culinary excellence and hygiene.

Ultra-sharp blades filleted, pared, sliced, diced, chopped, minced, and cut vegetables, meats, herbs, breads, fish and, at times, fingers. They flashed and menaced from under hot soapy suds that rose in the sinks where he toiled month after month, perspiration dripping from his forehead, on tired legs aching to sit down.

Little by little, frightening conglomerations of blenders, slicers, Turmix juicers, stand mixers; bouillon, stock, broth, spice, and yeast containers; frozen-cold, chilled, lukewarm-hot to boiling-hot liquids and solids . . . at last came into focus, alongside vinegars, cooking wines, cooking oils, and sherries.

Baked, fried, sautéed, boiled, broiled, simmered, braised, and slow-cooked vegetables; fruit, game, fowl, seafood, shellfish, and animal meats gradually made sense to Tell.

Allowed small breaks, he watched confectionary sugars, sweeteners, flours, eggs, and extracts transform into plated dessert delicacies under the hands of pastry chefs. Under the scrutinizing eyes of the chef de cuisine, which either approved them dismissively or disapproved them angrily, these plated creations passed or failed. The approved disappeared to the front room where patrons admired, savored, and devoured them with after-dinner liqueurs and coffees.

* * *

The hard-working stripling rose within a year to the unheralded status of *commis*, rewarded with his first prep-work task: peeling bushels of potatoes and dicing thousands of onions. Though devilish, there was method to the madness of the system. Young assistants learned knife control, and mentors discovered how skilled their charges might be with sharp blades.

Tell was next asked to boil potatoes, but not told how.

"My first day as a commis, the chef tells me, 'Make the potatoes for the night.' I tell him I don't know how, so he kicks me and says, 'You peel potatoes and you put them in a pot with salt and put them on the fire.' So I did it and half an hour later the kitchen fills with smoke. I didn't put any water in—he didn't tell me. He beats me for this."

No kidding.

His *chef de partie* berated him, *"Du bist dumm."* ("You're stupid.") But he never told his charge to add water and, instead, beat the boy twice a day. Still, the youngster would not quit.

Besides, there were other challenges for Tell to overcome. "When you put the food in the pot in the restaurant, you have to taste it first—to see if it's good, but I can't because I don't like onions. So he beats me, kicks me and says, 'Taste the onion.' I taste the onion and, ever since, I eat onions all the time. Maybe my mother should have done that and saved herself all the trouble with the cooking," Chef Tell recalled.

After a while, no longer scared and much more accomplished, Tell and his circle of peers shifted away from being the effects of their mentors. He devised nefarious returned "favors," which recouped morsels of dignity for himself and his fellow commis. There was the time he "accidentally" closed the freezer door behind the worst chef who taunted him and the other boys in the kitchen—an act heralded as the commis's rite of passage.

Tell, far right, and friends share a drink, 1969

"The guy never gets his master-chef degree, and I get to be the youngest one in Germany at twenty-four, but he teaches me to eat onions and to cook potatoes—what can I say?" he would comment years later to a journalist.

After another twenty-four months of solid apprenticeship, separated by one-month shifts spent working at different locations, Tell graduated the program and was recognized as a cook. The diploma in his hand allowed him to work hard throughout Europe for three more years in pursuit of recognition as a bona fide chef.

As he pursued the challenge, Tell's future played out well in his mind. His daydreams swirled with ambience. Hot and cool wall colorings and selected pastoral paintings mixed with avant-garde impressionisms.

Wide oak-floor planks, cool Italian tiles, and English linoleum grounded him. Classical German and multi-ethnic music soothed his tensions as much as they aroused his projected guests' appetites. Practical professional attire—polo shirts, aprons, and loose-fitted pants of wildly varying colors—completed the futuristic landscape in his mind.

Tell envisioned a professional world full of esoteric conversations among gourmands and—as equals—jocular repartee with the hoi polloi, cognoscenti, royalty, political insiders, celebrities, and blue-collar patrons. Added complements of imaginary food—memorable aperitifs and mouth-watering appetizers that accompanied stunning entrées and delectable desserts—completed the scenarios.

Well-selected spirits were standard fare within Tell's thoughtful feasts.

Every one of those postulated goals would become a part of the external dressings of his soul for decades to come, well before the spoils of television entered his dreams.

An invisible crystal ball, however, also played a part in Tell's personal world. It foretold tempestuous interactions, male and female, where tempers flew, betrayals stung, and lovers swooned. Volatile emotions ran the gamut from frigid cold through lukewarm to hot, boiling hot. The diversity of his exterior world would, in time, bring on both sublime moments and ugly emotions, though he could not foresee them now. Within his private world, Tell's clock ticked to reach one goal only: inner peace and understanding. The specter of the loss of his mother never strayed far.

The business side of kitchen work never appeared glamorous to Tell. Like many chefs, especially European chefs, he worked long and hard in, at times, out-of-control, extreme conditions. If he were to rise above the norm to executive chef, he would have to walk a finer, narrower line than his peers, propelled by self-discipline. As executive chef, he would be required not only to set an example with his planning of menus and cooking, but also to manage kitchen crews toward the attainment and maintenance of three-star rankings as overseen by Michelin.

Tell's qualifying years continued. Expletives screamed past him in several languages. He dodged plates of food and pots and pans—even knives—thrown at him day and night, month after month, for three years. Paid with occasional morsels of food, Spartan accommodations, and small stipends, he was rewarded at last with the coveted certificate and title of chef.

Later, he reminisced, "I am German. Over there they do things different. In my apprenticeship I was allowed to make any mistake—once. Then, the second time, they kick you where you don't like it."

Despite the circumstances thrown at him, Tell never acted out or showed a rebellious streak. Instead, with every obtuse turn of his journey, he redoubled his resolve and pushed after his dream. He stayed the course through a gauntlet of flying objects and dissuasive people, who tried their best to discourage him. He out-worked his peers and his handlers.

In what spare time he mustered, he rode a bicycle for pleasure in the countryside. However, Tell's competitive nature underscored all of his activities in or out of the kitchen. In 1958, the third year of his entry into the annual Stuttgart amateur cycling competition—he had placed in the finals every year—he finished as runner-up to the champion.

* * *

Tell Erhardt endured. Nothing fazed or deterred him. Cooking food well—making people happy—was his *sanity*. He could control that world. There he could use his personality, and he knew it. Though just past his teenaged years, he sensed the potential of his greatness the way a gifted thoroughbred senses the finish line before he enters the gate. He knew he could win; knew he would one day turn the high-stakes tables of fortune toward him. He knew and he vowed that the day the world acknowledged him, he would have justice for his mother's life and her trust in him.

In the immediate years ahead, Tell would have to deal with the rest of his apprenticeship tasks and requirements, and then somehow reconcile his strained relations with his father—a matter that would be settled by Fate.

12

FATE STEPS IN

"Fear machen Sie das Unmögliche tun."
("Fear will make you do the impossible.")
—German proverb

Mountaineers agree that they can learn more about a man's character in a few short days on a mountain than by watching him for years in his normal daily routine. According to Tell, his father and a half-uncle mountain climbed. On more than one occasion he shared with a close associate that an alpine tragedy occurred on their last climb together.

Details were not forthcoming from Tell. Indeed, some family members stated that there was never a half-brother, but Tell insisted at three separate times that an incident happened. What occurred, though? If there was a death on a mountain, did Max feel responsible for it? How might the events of that day have unfolded? Perhaps only some imagination blended with solid mountaineering data permits a glimpse into which mountain and what climbing methods resulted in a reunion for Tell and Max.

Serious mountaineering in 1962 in the southeastern German state of Bavaria could be found among several peaks, including Alpspitze, which resembled a solo pyramid rising to 8,595 feet. From the summit, the vista of blue-green rolling hills rising to snow-capped peaks rivaled those of the Blue Ridge Mountains in the eastern United States and the Rockies in the West. Though first flagged in 1946, by 1962 the mountain offered few *vie ferratas* ("marked routes"). The high-classed North face presented a climb with a great degree of difficulty and required the skill and trust of seasoned Alpinists formed into small teams.

On the day that Max and his half-brother might have climbed, before beginning the trad-climb (traditional team-climb) ascent before sunrise, the experienced leader would have double-checked the ropes, carabiners, chocks, and harnesses, as well as the approach, and monitored the local weather while the half-brothers and a fourth climber warmed up. Mountain equipment and Alpine lead climbing then was not as sophisticated as present-day twenty-first-century technology and methods, but mountaineering's known history went back at least three centuries.

Traditional climbing required safety training and coordination of efforts. Members conquered the summit together or gave up and retreated together in the name of safety. No self-respecting mountaineer would ever take credit for attaining a summit at the expense of the injury or death of one of his mates, and today was no exception.

The lead climber forged ahead for the attempt, belayed by Max and then his half-brother, followed by another skilled climbing guide who was the designated last man on the line that tethered the four team members.

The early portion of the climb on this morning transpired without incident. The sun slipped in and out of a wisp of clouds, and the wind blew soft and hard as the team scaled higher on the vertical wall. As noon approached, good progress had been made toward the top, and all anchors were holding well.

Without notice, the weather turned for the worst. A thick cloud cover darkened the sky. Thunder and lightning cracked the air, and a light mist started to fall just when the half-brother found himself in a precarious position on the siding. The sheer vertical plane in front of him led upward to a roof that the two ahead of him had traversed. With the sudden drop in temperature, his fingers numbed and his grip weakened; in short order, he was "pumped" (weakened).

The rock face felt like a sheet of ice. Unable to see his teammates above and only one below him, he could not signal directly that he was unable to move forward, backward, up, or down. Instead, he froze. A knot built in his stomach.

Max above him moved upward and felt the line tighten. He shouted to his mate below, but the wind moaned, and his call went unheard. One by one, the rest of the team realized there was a problem. At the lead's signal, climbing halted. They waited to hear a voice or an echo but heard only wind.

The distressed climber prayed for the sun to re-emerge and dry the wall or at least for the howling air to settle down. Instead, the weather worsened. Not resuming the climb could quickly remove any chance to make the summit. The probability that they could perish increased with each passing minute.

Seconds passed like hours as the embattled climber searched for an easier way to grip the wall and establish upward movement. Looking upward and to his right, he discovered a small area where he might wedge himself enough to relax his left and right side muscles by barn-dooring (holding on with his left-side hand and foot while the right side swung free; later, switching sides). To reach the spot, he would have to let go and swing free of the mountainside.

In a moment of wind stall, he made verbal contact with his brother above him, who relayed his message to the leader. Following the signal of three slaps of the rope, the team agreed, he would fly free. When he let loose of the wall, his weight would have to be borne by each climber above him. If no hold could be established within one or two swings, they would not be able to support him any longer. Of course, the strain on the upper anchors and the added heat drawn by friction to the rope presented additional challenges.

Rope slapped limestone three times. The man below called, "Belay off!" which meant he had freed the rope so that the swinging climber had freedom to move in a wider arc. The trade-off, however, should he fall, would be a longer and more dangerous fall with a greater potential for serious, possibly fatal injury.

Max's kin pushed off hard with both feet from the rock wall. At first he swung to his left, away from the spot where he wished to establish a hold. Meeting the cliff's face, he pushed off with both feet to increase his arc back toward his intended target. He came in too hard and hit the wall too hard and too fast to establish a hold. Luckily, though, he pushed away and swung once again to his left. As the anchored carabiner and the other climbers strained under the added weight, he pushed off a third time more gently. He sailed toward the wall slowly, but when he reached for the wedge hold, Fate stepped in.

A gust of wind fluttered his body like the slackening of sailboat mains. He twisted helplessly, which loosed the anchor from the choss it had been driven into, and he fell. Spinning like a top, he crashed back-first onto the mountainside. His arc was broken, so was his back. Dangling limply, he had no way to regain momentum or to help himself. Disoriented and numbed into an instant apathy, not thinking clearly, he reached for his pocketknife.

Muscles strained, chests heaved, and four hearts raced. Inhaling new air into their lungs, the team struggled physically and emotionally. Those above could not see directly what was happening below them. The teammate below gathered in slack rope as fast as he could so that he could make his way over to the helpless climber. An eternity of seconds later, horrified, he felt the weight peel off of the line and heard *"Auf Wiedersein,"* echo and ricochet off the stone wall as the hapless climber fell hundreds of feet to his death.

The wind kicked up, which spared the climb team from hearing the climber's fragile body hit the hard rock floor below them. Apart from each other on the sheer face, each surviving member suffered his grief alone and meditated in silence. Max stared straight ahead, unseeing, into open air. His mind rushed a blur of memories past his unfocused eyes and, when he thought of his two sons, he wept.

Ascending to the summit violated protocol and decency. The lead signaled a descent and the team roped down.

* * *

Did this event really occur . . . and in this manner? Unfortunately, the truth and its details rest with Tell. We can only assume that Max would have returned with his half-brother's remains and informed Tell. Presented with the news of his uncle's death, Tell might have wept and been consoled by his father. Unashamed and unaware of tears spilling down his cheeks, Max might also have asked his son for forgiveness for blaming him for Gisela's suicide.

And Tell might likely have replied, *"Wir alle tun, was wir für richtig halten in dem moment, vater."* ("We all do what we think is right in the moment, father.")

* * *

Whatever the reason, father and son forged a renewed bond. Tell corresponded and phoned Max on a regular basis. No matter how far away he traveled, he returned twice a year to see him.

After he retired from the newspaper in May 1975, Max accepted one of Tell's invitations to visit him in America. In October of 1983, within weeks of one of Tell's many visits to Germany, Max suffered an aneurysm and died, but not before he had observed how hard his son worked and how much he had accomplished.

"My father very badly wanted me to run his newspaper. Everybody else in my family is a doctor, a lawyer, or a vice president. I am the only guy who didn't get into 'anything big' in their opinion. But I have more cash than they all have together. They call me the 'black sheep,' but I love what I'm doing. I make money—I'm really well off," Tell told the media after his celebrated stardom soared.

13

HEART AND SOUL FOOD

"Ich nehme die Angst vor der Küche."
("I take the fear out of cooking.")

—Chef Tell

O nly through extensive training classes, hands-on experience, and passing the certification requirements and examinations do German chefs accomplish the extended knowledge and kitchen mastery that is the venerated status of *zertifizierter meisterkoch* (certified master chef). (In 2011, there were fewer than 100 Certified Master Chefs in America, only 320 in the world; in Germany, in Erhardt's time, far fewer. This rare status is a product of a much higher standard of a formalized training program.)

Legendary master chefs constitute a chain of illustrious masters of cuisine. "Prince of Chefs" Martino da Como—fifteenth-century chef to kings and the Vatican; "King of Chefs and Chef of Kings" Antoine Carême (1784–1833); "Emperor of Chefs" Auguste Escoffier (1846–1935); "Father of Modern French Cuisine" Fernand Point—1897–1955; "Dean of American Cuisine" James Beard (1903–1985) and television's *The French Chef* Julia Child (1912–2004)—were among the most highly regarded and best-known.

Da Como codified in writing the methods used to cook foods and train chefs as far back as the fifteenth century. Carême linked with da Como's work and advanced the records of culinary history and cook-training methods into the nineteenth century.

Escoffier brought Carême's historical works into the twentieth century up to 1935, at times with the help of the burgeoning newsprint media. To wit, in 1913, on the morning after Escoffier had served a refined banquet to 146 distinguished guests on board the Hamburg-American Line's flagship, *SS Imperator*, the Emperor of Germany, Kaiser Wilhelm II, invited him to breakfast. He wished to complement the chef for a strawberry pudding that the Kaiser had requested. Escoffier had named it Fraises Imperator, after the ship, the largest in the world at the time.

"I am the emperor of Germany, but you are the Emperor of Chefs," the emperor said.

Press personnel aboard ship latched on to the phrase. By the time they ported in Germany, the label had spread across Europe. Escoffier, already the acknowledged leader among chefs and heir apparent to founder of haute cuisine Carême, became the favorite of Europe's elite gourmands, and the new title stuck. Carême himself started his career arc with kitchen-boy chores in a cheap Parisian chophouse during the French Revolution—something akin to Tell's ignominious beginnings.

If da Como, Carême, and Escoffier developed and codified the leading cuisines of the world, it was left to Fernand Point in the twentieth century to lead the way to the establishment of *l'esprit du chef.* ("the spirit of the chef"). Point's *Ma Gastronomie*, the benchmark reference for French nouvelle cuisine, trained an entire generation of French master chefs to bring a generosity and hugeness of heart into food preparation. The making of master chefs, whose food would literally bring life and love to the table, advanced the chain of culinary excellence well beyond the earliest days of cooking. A chef like Chef Tell could not avoid use of Point's philosophy and textbooks, linking him to the chain of the great chefs.

Formally trained and certified or not, the turning of food combinations into avant-garde dishes remained the domain of certain chefs gifted with innovative genius, Tell among them. Up to the advent of cooking demonstrations on television, the general public rarely knew of such talents aside from word of mouth, print media, or direct experience.

Entrepreneur James Beard appeared in August of 1946 on American TV's first cooking show *I Love To Eat*, which ran for one year on NBC.

An American from Oregon, Beard brought French cuisine and cookbooks to America's middle and upper classes.

Julia Child—first and foremost a journalist—attended France's premier cooking school Le Cordon Bleu. She co-authored *Mastering the Art of French Cooking*, published in 1961. From February 1963, she was an in-the-kitchen TV personality and she won Peabody and Emmy awards. While Child's emphasis was upon French cooking, Chef Tell, also an Emmy Award winner, brought through syndicated TV not only German, but also French, Continental, and American cuisines to an audience *eight times* the size of Child's. Additionally, he toured the nation, doing live shows that brought thousands of paying customers and fans to his booths.

Child and Erhardt were ebullient TV personalities, which struck agreeable chords with the American audience. Yet, Tell was the first "rock-star" chef, according to former *Philadelphia Inquirer* food writer extraordinaire, Elaine Tait. She described Chef Tell's masterful skills: "Tell was the first of the great TV showman chefs and the only one whose food actually tasted good. He rivaled Julia Child."

Child and Tell shared a common philosophy regarding food: one should not fear it. "I take the fear out of cooking. You should play with your food," Tell emphasized to his audiences in the 1970s. Borrowing from Erhardt, Child stated in a 1990 interview, "If fear of food continues, it will be the death of gastronomy in the United States."

Common threads exist among all legendary chefs. They naturally have, or through training develop, a passion for food and for cooking for others. They possess skilled culinary knowledge, which allows them to control the kitchen environment and its outcomes to a precise degree. They suffer hardships, overcome obstacles, and still approach both food and living with decidedly *unserious* attitudes.

Master chefs have shared their unique sense of humor across centuries. Those who really knew their stuff blew off steam any way they wished. Strict and unforgiving in the kitchen, Fernand Point, accompanied by Paul Bocuse, his famous cohort and sous chef, ushered Parisian high-society elites into his kitchen, crowded them together, fed them his latest creations, and told them they were partaking in a survey. Bocuse meantime, hidden under the preparation table where they stood, whitewashed their shoe heels just for kicks. On another occasion, Point ordered Bocuse to paint the bicycle of a visiting gendarme pink while Point distracted the officer.

Of course, one bite of the food prepared by these geniuses—immediately they were forgiven. But, *Mon Dieu!* Inside the kitchen they were ferocious. In the kitchen their action was always hot and fast.

Such offensive behavior (to snobs) has led to the creation of gastronomic inventions that have stood the test of time. For instance, "blackened fish" was a result of Cajun Chef Paul Prudhomme's late-afternoon hunger pangs and his impatience with cooking time. Being a large man who loved to eat, he overheated a cast-iron pan when a reservation phone call distracted him. While trading anecdotes with his customer, he placed a fish fillet on the red-hot, heated pan, which danced on the heated surface and caramelized instantly. He dropped the phone, added a few of his selected spices, and ate lunch. He loved his new dish so much that he placed it on the menu of his restaurant that night! Asked to name the new dish, Prudhomme called it simply "blackened fish"!

14

TO WORK AND LIVE LIKE
A MANIAC

"Je besser das Hotel, desto weniger Geld Sie verdienen."
("The better the hotel, the less money you make.")
—Chef Tell

While Tell may have been a newcomer to the food industry when he began his apprenticeship, on November 12, 1962, he joined a heritage of almost five hundred years of food service forged on the spot where he worked. The Hotel Goldner Adler in Pforzheim, since the middle ages (1474), had offered beer and food to weary travelers.

The original building almost survived the war erect, but a February 23, 1945, air raid destroyed it four months before the war ended. It was the largest R.A.F. air raid on one area in World War II. Eighty-three percent of the town's buildings and 25 percent of its population—seventeen thousand people—disappeared in one night. Another thirty thousand people rendered homeless took their meals for months inside of hastily constructed public kitchens.

The German beer-brewing company Ketterer, which owned the site since 1901, erected the new building with the original name Gold Eagle emblazoned on it. Inside of it, Tell quickly progressed to *chef de partie* and was soon knocking out excellent dishes. His passion for the work grew past the verbal abuses, hot pans, and plates of food, which still came his way outside of the dining public's line of sight. The training manner was *Hell's Kitchen* long before the concept ever made it to television as a reality show.

The big deal was the first day Tell threw a plate *back*. The expectancy for cook-graduates was that they would spend six to eight months at different hotels and positions as they progressed over three years toward complete chef status. Tell's reputation for food-preparation excellence, knife skills, and an intense desire to learn preceded his training résumé and made him a sought-after sous chef among the better executive chefs of Europe, according to his letter of testimony dated March 15, 1963.

The venerable Hotel Krone, in the tiny town of Bad Liebenzell in the Black Forest, offered almost two hundred years of service through the same family lineage before Tell began his next workstation there on October 20, 1966. People booked nights at the Krone from near and far, not only to reap the benefits of the famous hot-springs (German "bad" means "bath" in English), but also to dine on its excellent food and be treated to some of the finest service available in Germany.

Tell continued at the Krone until he accepted a higher-ranked assignment at the Restaurant Fent in Berlin from November 16, 1964, through February 16, 1965. He may also have worked at the restaurant atop of Kaufhaus des Westens (KaDaWe—the best commercial retail store establishment in West Berlin in 1961), which offered the finest cooking and table service in Germany.

Demand for Tell's services expanded by word of mouth, and for short stints he worked in different countries. Along his path he left his mark on palates and patrons. People loved the six-foot-three curly-haired chef who appeared from the shadows of the kitchen and poured out lively jokes on patrons as quickly as he refilled their wine glasses—his clientele never minding the higher bar charges.

Television had not discovered Chef Tell, but European gourmands had. He was now an international culinary sensation on word-of-mouth reputation alone.

In 1962, the year that John Glenn soared into orbit in *Friendship 7*, President John F. Kennedy visited West Berlin to meet with Mayor Willy Brandt and discuss a Soviet military buildup in East Berlin.

Kennedy stayed at the Kempinski while in Berlin, and Tell anchored a small crew that offered large catering services there. As Fate would have it, Kennedy walked into the kitchen late one afternoon and struck up a conversation with the crew, Tell among them. He said he wanted to try some new foods. Tell and the others cooked up some "really hefty German food including pig's knuckles," which Kennedy liked.

A side-burned Tell holds court in the Kempinski kitchen.

In October of the same year, Kennedy confronted the Soviets, who had provoked the entire Western world into the Cuban missile crisis. A little more than a year later, he was assassinated in Texas. The incident was a matter of deep concern and cause for grief for Tell, whose meeting with Kennedy had fanned within him an intense desire to become a U.S. citizen. Hearing the news of Kennedy's death devastated Tell. This second important death in his life wounded him, and he sought relief from his feelings on top of a gasthaus bar stool.

Tell had been drinking for hours when he slipped into the driver's seat of his car. He knew somewhere in his mind that he shouldn't drive in that condition, but he wasn't in control. He didn't get very far. His car jumped the curb and crashed through the plateglass front window of a tavern across the street from the parking lot he'd just exited. Suddenly awake and alert, he knew he had to think fast. Stepping out of the car, he avoided the glass shards strewn across the ground, walked to the bar, and sat down.

"Bartender, bring me six shot glasses and a bottle of cognac," he demanded with cash in his hand. The bartender lined up the glasses and poured six shots of cognac, which Tell consumed before the police arrived.

"No, officers, he was sober when he crashed. He seemed very upset, like in shock, but he was sober when he crashed. He had a bunch of shots, though, before you arrived," eyewitnesses told the police. In front of about forty witnesses Tell had established an alibi. A DUI conviction at that point likely would have altered his entire career.

Sober the next day, Tell realized that he had gotten lucky the previous night. He decided to take a small vacation and headed to Max's home for some fatherly advice.

Shortly after, back on the straight and narrow, Tell won a large following among gourmands and captured the hearts of single women. Despite 80–100 hours a week spent at work in fast-paced kitchens, he made an impressive target for adventurous females with taste buds for a good man, but he had little time to indulge their whims—that is, until he spotted one particular blonde hair stylist in Bad Liebenzell in the spring of 1963.

Helga looked every bit the blonde bombshell that she was—Sixties-bob hairdo, svelte figure, fetching smile and eyes. The day she walked across the lakeside park in front of Tell, he was taken by how the warm hug of the sun's rays highlighted her beautiful features.

Helga, however, was not open to the upstart chef's advances. In fact, she was dating someone else. Although Cupid was in the air for Tell, who drove around town with the top down on his Mercedes 280 SL convertible to get her attention, her heart seemed settled elsewhere.

By leaving small notes every day at Helga's beauty salon workstation, each with slightly more information about how he felt for her than the last, Tell captured Helga's curiosity enough for her to wonder if he was for real in the kitchen. After all, a hair stylist stood all day long; finding a man willing to do the cooking was not such a bad offer.

Once the bait was set and the hook taken, Tell cranked the reel. In August of 1964, Helga relocated with Tell to Berlin and took a position at a high-end salon. Their romance blossomed. On November 12, 1964, they married in a civil ceremony before a Berlin court justice. The next two years proved to be a whirlwind of work and play for the newlyweds.

Helga and Tell

As Tell worked toward executive chef status, he cooked for the Queen of England—at least his team did. The Queen's meal protocol was rigid. Her meals were prepared in triplicate. Her personal valet alone served her, after he had pretested the food. No single chef could take personal credit for having cooked the Queen's meal in this wise. And the Queen never ate poisoned food.

According to Tell, he also worked short stints at the historic Strand Hotel in Stockholm, Sweden, and at a renowned French Alps one hundred-year old resort, L'Auberge Du Pere Bise, in the lakeside town of Talloires, France, where Bridget Bardot, Jean Paul Belmondo, and other world-renowned celebrities vacationed.

Those heady times filled with travel opportunities and romantic locales were tailor-made for a young couple in love, romantic enough to start a family.

Wedding Day

15

WAKE UP CALLS

"Sie schienen aus dem Nichts zu kommen."
("She seemed to come from nowhere.")

—Chef Tell

With Helga pregnant in October 1966, the couple opted for a return to the familiar small-town environment of Bad Liebenzell. Once there, they combined their August 1967 wedding ceremony with the baptism of their newborn son, Torsten, who would turn out to be Tell's only child.

Tell returned to the Hotel Krone, this time as sous chef. When Tell worked there earlier, well before his son was born, he often visited the owners' home and played with their son and his miniature railway display. Tell loved children, and the whole family liked him. Back then, sometimes on his days off, he took both of their children, Jürgen and Doris, to the public pool. At work with the same family again, he was more than an employee at the Krone; the owners considered him a part of their family.

On a gray winter day, the hotel owner's mother—an older woman without a driver's license—desired to get home from Bad Liebenzell to Calw (the birthplace of Hermann Hesse), which was only eight

Tell with baby son Torsten

kilometers away. With free time available between his morning and evening shifts, Tell volunteered to drive her.

Tell drove his compact hatchback Renault R4, mindful of his passenger seated beside him and the two others seated in the back.

Tell and Torsten at two years.

Though wind-driven, dry snow shifted across the pavement, the surface was straight and level. A woman driving a Mercedes car from the opposite direction blindly attempted to pass a truck in front of her, pulled into Tell's lane, and drove straight into them on the narrow road. In the horrendous crash, both vehicles were demolished.

Tell's passengers had not fared well. The elder woman, thrown from the car through the windshield, died on the spot. The passengers in the

Tell survived, three died

back seat suffered fatal injuries as well. Tell somehow survived, but not without permanent hip and facial damage. Surgeons replaced his left hip—which at the time was an adventurous surgery fraught with danger.

Given that there were no seat belts in use, only a miracle had saved Tell. Lying in a hospital bed, his face was wrapped and swollen—he would never look the same—so much that his father did not recognize his bed-ridden son on his first visit. Tell wondered why he survived. Mental impressions of his life to that point flashed through his mind—birth under bombs, mother's suicide, an uncle's demise, and now a first-hand brush with death coming straight at him almost harmlessly—nothing made sense.

Is some sort of angel looking over me? Am I missing something greater here? Tell wondered.

The unknown reasons as to why everyone else in that car had not survived the accident while he did haunted him as much as the suddenness of the accident. The unexpected turn of events scared him. With a wife and baby son to care for, he understood that this was no time to take chances. *Even kitchens where I work are dangerous places,* he thought.

The ugly scepter of Death had swiped its cold scythe across the familial ties between the Krone's owners and Tell's family. The raw scars and emotional memories would never disappear. Tell soon decided to move his career forward elsewhere. To his credit, his letter of testimony for his services dated April 11, 1969, continued his long string of recognitions of the glowing qualities that he had brought to each position held: quick to work, thorough with food preparations and cleanup, and extremely honest.

Tell heeded the advice he'd received from his father, "Get as much schooling as you can before it's too late; you may need something else to fall back on." Using what money he received from the accident settlement, he moved his family into the safe confines of the university town of Heidelberg for the next three years. There, he worked and studied hard for a better future.

Pipe-smoking survivor

16

PEPPER PORK AND GOLD

"Man kann sich eine Zukunft auf eine Ausbildung.'
("You can build a future on an education.")
—Max Erhardt

Master Chef certification—offered two to three nights weekly from six until nine and followed by more written, oral, and practical exams—required another three years of classes. Tell went for it, despite the hours he also poured into cooking locally.

By February 1970, he graduated from the local *Hotelfachschule* (cooking trade school), having passed all certification requirements for *Küchenmeister* (Master Chef) at the Industrie and Handelskammer in Baden Baden, a branch of the IHK Chamber of Commerce in Karlsruhe. He then lent his teaching skills to classes in the *Gewerbeschule* (trade school) in Calw to assist younger chefs with their apprenticeships.

In the same year, he captained the West German national cooking team of six chefs in the Cooking Olympics competition held during Oktoberfest, and his team won the gold medal. In the competition, Tell created a new dish, which he called SchweinePfeffer (Pepper Pork)—thinly sliced fresh pork strips cooked with chopped onions in heavy

Master Chef certificate

cream and oil, presented with sliced mushrooms, salt, and cracked peppercorns, cooked down (deglazed and reduced) with white wine and topped with fresh parsley. Later, the dish earned Tell a personal gold medal for Outstanding Performance in the International Art/Cooking Show in Stuttgart.

Capping a great year, Master Chef Erhardt took the prize of Germany's youngest-ever Chef of the Year. He stood at the top of the German world of culinary arts after his whirlwind of accomplishments. Any European restaurateur would have opened their front or back door and asked him to step inside and work for him if he would name his price; if he would tempt and tantalize their customers' palates and imaginations.

Tell opted to share his honors with his beautiful wife and son. Soon,

1970 Cooking Olympics

hard memories faded into the recesses of his mind, and he felt happy. He had survived long enough to create a family with which he could have a future. He was no longer alone and no longer hungry. That elusive peace he had sought for so long had *apparently* found a home in his life. What could possibly unsettle such a strong foundation bound to bring to his family fame and fortune in Europe?

In a word: infidelity.

21. BUNDESFACHSCHAU
für das Hotel- und Gaststättengewerbe
Stuttgart, 22.-29. Oktober 1970

URKUNDE

HERR FRIEDEMANN ERHARDT

erhält für
hervorragende Leistungen
bei der Kochkunstschau
eine

Goldmedaille

Stuttgart, am 29. Oktober 1970

Deutscher Hotel- u. Gaststättenverband e.V.   Preisgericht   Stuttgarter Ausstellungs GmbH
Bad Godesberg

National Gold Medal, Cooking Olympics

17

SOUR GRAPES TO LACE CURTAINS

"Ich habe ein Faible für Bekleidung aus Seide."
("I have a soft spot for silk clothing.")

—Chef Tell

A working chef approached by a beautiful woman is vulnerable. He is not just an artist at work, moving at great speed; he is often tired and defenseless. Sexual tensions stoked by alcohol lead to come-ons, which end up as affairs—not because the chef disregards women—because he cares *too much* to say no.

* * *

Despite several years with Helga and fatherhood, Tell faltered in the face of temptation. A woman named Ilse came after him, and together they bashed the sturdy keel of his marriage upon the jagged rocks of betrayal.

Upset and remorseful, Tell discovered too late that the disciplines of his training had not prepared him for the social pitfalls of his position. The conflicting emotions he felt were new and left him clouded and uncertain. Figuring he had no right to go back home to Helga, he asked Ilse to marry him. But she rejected him.

Alone and damaged, having no other choice, Tell admitted his sin to Helga. The damage to her heart and trust proved fatal. On August 4, 1971, Helga and Tell's vessel capsized—they divorced. Unfortunately, Torsten, too young to have any say, bore the brunt of the decisions they made.

Tell's right of visitations at a critical time of his son's life was limited to two days every two weeks. The best he could do to spend time with his boy involved trips to the local zoo. However, Torsten and Tell made memories together in the shiny convertible 280 SL Mercedes.

* * *

Tell sought redemption by pouring himself back into his work in Bad Liebenzell. In his free time he worked to master a second discipline— German wines.

German vineyards sheltered by the mountains of western Germany provided a great place for the young chef to study. Long hours absorbed in the study of the subtle nuances of German wineries and French grapes—France bordered the Black Forest region to the west—yielded rewards of taste and knowledge well worth his efforts.

Tell wished to be a good representative for his country's wine reputation and worked to play his part in its expansion. Because of postwar sentiments, although German whites were, in fact, very good, they were not considered among the best in the world. Over time, however, Germany approached the top ten of wine-producing countries in the world, generating in excess of 168,000,000 gallons annually from 201,000 acres of vineyards.

Tell studied every reference and history book that he could find on German grapes and wines. He spent every spare moment outside along the Rhine River. Vineyards there bore sweet, golden-colored *Müller-Thurgau* and red rust-tinged *Blaue Spätburgunder* (Pinot Noir) grapes and scores of other varieties worthy of the respected labels that were placed on their bottles. The grapes, he learned, were high in acid levels, making German white wines very crisp and dry. River-modulated temperatures complemented the slate-laden soil that absorbed the sun's heat and contributed to the elegance of the German wines Tell studied.

Wherever the wine experts of the area lived and worked, Tell created connections and absorbed as much as they would share with him.

On a Saturday in early July 1972, Tell walked among thousands of Freiburg residents and single-day tourists eager to taste the first vintages of the year. The free-market community in the heart of the wine-growing region hosted the annual event. The mood was festive and carefree, though everyone avoided falling or stepping into one of the free-flowing water gutters *(Bächle)* in town, lest they suffer the legendary consequence after falling into a *Bächle*—having to marry a Freiburger.

His wine tasting completed, perhaps with a glass or two of his favorites, Lauffener Katzenbeisser's Schwarzrieling and Canstadter Zuckerle—the latter named after the Stuttgart suburb where he'd grown up—Tell headed home in the 280 SL through the Black Forest at dusk. By day, the sunshine glinted between the tall conifers like reflections off brook riffles, by nightfall raindrops fell. Having secured the top on the vehicle, Tell turned on his wipers and maneuvered the twists and turns of the wet pavement with both hands upon the wheel. He was in a good mood. Feeling fulfilled, he whistled a few notes from his favorite Beethoven symphony, "Ta, da-da-dah . . . ta, da-da-dah."

As serendipity would have it, around the next bend, dramatic changes for Tell unfolded.

From the moment he laid eyes on the distressed beauty with a flat tire—the woman, not the car—Tell's journey through life was altered, although he did not know it at the time. He only knew what his eyes saw. The woman in front of him looked curvaceous under her rain-soaked silk blouse and shorts, and she looked like she needed some help. He slowed and pulled over to see what he could do.

Tell hopped out of his car and was rummaging through her trunk before they exchanged any words. In minutes, her car was jacked up about as high as her blood pressure. She scanned over her Good Samaritan's tall and tanned physique, thinking, *He's as German as they come.* She also adored his take-charge attitude.

With the flat tire replaced and the spare parts squared away in the trunk, Tell saluted the stranger and was about to take his leave when a lightning bolt flashed and cracked a tree nearby. The ear-splitting thunderclap frightened the startled woman, who pushed against him. A different kind of electricity rifled through both of them. Speechless, they kissed.

Tell broke away and asked her name.

"Janet," she replied in English, flustered. "I don't know why I did that."

"What? You mean kiss me? You were thanking me, right?" said Tell in German as he stepped away in the direction of his car.

Janet felt less embarrassed after his reply, but she could not deny the attraction she felt for the man who had come to her rescue. Despite the language barrier, they could communicate.

"You didn't tell me your name."

"Tell. My name is Tell. Everyone around here knows me. Just ask. I see you."

Janet was vacationing in Germany and was staying at a little hotel operated by friends of her parents. Later that evening, she sat at the bar and talked with them. A swarthy German blond entered and, after small talk, stated he wished to take her out. The proprietors said he was just being friendly, so she took him up on his offer, albeit with cautionary measures.

"I made him leave his license number and told them to call the police if I wasn't back in two hours. We went out for a drink, and there was Tell again," she said.

Tell walked into the café and found Janet seated with the other man. He invited himself to their table and soon discovered that the man was a blind date.

"I know this guy. He is so cheap. So I say to everybody we will go to another place and have a drink and dance. Then when we get there, I tell the bartender all the drinks are on me. Right away the guy switches from beer to cognac," Tell remembered.

Once the man had too many, Tell pounced. "I can't see you letting this drunken man drive you," he said to Janet. "Please, allow me to take you with me."

Janet followed without hesitation, since she would be one of several patrons that Tell offered to drive home that night. She had by now seen and heard plenty of evidence that he was, indeed, a known commodity—the man locals called their "favorite chef."

Tell recalled what happened next: "I drop everybody off, including my girlfriend, then I go back to that little hotel, and there is Janet still talking to her parents' friends. And I go in."

How they had met on the road, the coincidence of their meeting again the same evening, and the alcohol consumed opened Janet to Tell's soft embrace at her doorway. She asked him inside.

Near midnight, an amber glow from a street lamp streamed across her hotel room. Lace curtains fluttered softly. Lying by Tell's side, she told him her name, "Janet Louise Nicoletti, former Miss Philadelphia. Single."

They laughed.

Three months later, Janet and Tell decided to get married in America and announced their intentions to the townspeople. Not wanting to lose their favorite son and chef, the locals expressed overt resentment against Nicoletti. Tensions mounted.

"It was terrible in this little town because it was a resort, and I was the 'rich' American lady, five years older than he, coming to take their chef away. Tell was the big selling point of the main hotel restaurant. One man just walked up the street and started yelling at me—luckily I couldn't understand a word. Then he spit, right on the ground in front of me, and I understood that. I wasn't rich—I grew up in Germantown and my family owned a hoagie shop—but I did work for Marriott."

Tell put her on a flight bound for Philadelphia and soon after followed.

Tell and former Miss Philadelphia Janet Nicoletti

18

TRANSITIONING TO AMERICA

"Ich bin ein Koch. Die Messer sind für meine Arbeit."
("I'm a chef. The knives are for my work.")
—Chef Tell

As his twenty-ninth birthday approached, Tell sat alone in economy class on an Icelandair DC-10 bound for Philadelphia, Pennsylvania—his American dreamland. With two suitcases in the luggage hold and $600 in his pocket, he felt hopeful and happy. He didn't know that he was headed straight for a jail cell.

As a professional chef, Tell would never travel without his knives. Weary but happy, he stepped off the plane onto U.S. soil, retrieved his luggage, and entered Customs with his visitor visa in one hand and his custom set of knives packed inside one of the suitcases in the other.

Until the case was opened in front of the agent, he did not realize that he had forgotten to declare them. Asked what they were for, he told the agent in broken English with a heavy German accent that he was a chef and "the knives are for my work."

Wrong answer—naiveté just made a bad situation worse. For Tell, a spaghetti-western aficionado of sorts, High Noon had arrived.

Immigrants attempted to smuggle contraband into the country every day, and now a large German citizen with undeclared knives had entered America without a work visa. To the Port of Philadelphia agent, who could not look the other way, Tell was just another anomaly. He was taken into custody and hauled off to a Philadelphia jail.

Hours later, when Nicoletti bailed him out, Tell thought he was looking at deportation. Without her celebrity pull, he may well have been returned to Germany the next day. The misunderstanding cleared quickly once she came to his rescue, and he was allowed to remain in the States, albeit without his custom knife set.

How ironic was it that the very port that shipped millions of life-supporting C.A.R.E. packages to Germany, including assistance to the Erhardt family, almost became a career-killing nightmare for the exhilarated immigrant?

His dream-come-true-gone-awry moment averted, Tell felt like he owed Nicoletti big time. "When I come to America I can't speak English, so I need Janet to talk to me. I could understand her," he said.

Steadfastly sure that coming to America was the best decision he ever made, he continued to consider that fame and fortune would soon be his.

* * *

On February 20, 1973, Tell got a job through Janet's connections at the Marriott. He spent several weeks at the Chicago Marriott in April 1973 and in that short time was commended for his strong support. Beginning September 21, 1973, he worked for Marriott's Philadelphia Motor Hotel as complex chef in charge of four restaurants for six months at $200 weekly while waiting for his regular papers from Germany so that he could obtain a work visa. In that time, he fielded offers at $30,000–$40,000 annually, but time dragged on.

On a required trip back to Germany, he found that Marriott had been stalling the action to keep him working for them on a low wage. On February 25, 1974, having quit the Marriott position on the day he returned from Germany, Tell stood in Rittenhouse Square Park in Center City Philadelphia and stared across South Eighteenth Street at the famed Barclay Hotel. The heart of the city known as the "Home of the Liberty Bell" beckoned him to his next job interview.

September 21, 1973

To: Whom It May Concern

This is to certify Mr. Freidman P. Erhardt, is employed
with Marriott Corporation, at the Marriott Motor Hotel
in Philadelphia, Pa. in the capacity of Complex Chef,
who is responsible for food production for four restaurants.

Mr. Erhardt has been working for Marriott since
20th February 1973.

Respectfully,

Robert E. Gordon
Director of Personnel
Philadelphia Marriott

REG/b

PULCO / ATLANTA / BERKELEY, CALIF. / BOSTON / CHICAGO / CINCINNATI / CLEVELAND / COLUMBUS / DALLAS / FT. WAYNE / HOUSTON / LOUISVILLE
MIAMI / MINNEAPOLIS / NEW ORLEANS / NEW YORK CITY • ESSEX HOUSE / PHILADELPHIA / SADDLE BROOK, N.J.
SCOTTSDALE, ARIZ. • CAMELBACK INN / ST. LOUIS / WASHINGTON, D.C. / ANN ARBOR '72 / DENVER '73 / KANSAS CITY '74
LINCOLNSHIRE, ILL. '74 / LOS ANGELES '73 / MILWAUKEE '72 / NEWPORT BEACH, CALIF. '74 / PITTSBURGH '72 / TORONTO '74

Tell works for Marriott.

This is living, this is

Marriott

HOTELS

May 1, 1973

Mr. Friedemann Erhardt
Marriott Motor Hotels

Dear Tell:

   I would like to take this opportunity to thank you for
all of your help during the past several weeks. Your
professionalism and sincere interest in your job are to be
admired. Philadelphia should consider themselves very
fortunate to obtain your services and there is no question
in my mind that you can contribute greatly to their overall
success.

   Again, thanks for your assistance. It has been a
pleasure having you with us and we look forward to working
with you again in the not too distant future.

                    Sincerely,

                    CHICAGO MARRIOTT

                    Manfred Mork
                    Director of Food & Beverage

MM/cw

May 1, 1973: Tell commended by Chicago Marriott.

19

ONE DREAM COMES TRUE

"Endlich bin ich ein Chefkoch in Amerika."
("At last, I am an executive chef in America.")
—Chef Tell

Philadelphia's Barclay Hotel was one of America's most fashionable and elegant hotels—the place to dine in 1974. Anybody who was "anybody" stayed or dined there, as far back as the late nineteenth century. Irish-American millionaire, builder, and native son of Philadelphia John McShain owned the Barclay and hosted the city's most glittering high-society parties. McShain was a celebrity in his own right. He had a hand in the design and building of the Pentagon and Jefferson Memorial; the John F. Kennedy Center for the Performing Arts; the Library of Congress annex; Washington National Airport; and the 1950–51 reconstruction of the White House.

The hotel's guest list read like a Who's Who "A-List"—the Queen of England, several U.S. Presidents, Princess Margaret, the Emperor of Japan, local and national politicians, and as many Philadelphia, New York, and Hollywood stars as a galaxy might hold. The place known as

237 on the Square was the place to see and be seen, a home away from home for luminaries like Yul Brynner, Peter Ustinov, and Henry Fonda.

Standing in the park facing the Barclay, Tell also thought about the job interview he had earlier that morning. A history buff, he had interviewed for employment at the Downingtown Inn Resort, located west of city center.

Known as Milltown for its water mills, Downingtown during the Revolutionary War harbored food supplies and provisions for American troops under the name of Downing's Town, since Thomas Downing and his son, John, industrialized the mill sites. The resort's location situated on the spot where they built the first tavern on the unsettled western frontier, and near to Nicoletti's leased apartment on Philadelphia's Main Line, made the resort a natural first choice for Tell to seek employment. The Main Line, named for the Pennsylvania Railroad line, was a suburban enclave for some of the city's most affluent and influential residents.

Philadelphia's Channel 6 Action News interviews Tell.

Tell's interview at the resort, he thought, had gone well, but, in fact, he was turned down for reasons beyond his control: he had no experience with cooking prime rib, a specialty of the house. However, Nicoletti, a catering manager with connections at the Barclay, hoped the limelight would shine brighter upon both of their careers if Tell worked there. In turn, for her help in getting him out of jail the night he'd arrived, Tell felt he owed her at least the interview at the Barclay.

He crossed the street and walked through the Barclay's front door. Within minutes, his new set of knives was arranged on the kitchen countertop in front of him as he awaited the hiring committee's first request.

Barclay management liked to draw on talented personnel with obvious skills and enthusiasm, and Tell had both in spades. Twenty minutes later, halfway through the cooking audition, the executive chef held up his hand. He and his committee had seen and eaten enough. Tell was hired on the spot.

"The bearer of this letter, Friedemann Erhardt, executive chef has a position at The Barclay Hotel. [. . .] Your cooperation will be much appreciated," wrote William Trimble, general manager of the Barclay, to his executives on February 1, 1974.

Tell was at last an executive chef in America. By the end of the day, News Channel 6 aired the first interview and introduced him to Philadelphia. He didn't know it at the time, but they had set in motion a long string of television appearances that evening.

The Barclay

RITTENHOUSE SQUARE EAST
PHILADELPHIA 3

OFFICE OF THE
GENERAL MANAGER

AREA CODE 215
KINGSLEY 5-0300

February 25, 1974

TO WHOM IT MAY CONCERN:

The bearer of this letter, Friedemann Erhardt,

Executive Chef has a position at The Barclay

Hotel which requires him to travel a distance

of over a 100 miles per 24 hour period to satisfy

the requirements of his job.

It is essential for Friedemann Erhardt, to have

gas at all times.

Your cooperation will be much appreciated.

Sworn to and subscribed before me
this 25 day of Feb. 1974

Harvey B Gilbert

Notary Public
My Commission expires April 27, 1974

Sincerely,

William Trimble

William Trimble
General Manager

February 25, 1974: Tell becomes executive chef of the Barclay Hotel.

20

WHAT WERE THE ODDS?

"Never be afraid to try something different."
—Henry Fonda

A rabbit's foot, which Tell had kept in his pocket since he was a kid, had worked magic for him on many occasions. Inside the Barclay it worked even better. The good-luck charm placed him in the kitchen on the night an impeccably dressed gentleman, sporting a ribbon sash across his chest and a shiny medal around his neck, walked into the galley. The new menu had intrigued him, and he hoped to find the new European chef in the kitchen.

Tell inquired about the man's impressive hardware. *In perfect German*, the guest answered with a request for several German canapés and other dishes, which Tell hastened to prepare. The gentleman also explained that the medallion was a UNICEF (United Nations International Children's Emergency Fund, now United Nations Children's Fund) honor he'd received.

Under the watchful eye of Tell at the stove, the patron stepped closer to where the food was cooking and sniffed the aromas deeply. Waving his arms with a flourish and, with a smile upon his lips, he rolled his eyes up to the heavens. Tell watched him as he tended to the food.

The two dramatically different gentlemen—an ebullient chef with a thick German accent and an apparently straight-laced English actor (or so he would seem at first, until he made you laugh—and he could make anyone laugh)—were the odd couple.

The actor, writer, dramatist, and regular fixture on television shows and lecture circuits had earned three Academy and three Emmy Awards, a Golden Globe, a Grammy, and a BAFTA Award. He was nominated for two Tony awards, had received numerous governmental awards, and was also a composer of concert works and film scores. He correctly was singled out as a Renaissance Man. At the moment, though, he was both hungry and delighted as Tell placed before him, right there in the kitchen, an excellent presentation of the foods he craved.

Peter Ustinov was fawned over, not only for his deliciously dry humor and miraculous acting portrayed in *Quo Vadis*, *Spartacus*, and *Topkapi*, but also for his cerebral involvement on the world stage as Goodwill Ambassador for UNICEF. A raconteur, he delivered to Tell multi-accented, comedic impressions between large bites of food—a spontaneous roasting of Philadelphia politicians that he'd met. His audience of one, Tell, roared.

When he finished his monologue, Ustinov cocked an eye and stared at Tell. He pulled out a musical pocket watch from his vest pocket and said, "When the chimes finish, begin." Straight out of a Hollywood screenplay, the gauntlet was laid down.

Tell responded, "*For A Few Dollars More.*"

Ustinov laughed, "We shall, indeed, get along splendidly, young man." Both men, it turned out, were avid western movie fans.

Tell matched and raised the ante. While Ustinov ate, he turned the tables with a series of one-liners and ribald kitchen anecdotes. Ustinov laughed until his hankie dabbed at the tears in his eyes.

Laughter emanated from the Barclay kitchen to the wee hours of that night. Tell's rabbit foot was alive and well in America.

* * *

Henry Fonda noted the executive chef insignia on Tell's jacket as the two men rode the elevator. He made a request:

"Sir, when dining in my suite for breakfast, I usually dine alone, and it just bores me. Would you like to join me in the morning and keep an old actor company once in a while?"

Tell answered, "I tell you, Mr. Actor, Mr. Henry Fonda, I can even cook for you some special Eggs Benedict." Unknown to Fonda, Tell had been privy to a list of the actor's favorite dishes.

Fonda's eyes lit like fireworks, and he smiled, "I prefer Eggs Benedict. What do you say to 6:45 tomorrow morning?"

"Why so late?" Tell joked.

The next morning, and for several days after, Tell and Fonda conversed over breakfast. Fonda was nearly seventy but still a working actor. On recent days he had worked on a comedic western, *The Cheyenne Social Club,* with long-time friend and early-career roommate Jimmy Stewart. The movie—a romp depicting an aging cowboy's inheritance of a successful brothel—fascinated Tell, not only for its content, but also because of the way Fonda related its plot to him.

Fonda and Tell discovered they were quite alike. Each came from tough backgrounds, had made their own breaks, and loved to entertain. Each was renown within their respective professions. The exchange provided good company for Henry Fonda and a half-century of Hollywood anecdotes for Chef Tell. However, Fonda's final words in their last meeting perked up Tell's ears more than anything they had shared to that point.

Fonda shared with Tell what would later be his key to success on American television: "Never be afraid to try something different."

As Tell stepped off the elevator on the bottom floor, the actor's advice replayed in his mind: *never be afraid to try something different.*

* * *

What were the odds that anyone else other than Chef Tell might have stepped into such opportune meetings with Ustinov and Fonda? For that matter, what were the odds that anyone like Tell would?

In short order, the number of Tell's celebrity friends and acquaintances expanded. Among them was Yul Brynner, the actor born in Russia and educated in China who performed *The King and I* more than 4,200 times. He was a demanding guest with a penchant for one particular type of Washington State apple, which Tell took the trouble to find and keep on hand for him. Princess Margaret, the unpretentious Royal—her only peccadillo was fresh mint in her red wine—who found Tell's story-telling as charming as his cooking, said, "Whatever you would like to cook for me would be well suited to me, Chef."

* * *

Tell's favorite ride to the Barclay

Tell's days at the Barclay were numbered, however. The relationship between Tell and the general manager of the hotel broke down over minor disagreements, leading to a couple of incidents that gave management enough reasons to part ways with Tell.

"I walk through the dining room in my chef's uniform, and this is the greatest disgrace that ever happened in the history of the Barclay."

Tell was particularly proud of his uniform. "If I walk around like this, people think I'm a doctor because I'm dressed all in white, and they see a thermometer sticking out of my short pocket. It's a meat thermometer. And I go everywhere in my uniform. If people don't like it, tough. Somebody calls me to a party, wants me to come over for an hour, I go dressed like this. I drive to work like this. I move around like this. I shop like this. I am a chef, this is my uniform—this is a part of me."

Uniform or not, there was no getting around the Barclay's general manager. "Later, we fight about the menu—he wants stuff like chicken ala king. I tell him I will cook chicken ala king. I will cook anything. I just don't like it on the menu," Tell said. Instead, he presented French fare to the Barclay's diners.

About the same time, Marriott called and wanted Tell to work for them again. He told them he will never work for Marriott again, no matter what. But they kept calling with better offers with more money attached.

Meanwhile, Tell, the historian, soaked up every tale that he ever heard about elite Americans and their rags-to-riches histories. The phrase "Only in America" took on a ring of truth to him, for his life was becoming its living proof (little did he know how deeply). One of the couples he'd met in passing at the Barclay, Helen and Russell Baum, would figure prominently into his life in a few short years. In fact, several important people would become a part of his life.

21

THE FINE PALATE

"Chef Tell était une spéciale, homme très spécial."
("Chef Tell was a special, very special man.")
—Master Chef Georges Perrier

Authors and poets opine that the French are the most romantic men in the world. Certainly their cuisine is one of the oldest, their chefs among the most-respected. Peter von Starck, the son of a prominent Philadelphia lawyer, knew that when he hopped a transatlantic PanAm 707 in search of adventure in southern France in 1963. At the celebrity playground and dining spa in Provence, L'Oustau de Baumanière, he met Georges Perrier, who was an apprentice there.

Four years later, no French haute cuisine could be found in Philadelphia other than in two area gourmet restaurants. Only the bistro Janine et Jeannine, run admirably by Jeannine Mermet and Janine Etienne, offered French cuisine, although The Coventry Forge Inn, considered the area's first French restaurant, had been operated by brothers Wallis and Chuck Callahan in nearby Pottstown since 1953. Von Starck aimed to remedy the vacuum. He returned to France and looked up Perrier.

The twenty-one-year-old Perrier was, by 1967, a classically trained kitchen artist at Fernand Point's three-star, Michelin-rated establishment La Pyramide. Like Tell, he desired to see if he could build a following of his own as a chef. When invited by von Starck to open a Philadelphia restaurant with him, the opportunity to vacation in the U.S. and bring his skills for a year or two to Philadelphia was too good for Perrier to pass up. With von Starck, he planned an elite restaurant that would offer gourmet French cuisine in both classic and avant-garde styles right in downtown Philadelphia. The name they chose for the venture was *La Panetiére* (The Pantry).

Upon its opening, pent-up hopes for local haute cuisine burst forth from Philadelphians. They embraced the menu offerings of the two young men. Within a year, however, the successful operation split apart as the partners were unable to see eye-to-eye on future goals.

Von Starck moved the restaurant to Locust Street. Perrier stayed at the original location under a new name, *Le Bec Fin* (The Fine Palate). Later, with his reputation intact and needing more space, Perrier moved the restaurant to 1523 Walnut Street address, later renowned as one of the country's best locations for classic French cuisine and formidable desserts.

The advent of *La Panatiére* and *Le Bec Fin* signaled the beginning of a Philadelphia food movement, dubbed by *Esquire* magazine as the great "Philadelphia Restaurant Revolution." *Condé Nast Traveler* lent further credence to the uprising, bringing even more attention to the burgeoning world of gourmet cooking in Philadelphia.

Like Perrier, foreign-born master chefs Tell and Soren Arnoldi; Chef Nunzio Patruno and his partners; independent restaurateur Steve Poses; Chef Walter Staib; and Blue Bell Inn restaurateur John Lamprecht imported high-quality standards and introduced a multitude of cuisines. The revolution was underway. Like Perrier, several of their original plans had been to come and learn the language, enjoy a bit of America, and then return to their respective countries. However, with success in their wallets, they never looked back and never went home. Instead, they carved places in the hearts of Philadelphia gourmands only too happy to have found classic haute cuisine at home, rather than in New York City, a good two hours away by train, or Baltimore and Washington DC, equally as far. Perrier's signature dishes, *Galette de*

Crabe (crab cake) and *Quenelles de Brochet* (pike dumpling with mousse-line), and the uniquely talented skills of this core group of chefs, defined the foundation of Philadelphia's culinary rebirth. Asian-fusion master Susanna Foo would come along a bit later and complete Philadelphia's outreach around the culinary globe.

For Philadelphians, it would only get better from there.

2 2

CATCH A TIGER BY
ITS TAIL

"Grand, magnifique et lumineux."
("Tall, gorgeous, and bright.")

—Chef Perrier

Every chef has two goals—loyal followers and his own restaurant. Tell was anxious to step away from the Barclay's apron strings once he noticed he had groupies. His following was a mixed blend of generations of TV celebrities, movie stars, politicians (local, regional, and state), and captains of the corporate world. He put the word out among his circle that he wished to find a place where he could establish his own brand.

One day, one city official, who loved Tell's cooking so much that he wanted to be able to dine on it more often closer to his home, gave his favorite chef an inside tip. The zoning laws had changed close to where both he and Tell lived and a new Marriott Hotel would soon break ground there. He suggested what would be convenient for Tell would also be convenient for him.

"Perhaps one should at least check it out," he whispered. "I hear they'll put a new restaurant in there."

In late 1974, Marriott once again found the right price to get their man. Tell, at age thirty-two, became the executive chef of the restaurant inside of the brand-new Marriott on City Line Avenue. Within Marriott's system, he was listed a chef-trainee, but that was to assimilate him into their scheme as the executive chef without ruffling feathers. Tell didn't know it then, but his executive duties would reach far beyond the four walls of the Marriott in Philadelphia. Travel, lots of it, was already written into his Marriott agenda.

When the newly minted executive chef held his official grand opening on City Line Avenue, his fiancée was draped on one of his arms for most of the night. The leggy, dark-haired beauty with an engaging smile and pageant-winning good looks turned heads all evening, including that of Chef Perrier, who was a guest of Chef Tell.

Sacre Bleu! Qui est cette femme magnifique? (Who is this magnificent woman?), thought Perrier when he saw who stood next to Tell.

Janet and Tell engaged!

He could not take his eyes off her and he sidled over to introduce himself. He kissed the hand of the five-foot-nine woman towering over his five-foot frame and said, "*Bon soir, mam'selle.*"

When Tell's eyes met Georges' at the same moment, he welcomed the Frenchman's attention. After all, he thought, did they not both admire her good looks? Tell tested Perrier just the same. "What is the difference, Chef Perrier, between virgin olive oil and extra-virgin oil?"

Perrier pondered the question and replied, "Chef, I do not know this one."

"Extra-virgin means she brings along her sister," answered Tell with a laugh, ". . . I'm only sorry that my fiancée does not have one."

When Perrier looked around and then laughed, relief followed. Mutual smiles signaled a friendship in the making.

A Frenchman never forgets a beautiful woman. What impressed Perrier about Nicoletti that night would get summarized, years later, into three words: "Tall, gorgeous, and bright."

Perrier's conversation with Tell on opening night was brief, but the timing of their meeting was significant. Tell's acceptance of a TV offer to appear on the local show *Small Talk* would come just a few short months later. His career decision would not only explode Chef Tell's brand, but also have a positive impact on Perrier's, as well as the rest of the core grouping of Philadelphia restaurateurs.

Nicoletti brought over to Tell a man whom she knew could be of assistance to him. It was Herbert Engelbert, sommelier of the International Wine & Food Society of Philadelphia. The group was founded in London in 1933 by *Legion d'Honneur* recipient André L. Simon (1877–1970). The group's purpose was to bring together like-minded people devoted to going beyond the palate to promote and enjoy a healthy understanding of good food and wine. Philadelphia's chapter was founded in 1952.

In the course of their initial conversation, Tell happened to mention his love for cooking and eating wild boar, which greatly intrigued Engelbert.

"But wouldn't you have trouble finding a purveyor that carries wild boar, Chef Erhardt?" inquired Engelbert.

"Not at all, I know owners of game preserves that are located in northern Pennsylvania, right across from New York State. These guys have wild boar, and you can hunt," Tell replied.

"Well, then, I have a farm near Troy. We could stay at my place overnight and then do a hunt the next day," offered Englebert.

Early one morning in 1975, after the previous day's six-hour drive to the area and the payment of a $180 daily guide fee, the preserves' field guide took Tell and Engelbert to the location where they would most likely find a sounder of wild boar. Once there, he reminded them, "These animals are short-tempered and ferocious when cornered."

Tell got a little nervous when he realized he had only a camera in hand, albeit Engelbert had a hunting rifle. He asked the guide, "What do we do if they charge us?"

"Run, find a tree, and climb it as fast as you can," was the guide's answer.

"Holy shit!" replied Tell as Engelbert's finger twitched on the rifle trigger.

"Remember, Herb, you can't shoot just any boar," Tell said, "I know these animals and I will tell you which one to shoot for the dinner, okay?"

"Yeah, alright, Tell," Engelbert muttered as he looked around for a suitable tree to climb in case he missed.

The guide had explained back at the lodge that an average boar is three to six feet in length, runs fast, can weigh 110–200 pounds, and is coated with bristles and a deep mat of fur that covers dense bones. "Thus, gentlemen," he had concluded, "the intense challenge of your hunter's courage, since only a kill-shot will bring one down. Make your shot count."

The trio waited about thirty minutes before any sign of ground life appeared. The first sounder that showed up was made of five females. None were suitable for the hunt's purpose.

Suddenly, from a rise behind them, another five appeared—this time all male. At the same moment, the men spotted the sounder, its male leader charged in their direction.

"Shoot! Quick shoot!" yelled Tell as the lead male headed toward him.

"Which one?" Engelbert cried out.

"The second one, damn it! Shoot quick!" Tell dropped the camera and backed up.

Engelbert's shot rang true. The second male went down, and the others scattered away from the men. As the shot's echo rang in his clients' ears, the guide dressed the boar carcass in the field and handed the sides of meat to Tell.

Back in his kitchen at the Marriott, Tell's assistants prepped the dinner as he butchered the two-hundred-pound boar. His waitstaff set up the private dining room for the black-tie affair. Forty-five gentlemen members of the IW&FS entered the dining room on that night—"Boys' Night Out Tuesday"—and saw the massive, tusked, boar-head centerpiece that dominated the dining table. The boar head sported a bright red apple in its mouth and a German hunting cap with a note pinned to it that read, KISS ME—I'M GERMAN.

The conversation piece won kudos—a smash hit. Hearty repartee filled the night as the men dined on Tell's boar pâtè, followed by boar consommé, boar stew, and a reduced red wine boar sauce drizzled over inch-thick boar steaks. A different bottle of wine selected by Engelbert accompanied each course.

Due to the first dinner's success, several Tuesday evening gatherings of the IW&FS followed. "We had a fine friendship that really began with that wild boar hunt," Engelbert said. "…Tell was the kind of person, who, once you met him, you would never forget him."

Outside of his restaurateur duties, Tell taught cooking classes and at one point even opened his own cooking school. He taught throughout all of his professional life as a way of exchanging with others for some of the opportunities he received earlier. He also felt it important to help create a "trade awareness" of cooks and chefs as a profession worthy of any talented young person's pursuit. In America, unlike in Europe, kitchen talents were not being formally developed as much as he would have liked.

When the Bellevue Stratford hotel closed from bad publicity fallout surrounding the "legionnaires' disease" incident (later traced to bacteria formed in an underground shelter below the hotel and spread through the air-conditioning system), its retiring French chef was asked to teach for the Charlotte Albertson Cooking School.

He felt, however, that he was too old and truly wanted to retire. He suggested, "a young whippersnapper, Chef Tell." Tell taught sixteen times for Albertson's school and was "extremely well received with his gracious manner, good looks, and his ability to establish a rapport with the students," said Ms. Albertson.

Guided by highly acclaimed music engineer Joseph Tarsia, at Tarsia's Sigma Sound Studios located at 212 North Twelfth Street, a newly famous David Bowie and his band recorded their *Young Americans* album in August 1974. Ziggy Stardust and the Spiders from Mars, the group's latest stage persona, worked up an appetite recording into early morning hours.

Tell's reputation and skills were high on the list among Philadelphia concierges. Based on a concierge's recommendation, one morning just after sunrise Bowie's group descended upon Tell's Marriott kitchen like, well, like Spiders from Mars. They asked for service, and Tell put up a feast. The band and Bowie returned more than once for his hospitality, thanking him each time. Tell and his crew, as a result, catered several of the band's parties.

Philly concierges and taxi drivers took note of the master chef who delivered more than what people expected, even on short notice. Tell's reputation flourished and prospered in the city. Celebrity reservations poured in at all hours of the day and night.

Tell realized that the appetites of music stars and their engineers, as well as those of famous actors and politicians, would spread his brand far and wide. With hopes of a coming expansion, he designed a distinctive blue-on-white "Chef Tell" logo for his white chef's jacket. In short order, his celebrity influence burst far beyond the confines of Center City, and his brand recognition traveled coast-to-coast with him.

Of course, Tell couldn't predict his future. He had to concentrate on the tasks at hand at the Marriott where he managed fifteen phones, four secretaries, and six restaurants. "We served six or seven *thousand* meals a day in the Marriott—more in one day than I served all week in any restaurant. We had a conveyor belt for the plates—ten guys on it. One guy places mashed potatoes, another ten peas, another five carrots . . . meat and then gravy," recalled Tell.

Marriott kept its food costs down—a lesson not lost on the still young executive chef's fertile mind. But it could go overboard with the system. "Once we get a new manager of the hotel, and he wants me to buy undersized and un-graded tomatoes, so he can save $7,000 a year. I tell him this is false saving, but he doesn't believe me. Now I am getting fewer slices and rotten tomatoes, so I save them in a big stainless steel tray. Once a week, I walk into his office and say, 'Here are your tomatoes.' I teach him about false economy, but he doesn't like being wrong and becomes my enemy."

Marriott, looking to make both sides happy, had Tell train and mentor company executive chefs in different locations up and down the eastern seaboard, which took him out of town. In each location, he left behind better numbers than before, keeping the parent corporation happy.

On the other hand, Nicoletti remained home in Philadelphia while Tell traveled America, often for weeks at a time. Out of his sight, she met with therapists, who committed her to "rest" homes and prescribed "medications" that altered her already overwhelmed outlook on living. Grueling roadwork tired Tell, and home life wore down Nicoletti—these were mere glimpses of future challenges yet to come.

Still, Tell and his wife worked, saved, and, later, borrowed a $35,000 small-business loan—to open his own place, which had been a treasured dream of theirs.

23

PHILLY TEMPERAMENTS AND SYMBIOSIS

"In keinem anderen Ort der Welt . . . es ist unglaublich."
("In no other place in the world . . . it's incredible.")
—Chef Tell

Philadelphians would argue proudly that they were the toughest dinner crowd to please in the 1970s. After all, Philadelphia's heritage of cuisines and food innovations extended beyond the country's history. If you offered food to Philadelphians and wanted to be considered good, your stuff had to be more than good, day in and day out. In Philly you could be up and flying high one day—the talk of the town—the next day nobody would remember what you cooked for them. A tough crowd, high standards.

Philly was a tough town on several levels. Bribes were considered part of the toolbox and dirty politics a proudly upheld tradition. If you did good business in Center City, you clung to the right purse strings. The right money could buy you anything in this town. Conversely, without access to the right money, doors closed without explanation.

Philadelphia offered no handicaps. Here you *earned* your breaks. You made your own reputation, for better or worse. Ask the NFL franchise Eagles (only one winning season from 1962–1975); the NBA's 76ers (media-tattooed as the "Nine and 73ers" in the midst of a disappointing decade of seasons) or the NHL's Flyers (the team of "God Bless America," a.k.a., "Broad Street Bullies").

Beyond toughness, a spirit of creativity in Philly's long history reigned. The liveliness of the music produced by Kenneth Gamble and Leon Huff, writers/producers of Philadelphia International Records fame was "TSOP"—The Soul of Philadelphia in 1971. The O'Jays, Harold Melvin & The Blue Notes, Teddy Pendergrass, Lou Rawls, The Three Degrees, and Billy Paul, believe it or not, helped to make the food movement a reality. When the spirits of Philadelphia's music makers soared, the restaurateurs scored beautiful notes.

The active tones of the Philly sound brought people to a place where they felt nothing would stop them. "Ain't No Stoppin' Us Now" expressed this esprit de corps. No matter how many backstabbers wished to derail the coming "Love Train," the new cuisine scene in town grooved with the music scene. As people in Philly reawakened their spirits of creativity, they ate, drank, and danced with confidence again in local establishments. Favorite new places to be entertained and dined in Philly popped up, like the popular nightclub and Italian dining establishment The Monte Carlo Living Room on South Street. This would play an integral part in the formal establishment of the culinary renaissance of the city.

The upbeat chords of Philly music blossomed into restaurants and nightclubs across the city and state lines and then emerged nationally. Driven by Philly's musicians and restaurateurs, all eyes, ears, and palates tuned to Philadelphia. *Food & Wine* gave a nod to the emerging Philadelphia palate. The *Washington Post* averred the world might be witnessing a runaway pack of three cuisines, not two—"French, Chinese, and Philadelphia." To many critics, Philadelphia seemed to be "the center of a Great American Restaurant Boom," as New York food writer Jim Quinn wrote in *Philadelphia* magazine.

According to Quinn, all things were possible in this world. "Life, which is merely stranger than fiction, is always more complicated than journalism," he wrote. Taking a page from his logic, nothing could be weird about Philadelphia waking up and becoming the capital of a restaurant boom or the location for the emergence of a new brand of chef personality—embodied first by a German-American Chef Tell. After all, "America," as Quinn put it, ". . . was now a nation that jogs on its stomach."

The driving Philly character trait—to love or hate overtly—played a passionate game inherited from a well deep with multi-ethnic waters. Winner or loser, if you got Philly's attention and made them *like* you, Philadelphians would *love* you. They would deepen their passion for you. You always knew where you stood.

In most towns, only a small percentage of the dining public really cared beyond their taste buds what quality chefs put on their plates. Much less so than in Philadelphia, gourmands traditionally represented a minority. With food in Philly, however, high expectations among white- and blue-collar Philadelphians alike ran like a Mother Lode through the city's veins. Appreciation for cooking methodologies—classic, ethnic, avant-garde, fusion food, whatever—was a given in Philly. Here, the populace *wanted* to love their chefs as deeply as they loved their sports teams.

The City of Brotherly Love's food movement was seeded by its patrons as much as a handful of skilled chefs cooking within city limits— and as much by the *personalities* of those chefs as by Philadelphians' reactions to them. The city's lasting reputation as a gourmet town not only owed a large debt to its people of multi-ethnic origin, who will never be repaid, but to the *personalities* of the 1970s kitchen pioneers, who put the town back on the gastronomic map of the world—Chef Tell and his cronies. No doubt about it, Philadelphia's boom was all symbiosis.

Watch an old football game in Philly and listen when the crowd booed the Philadelphia Eagles (hint: it's when a conservative approach was taken to answer an opportunistic situation). Visiting coaches from other towns, brought in to run the Eagles, needed lessons in what Philly port stevedores knew as gospel—you don't keep all your body parts by acting timidly on the docks and you don't shy away from taking chances to win if you want to keep your job. Tell attracted a large following in the Philly area because he took chances wherever he hung his name out on a restaurant location. Still, at first he had to overcome his own upbringing.

"I was very temperamental when I came to this country years ago. When you come from Germany, everything is black or white. Either something is done the German way or it is wrong. If I would tell somebody something, I would say, 'We do it my way and there is no exception. Shut up, I don't want to know anything else.' I would get very obstinate if things didn't go my way. I wouldn't consider other people. I would say to myself, 'What the hell? I'm the chef.'"

But he got upset stomachs, headaches, and didn't like his job. He thought, *I better do something*. When he did, he ended up more open to suggestions, more flexible.

Because he was always in the news, food-news-loving Philadelphians followed Tell's career. The *Philadelphia Inquirer*, through their scribe Elaine Tait, inked newsprint about Chef Tell every time his career took a new turn. Tell was easy to write about, since he was always pushing some new envelope—a new dish, a new twist for the restaurant, or just tooling around the area at high speeds on his super-charged Kawasaki, which he rode to work daily. A writer's passion and imagination could really take off on the magic carpet that was Tell's flamboyant, flying silk scarf.

But his six-foot-three size and stern face had people thinking he was more serious than he actually was, and he knew it. "Some people take one look and freeze. If I don't smile, I look really mean. People say, 'He has an accent, he is German, he is mean.' But I shrug it off."

Eventually Chef Tell's personality had so changed that when he met another group of Germans, and watched their autocratic, cold demeanor, he had to admit, "I can't stand them."

Pathways to Philadelphians' wallets, purses, and palates opened to Tell as long as he gave them a place they could eat his delicious food and as long as he made his celebrity personality available to them firsthand.

Tell's keys to success in Philly included younger-generation residents from all walks of life who were attracted to him. Following the trends, mingling with hard-working blue-collar people—the inner make-up of most of the city—kept Tell at or near the top of the Philly food chain. Like a chameleon, he changed as much as the public environment changed. With vision and personality, Tell knew with his peers that the dollars this city handed out came from generations of people who wore their sleeves rolled up and whose sweat poured off their brows. He looked forward to putting his name over his own door. Yet, though he would have that, changes in television were underfoot across the nation that would arrive at his doorstep in the form of an opportunity he had not included in his dreams.

24

A MEDIA-ORIC RISE

"Plötzlich weiß jeder, mich."
("All of a sudden, everybody knows me.")

—Chef Tell

Five years back in 1970, TV airwaves were glutted with nationally syndicated reruns and programming which, while very lucrative for the networks, were too expensive for local producers to compete against. A level playing field for local producers simply did not exist. With the passage of the Prime Time Access Rule, Congress mandated the syndicated television market to allow access to local programmers. At its enactment, the legislation leveled the field and made room for TV shows like *Small Talk*, sponsored by Weight Watchers of Greater Philadelphia, and *Dialing for Dollars*, which began on radio in 1939. Even Janis Joplin sang about it in *Mercedes Benz*, "Oh Lord, won't you buy me a color TV? *Dialing for Dollars* is trying to find me."

In 1974, Philadelphia's Channel 29 carried its local-feature, afternoon show *Small Talk* in black and white. WPVI-TV, ABC's Channel 6 in Philly, televised an hour show *Dialing for Dollars* in the mornings five days a week, 10:00 to 11:00 a.m. The appeal was simple: at the beginning, a live show host announced a daily dollar amount a viewer would win if the correct amount was guessed on a random phone call during the show. Once the daily dialing game was played, the rest of the show continued with live celebrity interviews, cooking segments, and demonstrations of featured products, such as recipe books, sets of knives, and more. Advertising in this manner increased ratings and revenue dollars for the local TV station since more people watched the show.

The show's executive producer in 1976, Art Moore, who was working to change the *Dialing for Dollars* show into *AM/Philadelphia*, contacted the Marriott on City Line conveniently located right across the street from his studio and asked an executive chef to do a segment. The part would be an unpaid appearance. The initial chef approached refused to do the show without pay. Tell, however, having overheard the proposition and remembering Henry Fonda's advice, volunteered for the segment. "I don't care if I'm not paid. I'll do it."

Channel 6's *Dialing for Dollars* producer Moore took notice and offered Tell an opportunity to cook on-air if Marriott would provide the food. Marriott was receptive, and Tell's first ninety-second TV cooking demo aired. The station received a flood of phone calls. Half the viewers liked the novelty of his having to cook in ninety seconds or less and they liked Tell; the other half complained about his thick German accent and the speed at which he talked.

When eight hundred letters from the audience deluged the station after airing the one test segment, Moore decided to air another segment, albeit after he and Tell had worked together to improve his speed of speech delivery and, of course, do what they could about the accent.

"We created the show and went looking for a chef to do a cooking segment. Fortunately, after the initial trial, we found we had a chef on our hands who understood the importance and potential of television. Tell 'got it' right away. Even though we prodded him about his accent and joked with him, he rolled with our advice, which helped create his banter on-air with the audiences," said Moore, who further commented upon Tell's personality. "He had a charming, ebullient personality. He was smart, and we saw that what he did worked."

And what Tell did was think on his feet and tell the audience what he was thinking: "People ask me, 'Can you freeze it?' I say, 'Sure, you can freeze anything. . . . It isn't until you thaw it that you run into trouble.'"

One of Tell's earliest taped segments

Their switchboards lit up again after Tell's segment. Ratings climbed off the top of the charts. The concept took off. Moore moved Tell over to the newly formatted show once it started in May 1978. Tell became the resident chef of the program. His monthly appearances multiplied into once-a-week segments, and then to three times a week. The number of fan letters and recipe requests expanded over a three-year period.

Channel 3's popular Group W syndicated show *Evening/PM Magazine* also took note of Tell's success and they offered him a coveted slot. Their show's executive producers called for local hosts—in California Jan Yanehiro was the first co-host—to air five to fifteen minute, on-location segments about local people doing newsworthy things.

Here was a perfect venue for Tell's cooking demonstrations and Tell's personality . . . and a perfect fit for the newly popular show. Syndication allowed for local-feature story sharing among other stations on the network anywhere in the country. Local segments starred local talent and became breeding grounds for on-air talents like Leeza Gibbons and Matt Lauer.

Summoned to an open-air audition in Rittenhouse Square Park across from the KYW-TV building in 1977, the newlywed Tell pitched the camera empty-handed—no props; only personality and imagination. His *Dialing for Dollars* experience paid off: Tell won the audition. While he had to leave *AM/Philadelphia*, since he was aired in prime time access periods on the new show, he soon was on-air in thirty cities. Eventually, 40,000,000 weekly viewers in 114 cities watched him cook three times a week. By the end of the 1970s, *Evening/PM Magazine* ran all over America, and Chef Tell cooked to a nationwide audience. Regular personal appearances on other TV shows like KYW's *The Mike Douglas Show*, *The Dinah Shore Show*, *The Merv Griffin Show*, *The John Davidson Show*, and live cooking demonstrations in shopping malls all over the country followed.

Sarah Casey, food editor for Philadelphia's the *Sunday Bulletin* on September, 18, 1977, wrote, "There's no rest for the Bionic Chef . . . the only way Erhardt does everything without collapsing like a sunken soufflé is because apparently he does not like to sleep."

"I take three days to tape three weeks of shows. Then I travel all over the country to give cooking demonstrations," Tell told reporters for the *Buffalo Courier Express*.

Tell's personality was perfect for the television medium and live venues. He cooked fast and was humorous. His signature, German accent in ninety-second and five-minute segments caught on with a cavalcade of fans all across the nation. They wrote him more than one thousand letters weekly and thronged to his live shows. In Capitol Center in Baltimore, Maryland, Tell drew twenty thousand people to his five live cooking shows in one weekend.

A new breed of TV star was born—the TV showman chef, and Chef Tell Erhardt was its pioneer.

Evening/PM Magazine was thrilled with their new "star," who in 95 percent of their syndicated outlets drew up to a 50 percent market share. Tell was mobbed at airports and required police protection—*for a chef!* Local media stations conducted "Chef Tell Look-Alike" contests in Detroit, Michigan, where he appeared on the popular morning show *Kelly & Company* and in Greensboro, North Carolina, and Dallas, Texas.

Tell's appeal crossed gender and generational lines of television viewers. He was masculine, of sturdy build, and comfortable in the kitchen. Kids thought he was the Swedish Chef from *The Muppet Show* (he wasn't, according to Jim Henson's company), and homemakers loved his teaching methods and simple recipes.

"If a housewife sees me do something in ninety seconds, they figure they can make it in five minutes," Tell said. "Most recipes are overcomplicated, anyway."

Amazingly, Tell had no clue as to how extensive his influence was at the time.

"All of a sudden, everybody knows me. Everybody's my friend," wrote Erhardt. "I just couldn't believe it."

Embracing the camera

The idea of a chef cooking on TV, although not entirely new, was a welcome novelty for viewers attracted to Chef Tell's lively segments. Like whipped cream on a sundae, his humorous lines were sometimes over the top. For example, "Why are radishes red? Because they are ashamed they're so small and hard." But his one-liners only added to the viewers' interest. Tell was different, and he was fun.

"I tell my chefs to wrap up the fish in a newspaper and throw it at me, that way I can say, 'I caught it,'"—one of his throwaway lines as he prepared his food. Schmaltzy, but it worked. His fan base kept growing.

"Tell could cook fast and talk non-stop at the same time—an unusual skill," noted up-and-coming TV personality, Regis Philbin, at a road-show convention. The combination made for interesting television.

Back home, Tell's shows continued to catch the eyes and ears of food writer Elaine Tait in Philadelphia. She perceived correctly that this TV showman chef could explode Philly's restaurant scene. She jotted a memo on her pad to meet with Tell as soon as he returned to town.

25

ELAINE TAIT, THE INQUIRING PHILADELPHIAN

> "Chef Tell was the only TV chef whose food
> actually tasted good."
> —Elaine Tait

Elaine Tait filled dining and entertainment column inches as far back as 1963 for the *Philadelphia Inquirer*. She wrote as the newspaper's food writer and restaurant critic at-large. By the time Tait's column opened, inner-city Philadelphia and its handful of restaurants had dissolved into the quiet mourning of something lost, like so many other cities around the nation. Urban flight in the late 1950s and early 1960s had decimated much of the city's inner identity and culture as the suburbs became more popular.

When *American Bandstand*, Philadelphia's wildly popular music and dance show fixture since 1952, took its production studio lock, stock, and barrel to Los Angeles in February 1964, the Center City's local entertainment and sports scene lapsed, and several restaurants folded in its wake.

Worse, with the peak of the civil rights movement and passage of the Civil Rights Act of 1964, morale should have been at a high, but the flight of white families to the suburbs left a vacuum—a economic base that lowered the morale and expectations of the remaining inner-city residents. Frustration peppered the malaise. Parts of the city were tinderboxes itching to break out in flames on August 28, 1964. The inevitable spark came soon: an incident of police brutality brought public outcry, and riots erupted, destroying many North Philly businesses along Columbia Avenue. To this day, that section of the city has never recovered from the self-inflicted devastation.

Tait wrote about food right through the heat of that toughest of Philadelphia summers. She loved what she did and took a hands-on approach to her work. She ate, cooked, and wrote right inside of her subject's restaurants. She kept large segments of city people hopeful for better times and put bodies in the seats of local restaurants. Her words in print—gospel to her congregation—made her a must-include on the list of people who spearheaded the food renaissance. Tait's powerful prose influenced her readership and heralded the arrival of the chefs who collectively were the most influential circle in Philadelphia's long, gastronomic history.

Tait's time track, and that of the chefs destined to make history in Philly, converged in the mid-1970s. Together they saw an opportunity to make dining out the new, main entertainment in the city. They realized that to reach such a goal, they would have to become a well-coordinated team. Each member would play his or her part. They would put their noses down, work diligently in their kitchens—Tait either in someone's kitchen or at her desk—and cooperate in a spirit of brotherly love.

Tait, the chefs knew, was the one person they could trust to chronicle their run for the prize through her public journal at the *Inquirer*. She got the ball rolling with Chef Tell, whose star shined brightest at the time.

"Chef Tell, did you find Philadelphia, or did Philadelphia find you?" asked Tait.

"Philadelphia found my family back in the 1940s when C.A.R.E. packages arrived from here and helped us survive," Tell replied.

"Could you say, then, that you tasted our food well before we tasted yours?" she asked.

"Sure. By the way, have you been to my restaurant?"

Tait dined anonymously in restaurants before she wrote a column on a restaurant, but she was also known to get closely involved with a chef's food to understand it better, once she knew the quality was there.

"You know I can't tell you that directly, but now that we've met, you'll know when I'm there if you're doing the cooking. My friends tell me what you cook on TV is better live. I'd like to come to your restaurant when you're there, maybe even into the kitchen to see how you work."

"Come anytime. I will show you how we Germans cook."

"German food?" she asked.

"Anything you want—I can do it," Tell assured.

Tell got along with her because Tait got along with most restaurateurs and chefs.

Tait's interest in Chef Tell's emergence amid the arrival of other capable restaurateurs would prove just as vital to the Philadelphia food renaissance as what came out of their kitchens. She wrote about food and wine and restaurants so very well that by the 1970s, her loyal readership hung on every column inch she wrote to know where to dine. In Tait's case, the power of the pen led to the knife, fork, spoon, even the chopstick.

What spilled from inside Tait's fertile, Lithuanian imagination was ensconced in a basic understanding of food preparation, which she learned by doing. No dilettante hack, Tait delivered the real deal with her opinions because she worked hands-on in the kitchens with the chefs. Her discerning palette of words and sentences were brushstrokes—tones and patinas that moved readers out of their homes and into local restaurant chairs. If Tait told her gourmand *Inquirer* subscribers to eat at Chef Tell's, they flocked there and were not disappointed.

"His sharp knife work, cutting wit, and easy recipes made him an indelible fixture of TV pop culture," she reported. In turn, Philadelphians set the channel dial on their TV sets to Tell's segments and lined up outside of his restaurants to watch Tell in action and to taste what was worth the wait.

Tait's column multiplied customers exponentially into places like Tell Erhardt's International Cuisine on Main Line, Perrier's *Le Bec Fin*, Nunzio Patruno's Monte Carlo Living Room, Steve Poses's Frog, John Lamprecht's Blue Bell Inn, and, later, Susanna Foo's Asian Cuisine to dine on new and exciting Philadelphia-style dishes created within different cuisines.

Georges Perrier said about Tait: "We loved Elaine Tait. She loved to come inside the kitchen, loved to learn the cooking."

The group goal to make dining the number one entertainment in the city became a reality in the 1970s when the offspring of old-money denizens from the suburbs of Berwyn, Devon, Strafford, Wayne, Haverford, and Ardmore—the whole Main Line—embraced Tait's recommendations. Tell's recipes, and the wine and food presentations of restaurateurs across the spectrum of the city's rainbow of food establishments, benefited the same palates.

Tait was genuine. When she picked up her pen or pressed the keys of her typewriter, she first washed flour residue off her fingers and set aside her apron. If her column review was submitted with smudges, they were probably grease spots from leftover orts picked up in a kitchen.

Georges Perrier spoke for all chefs when he said, "It was a love affair with Elaine Tait that we had. We would teach her how to cook. She was very smart. She loved food and was interested to see how it was done in the kitchen."

Tell concurred, "Elaine was a major player in Philly. She was the first really good food writer for the *Philadelphia Inquirer*. Importantly, she never hurt a restaurant with her writing. She was fair."

Tait won the coveted Vesta Award for outstanding food pages during her residency with the *Inquirer*. National editors took note of her body of work and often published her articles in the *Philadelphia Daily News*, *Condé Nast Traveler*, *Food Arts*, and *Food & Wine*.

America's bicentennial approached and much of the nation's attention centered on Philadelphia and the mixed heritages of the city's people. What Philadelphians made of their city would be cause alone for admiration, but the rise of a group populated by the best chefs and their associates, rallied together by a non-chef with an exquisite gift for taste—that would be over the top different.

2 6

CHAINE-CHAINE-CHAINE

"Den dag du stopper læring er den dag, du skal forlade køkkenet."
("The day you stop learning is the day you should
leave the kitchen.")
—Master Chef Soren Arnoldi

R ussell Baum, a businessman from Michigan, had become a
Philadelphia resident in the 1960s. Partial to spending his
money in restaurants for business and pleasure, he was a
food and wine gourmand who possessed a golden palate. His
wife, Helen Baum, shared his interests and tastes.

Baum's palate was so fine, and his penchant for telling the truth so
solid, that both Perrier and Tell, once they discovered him among their
patrons in the 1970s, invited him to test new dishes in their kitchens
on a regular basis. He gave them his honest opinions, even if most of
the time they were mere validations of what the chefs prepared. Baum's
subtle changes suggested different accompanying vegetables or, at times,
a different sauce.

In time, conversations with Baum and the chefs centered on their
ambitions for the Philly culinary scene. Baum, who possessed a per-
suasive, likable manner, had a reputation for getting things done. His

powerful food industry connections included at least two presidents of the prestigious Culinary Institute of America (CIA), arguably the premier culinary arts educational institute in the world.

A fortuitous meeting occurred in 1973 when Jack Rosenthal, cofounder of the CIA, also president of the institute from 1965, met Russell and Helen Baum at Steve Poses's new storefront establishment, Frog, downtown at Sixteenth and Spruce streets. Sensing an historic opportunity, Rosenthal wanted to contribute to Baum's intentions to enhance Philadelphia's dining sophistication.

Baum couldn't have found a better friend. Rosenthal had defined and set culinary training into motion in the United States through the CIA. Baum would be able, with Rosenthal's assistance, to influence many notable trainees from the CIA to work in the Philly area upon their graduation. Chefs well versed in food preparation, cooking, pastries, and kitchen management, if flooded to the area, would further strengthen Philadelphia's rise.

Rosenthal also had plans for Baum. He asked him to research an international gastronomic society, the *Confrerie de la Chaine des Rôtisseurs* (literally, Brotherhood of the Guild of [Goose] Roasters). Rosenthal suggested to Baum that a Philadelphia *Chaine baillage* (guild chapter) might be set up to help advance their mutual plans.

The historical brotherhood, which restarted in Paris in 1950, was based on a royal guild of goose roasters chartered in 1248. The original guild brought together food industry people who wished to share their interests of cuisine, wine, and fine dining in a spirit of camaraderie and cooperation. Its membership was composed of kitchen professionals and related associates with similar values.

Baum did not overlook Poses that night. Poses, an alumnus of von Starck's *La Panatiere* brought French-influenced, American, and Southeast Asian/Thai cuisine, as well as what was arguably the best wine list, to town. A 1960s carry-over, Poses catered to Main Line offspring buying and renovating downtown town houses for an inner-city lifestyle that was different from their parents'. Poses struck the Mother Lode with his wildly popular restaurant, and Baum knew it. He also knew that any sustained rebirth of cuisine in the city would require the capture of fresh, young hearts and minds.

Planning and research became reality for the Baums the day they picked up Rosenthal for a drive to Reading. The occasion was the annual hunt and harvest of wild mushrooms sponsored by the

Chaine Des Rôtisseurs logo

restaurant Joe's in Reading. Joe's featured mushroom-based entrées year round on its menu, and the Baum's knew it was a favorite of Rosenthal.

Rosenthal opened the door to his apartment and greeted the Baums with two glasses of the white burgundy wine he had chosen for them at their first meeting at Frog almost three years earlier. The wine had not gotten much of their attention that night, but now, more properly aged and chilled, its cultivated balance bloomed.

"The taste is exquisite, Jack," Helen remarked.

"It is, Helen," said Rosenthal.

Russell took it further, saying, "That's the Corton-Charlemagne we had at Frog."

"My, my, Russell, you do have a discerning palate!" said Rosenthal, ". . . and a good memory, too." He had not mentioned the brand the night they first met.

Rosenthal had been looking for a trustworthy and knowledgeable partner to manage his planned *Chaine baillage*. Having Baum do research on the society had been a test. He knew now why he had felt he had found the right man to head up the *baillage* earlier.

Baum accepted Rosenthal's offer and agreed to be responsible for the quality of the group's membership. He drew up a list of the best restaurateurs and chefs in Philly, Chef Tell among them, and invited them all to the first annual induction dinner, which was to be held in November 1976 at Chef Nunzio Patruno's Monte Carlo Living Room situated at Second and South Streets. The place had a nightclub on the second floor and a trattoria dining room perfect for the meeting on the first.

Rosenthal and Baum named another Philly master chef, Soren Arnoldi, as chef de cuisine for the upcoming event. Arnoldi, who once reminded his son, "The day you stop learning is the day you should leave the kitchen," was a chip off the block of training from which master chefs Tell and Perrier were drawn. He was well liked, a formidable chef with a positive attitude. Arnoldi aimed to impress the *Chaine* dinner guests on the night, which included Chefs Tell, Perrier, Arnoldi, Patruno, Mermet and Etienne. Poses, Rosenthal, the Baums, and restaurateur Jay Guben of Striped Bass completed the group.

Baum's tone and the enthusiasm of the first inductees created an ambience so favorable that for years to come more than a hundred prospective members joined the waiting list for the *Chaine's* annual dinners. After the multi-course dinner, the newly admitted members pledged their energies and time to work in concert for their mutual benefit and for Philadelphia's reputation.

Chaine camaraderie led to lasting friendships and cooperation. To the restaurateurs, a group where they could cooperate, learn, and share each other's skills and knowledge just made sense. One only had to look around Philadelphia to see that the ethnic segments of the population pretty much kept to themselves. Without the *Chaine,* the renaissance would have devolved into a disjointed business-as-usual culture of competitiveness. Instead, when Perrier saw that Patruno made black noodles with inks, he could pick up the phone and find out how to make them. If Patruno called Tell to inquire if Ninth Street Brand sauce was better than another, he would get an honest answer. *Chaine* chefs spread their wealth of resources among the membership.

Truth be told, they had all along been *willing* to share what they knew with each other—now they had common ground to make it happen. Precisely because they had come from such diverse backgrounds, an unspoken, strong, and common sense of community developed in Philadelphia's *Chaine.* The spirit of *Chaine* cooperation—really a mirror of the spirit of the people of Philadelphia—trickled down to the dining tables and accelerated the rebirth of the city's pride—a time-tested pride that ran deep for Chef Tell.

27

A MELTING POT OF
INNOVATIONS

"Chef Tell was kind of our local Paul Bocuse*."
—Elaine Tait

Though Tait preferred to compare Chef Tell with the renowned *French* chef, Bocuse, Tell aligned with Pennsylvania Dutch clans, who were descendants of emigrants from southwestern Germany. These immigrants established Pennsylvania roots in the seventeenth and eighteenth centuries and influenced the city that the Quaker, William Penn, founder of the Province of Pennsylvania, had brought into being on the Delaware River on October 27, 1682—Philadelphia (from the Greek, *philos*, "love" or "friendship," and *adelphos*, "brother").

Of course, in this city, which was one of the nation's many capitals during the Revolutionary War, America's *most* famous leaders, the Founding Fathers of the United States, signed the nation's Declaration of Independence on July 4, 1776, and the Constitution on September 17, 1787.

---

*   prominent French Chef and co-founder of nouvelle cuisine

Philadelphia cradled the arts from its inception. Artists of great skill were respected and honored in the city. Young minds such as Benjamin Franklin, inventor of the lightning rod and bifocals, publisher of *Poor Richard's Almanac* and *The Pennsylvania Gazette,* found safe haven here. Edgar Allen Poe and Betsy Ross became residents. In 1805, painter Charles Willson Peal and first major American sculptor William Rush founded the Pennsylvania Academy of Fine Arts, the oldest in the nation. The Philadelphia Sketch Club, one of the country's oldest artists' clubs, also made Philadelphia home.

After the Civil War, Philadelphia reconstructed with more outdoor sculptures and murals than any other American city. In 1872, the first private association in the United States dedicated to integrating public art and urban planning began—the Fairmount Park Art Association. Fairmount Park was the largest landscaped urban park in the world.

This haven of freedom yielded more public art than any other American city. The Academy of Music and the Walnut Street Theatre— not only America's oldest theater, but also the nation's oldest continually operating opera house and largest subscription theater in the world— both operated in the city.

Philadelphians' love affair with the arts continued through the two hundred years that intervened between the nation's birth and the day Tell was commissioned for one of the city's most memorable celebrations. In the bicentennial year, on March 24, 1976, the Academy of Music threw a birthday party for Arthur Rubenstein, his eighty-ninth, for which a birthday cake was commissioned to Chef Tell. With the help of his crew, Tell turned out a five-hundred-pound, life-size replica of a grand piano, with 110 white keys and 55 black keys made of marzipan. The cake had to be assembled onstage. Rubenstein was so taken by the realistic rendition that he requested Tell and crew to take a bow. When they bent over, Rubenstein swiped a finger across a key and licked it just to make sure the piano was, indeed, only cake. No fewer than 3,300 attendees ate cake that day.

Philadelphia filled a melting pot of food innovations. The 1930s creation of the cheesesteak, influenced by the city's Italian-American population, debuted at a hot dog stand run by Philadelphians Pat and Harry Olivieri. Any righteous disciple of the famous sandwich knew its ingredient list by heart. To be considered authentic, an Amoroso Bakery bun from Philly held the meat, onions, and peppers, which were smothered with another local creation, Cheez Whiz.

Salted soft pretzels—a southern Germany, centuries-old tradition sold from street carts in the city since 1851, with or without yellow mustard—remained famously emblematic of Philadelphia's street cuisine, along with the hoagie, scrapple, and water ices. Tastykake Bakery products extended the menu from retail shelves.

No wonder the food renaissance sparked to life in this magical city. Philadelphia's fertile ground openly embraced the likes of its chefs with their food sensibilities and flairs for innovation. These chefs were, in a much larger sense, cooperative players in an age-old play springing from a deeper well than their lifetimes. They were not only geniuses, but products of their environment. Like excellent soufflé, the heated oven in which they were placed was protected from outside drafts, but the separate ingredients still had to rise together.

To combine food as entertainment with notions of American freedom was not too far-fetched for Philadelphians. After all, human bodies perish without sustenance, and a people without freedom ceases. Restrain the chef and you restrain humanity. Set him free and you release creativity. The passions infused into plated foods enter the populace. Food is fuel for the human body; and *artistically crafted and presented food* is fuel for the soul—a symbiotic sustenance of ideals.

"Chefs are artists, who bring innovation, invention, and structures of taste that play with your mind, your eyes, and your taste buds," said Chef Patruno as he recalled, after thirty years, his first meal cooked by Chef Tell: "The great rack of lamb that he produced—his lamb was perfectly cooked medium-rare with a light mustard crust and au jus—his asparagus and Vienna-scalloped potatoes—very classic—done to perfection. And his desserts—*his desserts!* The Sacher torte was just as Franz Sacher developed it in 1832 in Vienna. Linzer tortes . . . apple strudels with crème fraiche on the side, tart from northeastern rennet apples—*oh my!*"

Chef Tell wrote, "There are two passions with food. The first is to enjoy eating and savoring it. The second is to cook food for others." That second passion might appear most anywhere.

28

WORK HARD. PLAY HARD.

"Schau, was sie während ich weg wargetan."
("Look what they did while I was away.")

—Chef Tell

One Friday morning in late March of 1976, a German-American boy living in a suburb town of Philadelphia uncovered his passion for cooking. Freddie Duerr's discovery would lead him directly to Chef Tell.

Duerr had watched Tell many times on television. The segments got him thinking about his future until that Friday morning when he turned his bicycle away from high school and peddled toward the Tremont Hotel in Lansdale. He was hired on the spot as a pot washer for $2.85 an hour. Though just a fifteen-year old high school student, he reported for work at 6:00 a.m. that Saturday. After a month, when the regular sous chef turned sick, Duerr got his first chance to cook. He didn't do too badly for a boy who attended classes all day and worked at night.

With hard-won months at the stove under his belt, Duerr moved on and cooked at the Century House restaurant closer to his home in Hatfield. There he came under the watchful eye of Executive Chef Horst Herold, a long-time friend of Tell's.

The following February the laid back Herold and Tell were chatting at a table in Herold's restaurant when Duerr walked over. Herold introduced him, and Duerr stood starstruck in front of his TV idol—his first encounter with any celebrity. Upon Herold's recommendation, Tell opened the door to the possibility of making Duerr his apprentice one day.

* * *

Chef Tell's International Cuisine in Germantown, PA

The eponymous Tell Erhardt's International Cuisine took up most of the first floor inside the 1864 colonnaded Chestnut Hill Hotel in historic Germantown.

A mélange of dining rooms with high ceilings, stained-glass transoms over tall windowpanes that faced the street and wooden tables and chairs, the rustic colonial-style tavern was located in an area once considered wildwood. In Tell's time, it had become an enclave of the affluent.

Seating accommodated about one hundred, and there were two main seatings at six o'clock and nine o'clock. Two of Tell's "rules of the house" were: "no salt and no pepper on the tables," and "expect vehement opposition for all requests for steak sauce or ketchup." However, one all-important caveat overruled those rules, "The customer is always right. I don't care what he says. A restaurant is a business."

Tell left no stone unturned: in the company of his new bride, he had the place blessed by Father John Casey of the local Our Mother of Consolation Church six days before the opening. He also made his featured dessert the raspberries over ice cream with hazelnuts dish that Nicoletti loved.

The good Father's blessing must have worked: Tell's place was a roaring success right from opening day, Wednesday, March 9, 1977. An average of seven hundred meals in a five-day week grossed $500,000 the first year, and this would trend upward of $800,000 in the following three years.

Why not? The food was nearly always the freshest possible and cooked by a master chef aided by a complement of three sous chefs that he had personally hired.

"I first interviewed with Tell sitting at his crew break table. I told him casually that I was currently working under a chef who had worked with him at the City Line Marriott. He immediately corrected me, saying, 'Chef Winkler worked *for me* not with me!' Tell never missed a detail like that. He never forgot names, either—that was Tell," recalled Sous Chef William Reagor.

Tell worked from a personal instinct that worked like a compass. When he hired Reagor, he knew precisely how he would fit into the ideal scene he envisioned.

"Chef Rene (Plattner) loves to fish. He finishes work at eleven-thirty or midnight and then gets up and drives around in his jeep to fish at five a.m. He likes the surprise and imagination of fishing. He is trained in the European way like me—but more with the nouvelle cuisine, with the lighter sauces. My other chef, Ted Gawarzewski, is like one, two, three—everything he does is exactly right, exactly the same, time after time. So, they are balancing out in the kitchen. You need the steady chefs and you need the imagination. An executive chef needs good sous chefs. These I hired," said Tell.

Reagor got the job, although he was low man on the crew of three sous.

"My senior was Gawarzewski. He was another gentleman that I knew from the Marriott who commuted from Camden every day and always dressed to the nines. The other, Rene, was from Basel, Switzerland. He was more casual in his approach to cooking but still a 'stick' to work with, the way I saw it," added Reagor.

Tell selected his own ingredients early in the morning at the central Food Distribution Center in Philly because he could control costs better that way. Later in the day, unafraid of a little heat in the kitchen—1400 degrees to be exact—from his three custom stoves lined up side by side, Tell and his sous chefs cooked for hours on end, their faces illuminated and reddened from the open flames and heat.

Chef Tell cooked the way he drove. "I only have two speeds," he said, "stop and fast." The way pans flew across the hot stoves at lightning speeds, which the high heat demanded, testified to the veracity of his personal statement.

"You will see, I'm a *fast chef.* I drive a supercharged BMW with a special spoiler in front from Germany and a racing steering wheel. At 130–140, you just take your hands off the wheel and it just goes straight," he reminded anyone within earshot. To prove his point to a journalist one morning, Tell told him, "Today we cook omelets for a party of forty—you will see."

His observer watched as Tell churned out the forty omelets—150 eggs—at a mind-boggling clip. Loading three large pans at once while Reagor brought out nine plates from the hot locker, Tell shook the pans sideways, sending the eggs across the surface. Then with three slight flips of the wrist, he curled one edge before placing the pan over the hottest flame of the 1400-degree stove for a moment. Another flip and the curled, fluffy omelet fell onto the prepared plate, with two more close behind as the original pan was refilled with the mix. The flow never stopped until the forty dishes were finished, garnished, and spirited away from the kitchen. The clock had hardly moved. A stopwatch might have been a better instrument to measure the production speed at which Tell performed.

"Thirteen minutes and 55 seconds! Forty omelets! Sh**! That's why in my BMW my short wave handle is 'Short Order One.' *Cooked to order!*" said Tell.

* * *

International Cuisine's staff of twenty-eight people included three experienced line chefs, a pastry chef, two station cooks for cold dishes, two apprentices, a manager, a maitre d', four dishwashers, a general secretary, a mail secretary to handle the overwhelming incoming mail, a cleaning woman, and three cleanup men—all, for the most part, twenty- to thirty-somethings. Eight undergraduates between collegiate semesters or newly graduated worked the front room and were well paid, better than most chefs in the area other than Georges Perrier.

Despite Tell's regular schedule of television—every Friday he appeared on *Dialing for Dollars*—and cooking demonstrations across the country, he selected his chefs with accuracy and trained his staff well. They were expected to adhere to a strict regimen, including the budding kitchen star, Alison Barshak, who would later also see her star rise to fame.

Tell expected personnel to arrive on time, ready to work. There was hell to pay if someone was tardy. Simply good professionalism, it was also in Tell's basic German nature. German train stations listed arrivals to the minute. If a 14:11 arrival was posted, the train arrived exactly at 2:11 p.m. If a 14:17 departure was posted, the train left at that time.

Tell expected the same exactitude in every aspect of his operation, "The customer has to be right. If I don't do it, somebody else well. If the phone rings more than twice, and the caller is not greeted warmly—the reservation and phone number noted in a book that others can use to confirm the reservation the day of arrival—I blow my top."

When customers arrived in Tell's place, they were greeted *nicely* and taken to their table. If not ready, they were directed to the bar where a round of drinks was picked up by the house and then they were taken to their table. As for the dining party seated earlier, Chef Tell forbid them ever being asked to leave.

"What am I going to do? Some guy talks to his girl so he can get laid, and I tell him he takes too long? He doesn't score, and I lose a customer."

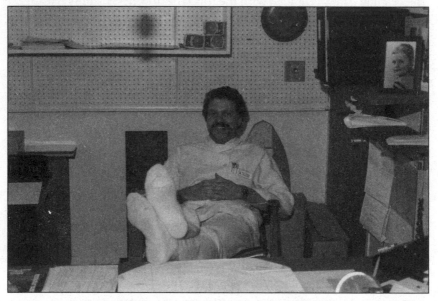

Tell takes a breather at Chestnut Hill.

A year and six months after opening, Tell shut the restaurant down for a month. An annual tradition started in September 1978, with a one-month sojourn to the vineyards of Napa Valley, California. Tell flew straight to Napa with a couple from the restaurant, Johann (his maitre d') and Cristl Eggstein (a waitress), while two other women who worked on the crew, Barbara Schnoor and Liz, headed to southern California first before driving north to rendezvous with them. Such a trip was the only way to work vacation time into Tell's busy schedule. Each year, he trekked to a different part of the world and mixed fun with homework.

Tell's International crew members enjoyed loads of fun, but they worked hard to earn it. Their days began early. Tell, being a morning person, was up at 5 a.m. and at the restaurant by 6. He fired up the stocks before taking inventory of the walk-in box to determine the daily specials, often accompanied in the work by his sous chefs. Food prep in the morning almost always was complete by 11 a.m., well before the first customer walked in for lunch. No food scrap went unused.

"It costs me $120 for a leg of veal. It costs me $130 for the whole side of the same veal. Rene, my Swiss sous chef, cuts it down for me, along the muscle, takes out all the tough parts, makes the bones small. We make roast veal or we stew parts like the frincandeau, in a dark stock with mushrooms, cream, and then top it with a hollandaise—a beautiful appetizer. We use it all, at times browning, deglazing, and reducing to get a real stock, a chef's stock."

Tell's "gofers" began early, too. At least one cleaning staffer worked with him in the mornings. He relied on such help for chores that needed attention when he could not get away from the prep work. Bob the Pot Man, for instance, would have cleaned all of the pots and pans well before the first customer came through the front door.

* * *

Occasionally, on days the restaurant was dark, Tell went out on errands, stopping in local shops for conversation.

"Jeannette, how are you today?" Tell asked the pert Irish redhead working the early shift at a local coffee shop.

"Pretty good, Chef." Without asking, she poured strong hazelnut-flavored espresso into a cup up to half and filled the rest of it with Half & Half before she handed it to him.

"Hazelnut and Half & Half, as you like it," she announced. Tell half-replied by reaching in the direction of the cup on the counter moving toward him. He had spied a woman sitting alone and reading a news-paper and he wished to meet her. He took his cup and walked toward her; the young, redheaded barista half-listening after Tell sat down and delivered his opener:

"Do you ever chop radishes? Thanksgiving is coming."

He sipped his drink.

The redhead at the counter twirled and snickered into her fingers pressed against her upper lip. She tried not to laugh aloud, knowing what was coming next.

The distracted woman lay her paper on the table and looked at Tell, "What?"

"Do you ever chop radishes?" he repeated.

"Okay, I'll bite. Why do you ask?"

"If you chop radishes you need to use your knife carefully. Have lots of bandages nearby, because radishes are red, and you don't find out you cut yourself right away."

He sipped his drink again.

The woman, not seeing where the conversation was going, smiled as best she could—*Are you kidding me?* written all over her face. She was about to return to her paper when she suddenly recognized Tell.

"Hey, you're that chef."

Tell smiled and said, "Chef Tell."

"I have a question for you about 'turkey day' preparations. Do you mind?"

Didn't I just give you a Thanksgiving tip? he thought.

So the conversation went. Next thing you know, on a napkin Tell wrote out a recipe for a complete turkey dinner. The woman sat back awestruck. Having forgotten all about her newspaper, she stood and, clutching the napkin, left with a wide grin plastered across her face.

Tell turned toward the counter and located the redhead, who was shaking her head. "I try to make some morning foreplay, and all she wants from me is turkey tips. What's going on here?"

Back at the restaurant, banter was discouraged. As waitstaff clocked in, Tell's kitchen remained as quiet as a Catholic church during confession. His rule of silence in the kitchen during prep and service hours, except for chef communications as needed, kept noise to a minimum in the high-speed environment.

Tell's voice covered the silence upon his return to the restaurant, "Okay, everybody, you think you could get dressed? Looks like the Village People in here," before he apprised the staff of special-guest parties for the day.

During food service hours, the kitchen crew moved, cooked, plated, and delivered. They attended to either Tell's personal directions or to policy enforced through his sous chefs. Produce a subpar dish, miss a garnish—there were a thousand ways to mess up—and the atmosphere turned into a *Hell's Kitchen* drama, except that Tell's bark hurt worse than his bite on most days.

A Chef Tell restaurant harbored a team-effort culture. The crew worked hard for every customer, knowing the tip pool was going to be shared among the entire staff. The customer, always right, was their paycheck. The team worked together, and Tell credited his team members where due. International Cuisine earned the coveted Cordon Bleu Award for excellence in dining four times and was credited with a top Four Stars rating by *Philadelphia Magazine*. Tell gave credit to his staff, but he always promoted his brand as well.

"Look at what they did while I was away—Chef Tell cooking delivers," he would say, even as he pointed to the trophies, framed magazine article covers—including the *Philadelphia Magazine* story by Jim Quinn "Hail To the Chef," photos, and letters of commendation.

Philadelphia Magazine features Tell in 1979.

29

GOURMANDAISE: THE FRIENDSHIP DRESSING

"Was ist der Unterschied zwischen einem Koch und einem
Küchenchef? Über $ 100.000 pro Jahr."
("What's the difference between a cook and a chef? About
$100,000 a year.")

—Chef Tell

C hefs Perrier and Tell never cared about awards, truth be told. Those were the trappings that came with the job. Their motivation was the work. The creative challenge alone was prize enough, although a little friendly competition in a light-hearted way was acceptable between them.

They had met several times at various functions—*Chaine* dinners, anniversary celebrations of other chefs, grand openings, and the like. The opening of Tell's place in Germantown brought them together for a lengthier time than most of the other events. Here, in a historical location where American volunteer troops had gathered to regain purpose and provisions before doing battle again, Tell and Perrier formulated a friendship that would last for thirty-three years.

Cordial as friends can be, they exchanged a lot of cooking knowledge between them. They were, however, not above trying to outdo each other with their output from their respective kitchens. Tell cooked for Perrier, as Perrier put it, "Of course, because I dined at his restaurant several times."

Tell put it this way, "Of course, Perrier came for my cooking, often. He knew good cooking."

When Tell visited Perrier's establishment, it was to observe first hand in the kitchen avant-garde French methods of food preparation. Try as he might, according to Perrier, "Tell never got the hang of cooking in the avant-garde French manner with French ingredients."

Tell learned a lot from Perrier, enough to poke fun at Perrier in later years; enough also to respect his talents and request his services in the Cayman Islands when French cuisine was the preference of Tell's VIP guests at special events. The respect was mutual. Perrier also pitched in to assist Tell at *Chaine* picnics. The real difference between the two chefs was the ingredients with which they worked and their methods for handling them.

German cuisine brought local game and livestock meats, sausages, potatoes, pickled foods (like sauerkrauts), vegetables, and breads to the plate, but not much else. With limited access to large waterways, prehistoric Germany ate foods that were bland or that had been pickled for use at later times. The short German growing season—Germany shares the same long summer nights and cold, snowy winter latitude as Newfoundland—unlike that of the Mediterranean countries to the south made for a disadvantage that limited their livestock provisions and dairy product production. Requirements for feed were year-round, but agriculture was limited to early-season wheat and barley. Relations with the Romans brought additions of oats and rye—staples for breadstuffs.

The nature of Germany's weather determined its spices and limited them to salts, mustards, parsley, celery, and dill. While the Romans cultivated fruit trees and exported their seedlings and growing methods to Germany in early centuries, sophisticated spices—basil, anise, rosemary, marjoram, cinnamon, and the like, which Germans used in later centuries, from the 1400s—were items of commerce funneled through the trading city of Cologne, prominent because of its Rhine waterway.

French cuisine, however, boasted a wider variety of foods than German due to the country's geographic medley, milder climates, and widespread access to the sea. Emphasis on local, fresh foods determined regional specialties. Milder climates extended milk production which, in turn, produced more cream, butter, and cheeses—traditional staples of French cuisine. To the south, the proximity of Italy's growing climates brought olive oil, herbs, and tomatoes to French cuisine, further expanding the French chef's repertoire.

No real argument existed between Perrier and Tell as to whose cuisine was better. They cooked whatever was available and fresh. However, German cuisine was never cloaked by controversy, which was not the case for the French.

The French palate supported national recognition for *pate de foie gras* (fatted goose and duck liver) on French tables, but the process of force-feeding corn to millions of ducks annually—long-considered inhumane in some circles—brought ongoing controversy and remains a shroud over the magnificent gastronomic history of France. *Pate de foie gras* became synonymous with the French, even though historical facts belie that connection. Forty-five centuries ago, the Egyptians enjoyed the dish, and the Romans wrote about it in the second century. After the Roman Empire faded, the Jews kept the tradition as an alternative to cooking with butter and imported it to Germany and France when they migrated to those countries.

Tell and Perrier both offered *pate de foie gras* on their menus. For them, cooking and dining was about pleasing the palate different ways through food preparation, excellent presentation, and crafted innovation. Their alignment as both chefs and friends stemmed from one time-honored purpose—to please palates. Controversies that stemmed from sources outside their realm were not able to penetrate it.

From the beginning, the two master chefs blended as one might blend ingredients for a good hollandaise—carefully. Their affinity coalesced around foods, but their training enforced different approaches to ingredients. In Perrier's words, "Tell cooked sophisticated. He knew classic French but he never did avant-garde French. It was not his fault."—a true Frenchman's turn of phrase, penurious in his praise, yet rooted in respect.

Tell could be just as direct about Perrier's cuisine. "Marinate a chicken in a nice wine overnight, and you have French pheasant," he once confided (in jest) to a sous chef.

They attended the same parties, tasted the same foods, and kissed the same women—on the cheeks only—but they only cooked for each other in public.

"Privately it never happened," recalled Perrier. "Additionally, I must say, Tell knew wine. When you have the 'taste,' you can do it all. It is not difficult to know what to drink with what foods, because the palate is unerring when you have it. Like a musician who has a good 'ear' for the proper notes and chords to play, Tell had the ability of taste that rose above the common man or chef."

Often, beauty is the real inspiration in the kitchen—beautiful women inspire chefs to make beautiful food. But these two chefs pursued aesthetics with very different career choices, albeit with vigor. Perrier kept to "cooking and working like a dog, although I was younger and could work many hours back then." Tell traveled everywhere and was a household celebrity on TV and in convention centers, telling the world, "I see you!"

Tell and Perrier were left to wonder about the other, *How did he do that?* On that they agreed. The answer, of course, was part serendipity, part personality, part individual skill and, for Tell, the luck of that rabbit's foot in his pant pocket.

Tell's TV career expanded and was in full swing in 1978. Tell had tied the knot with Nicoletti almost a year ago by now, but it was a loose binding. Tell worked on the road more than two hundred nights a year. Nicoletti, after early interest in traveling with her husband, remained home in Philadelphia and wondered what she should make of all the fuss. That is, when she surfaced from the effects of her psychiatric drug prescriptions, which were far worse than Tell ever suspected since their earliest days together.

To make matters worse for Nicoletti, when Tell returned to town, he was rarely at home with her. He spent most of his daylight hours taping shows, prepping foods, overseeing his restaurant, and teaching classes in Chestnut Hill College with another cooking instructor/partner Hermie Kranzdorf.

Kranzdorf had trained under some of the biggest names—James Beard, Diana Kennedy, and Jacques Pépin—and had already put in two years working for Tell as his pastry chef when she was asked about who her greatest instructor was.

"Tell. It's not just what he knows; it's how well he gets the message across. He's a fantastic teacher, he really is."

Capitalizing on his growing TV popularity in 1979, Tell and Kranzdorf successfully released a local book, *Chef Tell Tells All*. The publication displayed how to get fresh food from the market to the table, but recipes took center stage. Many dessert recipes were included in the publication because, in Tell's words, "What people eat last, they remember first." By the turn of the decade, Lobster Chef Tell's Way—butter flied and broiled lobster tail stuffed with chunks of crabmeat under a beurre blanc sauce—was one of his most popular recipes craved by the book's readership.

Tell's book cover photo

By the 1980s, Chef Tell's personal appeal exploded. His unique phrases, "Very simple, very easy," and "You do like this; you do like that!" were household staples. His signature salute, "I see you!" echoed everywhere. To the world, Chef Tell was rockstar, culinary royalty.

When he looked in the mirror, though, what he saw was a common man who felt empty inside, knowing his mother couldn't share his success with him. He never got used to it. His celebrity activity on-camera was an acquired skill. True, opportunity arrived at a time he was ready to receive it, but the TV persona of "Chef Tell," the lines and the jokes, were well-rehearsed methodologies passed on to him from professional consultants, who knew the small-screen craft that was early-television.

Tell Erhardt looked in the mirror and saw his private persona, but also saw the public image in the mirror and wondered, *How do I continue to be 'Chef Tell?'* Tell would practice his lines and gestures so he could impress his viewers as a professional chef.

Off-stage, however, Chef Tell was just Tell—a man of simple taste with an impeccable palate and, really, a heart of gold.

"People always want to take me to a German restaurant. If I want to go to a German restaurant, I can go to Germany. In Shreveport, people wanted to take me to a French restaurant. I don't want French food in Shreveport. I say, 'Take me to eat catfish.' So we go and have catfish and coleslaw and beer—one of the best meals I've had," Tell said.

Before a repeat television appearance on *People Are Talking* in Baltimore, Maryland—a town known worldwide for its crab dishes—a reporter asked, "What do you usually order when you come here, crab cakes?"

"Polish food," Tell said.

Pressed with ". . . not crab cakes?" Tell—tongue firmly planted in cheek—replied, "I don't fool around."

There was, however, only so much "road" a man could take without a break. Tell longed for the comforts of home and the camaraderie of friends. He would soon meet an individual who would become his friend and a fellow member of the *Chaine des Rôtisseurs* and who would share with him a common passion for good food and intellectual stimulation.

3 0

A COMMON PASSION
TO COOK

"Ich nehme die Angst aus der Küche."
"I take the fear out of cooking."

—Chef Tell

usanna Foo met both Perrier and Tell at the 1980 *Chaine* dinner
that Tell hosted at his restaurant in Chestnut Hill. Foo attended
because her noted skills as a cook had come to the attention of
both Russell Baum and Jack Rosenthal, who invited her to join
the *Chaine*. During the course of the evening, standing between the two
chefs for a photo-op thrilled Foo; however, the food that was served
impressed her more.

"Chef Tell—his food was really good, really unbelievable," Foo
recalled.

At such professional functions, members made time to relax after
dinner. They repaired to the bar for drinks and lit cigars, especially the
Europeans, and often traded passels of ribald jokes. At such a time, a
married woman with children like Foo would have little choice than to
retreat to her hotel room for the rest of the evening. But the night turned

out differently when Tell took note of her predicament and paid her the courtesy of conversation away from the smoke and noise, an appreciated gesture.

Baum and Rosenthal joined Tell and Foo and talked about the role of the *Chaine* in Philadelphia. Foo averred that she could see how *Chaine* dinners opened opportunities for members to meet and help each other, as well as observe and experience the foods that other chefs prepared. While Baum and Rosenthal lead the charge to get Foo to join the group by encouraging her to take up the challenge of hosting one of the annual *Chaine* dinners, Tell harbored another reason for her to join. Peking duck was his personal favorite, and Foo's notable Peking duck dish was on his mind.

Although unlike Chef Tell's journey, Foo's way into the kitchen was just as fascinating.

* * *

Susanna Foo knew the indigenous herbs, spices, and grains of China during her childhood in Formosa (now Taiwan) but she had not felt a passion to cook at that time. The thought still had not crossed her mind to learn the trade, until Wan-Chow Foo, her mother-in-law, taught her Hunan-style cooking in Philadelphia. When Chao Su, her cousin, showed her the delicate nature of Chinese Northern pasta, a seed of creative possibility sprouted within her, which eventually brought her to the attention of Baum and Rosenthal, and then to Tell's restaurant in 1980.

Although inspired by the camaraderie of the *Chaine*, an unexpected 1984 trip to France with friends really changed Foo's world. Russell Baum observed in her "a cook with great talent" and invited her to travel with him and his wife. During their two-week working tour from northern France to the southern regions, the trio tasted their way through several top-rated Michelin three-star restaurants. Foo came to recognize three things on that trip—that Perrier's culinary wizardry equaled that of any three-star chef; that Tell's food was equally amazing; and that she did have a passion for what she might achieve as a chef/restaurateur. Now that she felt a dedication to cook on her own terms, she resolved to return to Philadelphia and learn whatever she could about the culinary arts.

Back in the city, on the advice of Russell Baum, Jack Rosenthal arranged for Foo to attend an eight-week course in cooking fundamentals and sauce making at the Culinary Institute of America. Her short time at the CIA opened her eyes to a whole new world. Her fellow students were, in her eyes, "professionals in the food business," and the environment energized her. After morning classes, she spent extra hours inside the institute's library and absorbed as much information as possible.

Rosenthal believed, as told to Elaine Tait, "that a marriage of French techniques with Chinese ingredients would produce marvelous offspring," and he affirmed, "Susanna Foo can produce such a marriage." He admired her progress and watched her blossom into "one of the best chefs I've ever known."

Chef Perrier invited Foo and her husband, Hsin, to open a new restaurant in her name right across the street from his bistro. Once opened in 1987, her new Asian fusion cuisine menu creations made history with her name over the door.

Foo cooked food on her terms, which meant she drew from the French influence she experienced but cooked decidedly Asian. Her innovative dishes were stunning. They were visual and they were something new—an *original fusion* of method and ingredients from two cuisines worlds apart. The breadth of her imagination was a breathtaking breakthrough on the culinary scene. For example, Foo might bring together water chestnuts with arugula and balsamic to produce bitter and peppery tastes with walnut overtones, rather than sweetness. The effect was healing or soothing for the dining patron. Foo was not only pleasing the palate, but soothing the soul.

Philadelphians embraced Foo the way Hsin embraced the recommendations of a young, professional female wine representative of a local wine distributor. The quiet beginnings of the restaurant's wine cellar included one wine, Blue Nun, and a lineup of beers. The wine rep, Bunny Kule, recommended a Kenwood Chenin Blanc, which, years later, would remain as fond homage on the wine list.

Not long after finding an enthusiastic patronage in Philadelphia, Foo embraced a much wider sphere of influence with her kitchen output. In 1988, *Esquire* magazine would name Susanna Foo's Asian Cuisine one of the country's best new restaurants. In 1989, *Food & Wine* would call her, "One of America's 10 Best New Chefs." *Gourmet* magazine would write, "[Foo is] truly one of this country's best chefs."

Beyond the hoopla, like her friends Perrier and Tell, Foo preferred just to cook, and most of all, she loved to cook for her peers.

"Almost every year I had to do at least one dinner. I would have to plan and think it out for a month before, which was always good for me because it pushed me to do something new. If my food was a hit with the *Chaine* members then it would be added to my menu in my restaurant," said Foo. "This came from Russell Baum and Jack Rosenthal, and from the night I met Tell, and we talked. Tell was always upbeat, pleasant, and he never complained. My relationship with him was a kindness for me."

The circle of key players in the food renaissance movement was completed when Foo added her cuisine to the slate of menus available to Philadelphians. All major cuisines were now available to gourmands from within Philadelphia's city limits.

31

TOO MANY TEMPTATIONS

"Ich dachte, ich könnte ihr helfen aus ihm heraus . . .
deshalb bin ichgeblieben."
("I thought I could help her out of it. That is why I stayed.")

—Chef Tell

With only twenty-four hours in a day and only seven days in a week to be an expert chef, restaurateur, TV personality, cooking instructor, author, cooking demonstrator, and husband, something had to give in Tell's workaholic lifestyle. The limelight that his wife had wished would fall upon both of them failed to shine upon her. Aside from her beauty pageant success, not much else had happened with Nicoletti's career, which was eclipsed by her spouse's. Instead, twice in 1981, prescription drug–related incidents nearly took her life when he was out of town. And when he was in town, she had already attempted suicide twice.

Nicoletti's troubles were a minor reflection of America's growing affectation with drugs, street or prescription. The scourge had been building since the press glorified street-drug use and LSD in the Sixties. Perhaps Nicoletti was only a product of her environment. A deluge of media brought pharmaceutical drugs into America's living rooms and into doctor's offices. Under the care of "professionals," an unsteady Nicoletti was vulnerable to their "diagnoses," which in any case did not improve her underlying conditions.

Studio 54's popularity was in peak form in Manhattan in the 1980s. Magazine articles made the lifestyle look glamorous, but they didn't show the downside. People that could afford the toys and lifestyles like the celebrities wanted the same. Unfortunately, although Nicoletti's shopping list did not include the popular nose candy, cocaine, the list did include prescriptions for new drugs, which most lay persons would find difficult to pronounce, let alone understand the risks. Tell was unable to stop the nightmare that started in doctors' offices when he was away.

"I tell you, once I knew about it, I thought I could help her out of it. That is why I stayed as long as I did, but I was busy most of the time," Tell confided. "Besides, to tell you the truth, it just scared the hell out of me. It seemed in a sense that I had married my mother."

Tell's International Cuisine in Germantown continued to be a big hit. The food was good, and diners lined up after Tait's strong reviews and the Cordon Bleu awards were publicized. Money, accolades, and celebrities—*Saturday Night Live's* John Belushi and Dan Aykroyd, Mayor John Daly, and Senator Arlen Specter among them—poured in. Life was good.

Tell was not immune to the pressures to conform to what had become a passionate part of the American celebrity lifestyle. He could afford to pay for just about anything he wanted. He experimented with recreational drug use, which put him in a bad place mentally. Still, any alleged drug use apparent to others inside the food business, if not to his patrons, remained publicly unproven.

Years later, when confronted with an investigative reporter's probing questions, Tell replied, "Sometimes, I thought back then, 'Should I buy a pound of coke and O.D. (overdose) or blow my brains out?' Knowing Tell's ironic in-your-face humor, and his short attention span when faced with inane, media questions, he had likely not told the truth and simply added fodder to the publicity mill, which brought in more customers.

Considering the widespread prevalence of drug usage at the time, did it even matter?

Tell had it all—a winning reputation, money to burn, a comfy residence, and a custom Kawasaki 750 in his garage. His Renault days in Germany's Black Forest were long gone. In the 1980s, the workaholic chef added German and American engineering in the form of a sleek black Porsche for play time and a Ford Bronco and GMC trucks he commandeered for work, later adding a gorgeous Mercedes sedan to the mix. In his closet he kept one hundred shirts, fifteen suits, and forty pairs of shoes. Eventually, he would accumulate as many as twenty thousand bottles of wine in his cellar.

Tell worked his tail off for every bit of what he earned. Touring in a different city almost every day was grueling work. He had two morning and two afternoon cooking shows daily, which paid well, and radio show appearances in between that sold books.

Off-stage at the end of the day, there was very little to do for entertainment other than to find a group of people from the venue to hang with, dine out, or party. When in the Carolina's, Tell could be found on Jimmy Dean's large boat offshore. In the Miami area, Tell partied at Jimmy Buffet's place down in South Beach. In fact, if he had the chance to be there for a whole weekend, for sure one of three things—at times, all three—was going to happen: he was going to get drunk, stoned, or laid.

Other top restaurateurs in Philly, unlike Tell, were too busy to lift their heads up much from inside their kitchens and they could not hope to follow all of Tell's peregrinations, but the gossip grapevine—remember, the culinary community was a small one with close ties—would know if there was any dirty laundry. If there was any truth to the rumors that Tell had frayed around his edges, tattered with jagged cuts from the serrated blades of black journalism, the "news" would have spread all over the restaurant community's back rooms faster than printing presses could roll out copies onto the streets. It never happened.

Skulking reporters and food critics—prowling for a story as juicy as one TV celebrity chef nose-diving into "rock candy"—would have loved to write the headline or hit the airwaves without remorse, but that never happened, either. In his own way, Tell was just as busy as any other top chef in America. The best of the best, Tell included, were far too busy with their respective food operations to experiment beyond what helped them work more with better results in their competitive world.

But hell, let's be frank here: Philadelphia chefs of that era might easily have experimented with substances beyond what filled wine glasses at their parties. All of America was flying high; people just weren't talking about it.

The true story on Tell was that he tried on occasion what was available, but in moderation. Those who knew him personally knew that he would offer what was current to customers and friends far more than what he ever might have ingested. He understood firsthand much was at stake to not slip overboard and drown in a world of drugs, which he could easily have afforded. One bad publicity event or article alleging substance abuse on his part would have brought him revocation of liquor licenses and restaurant closures. The abrupt slam of TV studio doors and endorsement contracts would have been deafening.

If that was not enough incentive, the near-death of his wife, Nicoletti, fit the bill.

* * *

When news arrived of Nicoletti's second suicide attempt, Tell was working on the road. He dropped his itinerary and flew to his wife's side, expecting to find a weakened and defenseless Nicoletti. However, rumors of infidelities had arrived before he did. Nicoletti had filed for divorce. She served him with the papers and sent him packing back to his scheduled workload.

Tell never changed his behavior pattern, despite the pending divorce. The only thing that changed, when Nicoletti confronted him, was the depth of his personal disappointment on two counts: the thought of divorce dredged up deep memories that included his mother's depression and her lifeless body, coupled with his emotional hopelessness with regard to Nicoletti's state of mind affected by the prescription drugs.

From the beginning of the divorce process until the bitter end years later, Tell—not his "Chef Tell" persona, which was the life of the party and thrived on publicity—continued to be the man most likely to step off the stage away from the footlights. Tell was the guy that used the same exit door as the audiences who came to see Chef Tell. Outside the glamour and glitter, road shows were daily grinds of room service, a little TV, and sleep—which was never enough, when he could get it—until the next day and another flight to another town and a different show.

A reporter asked him about road life and what was home for him. Tell replied, "I have a good support system there. People take care of my house, my plants, and my cats when I'm away. I don't have to be Chef Tell with them. My lady friend is there." And then he opined, "You go on the road all the time and if you believe your own publicity you could go crazy."

The show had to go on, but it took a toll on Tell. He began to feel the urgent need to find someone he could trust as a safe companion.

Repeating what had worked for him earlier, Tell reacted to his challenges by working more and taking on more responsibility, not less. He never shrank from the demands of living his lifestyle; he did give back to his profession. By making a simple enough computation—if you're having trouble with one area, take on two—he found he could boost his morale and keep on doing what he had to do. He expected to not only find peers he could relate to, but also more control, when he assumed extra duties within the *Chaine*. In 1981, he became the *Chaine's Conselier Culinaire* (Professional Officer), a position he would hold until 1988.

Tell's career was speeding, but it was about to rev up to even higher rpm's. Another new toy in the garage would help him ease what he missed at home.

* * *

Footloose and fancy free again, Tell made the most of what Robin Leach would call "champagne wishes and caviar dreams." And he didn't mind showing off the spoils to his friend Perrier back in Philadelphia.

The year 1981 saw the last production model of the limited edition 450 SEL 6.9 Mercedes come off the line. Only four were built in the year, adding to the 1,812 previous. Tell—he shared with others—purchased one after being invited to do so by Daimler Benz. In the words of David E. Davis, contributing writer, editor, and publisher at *Car and Driver* magazine and founder of *Automobile* magazine—and, according to *Time* magazine, "the dean of automotive journalists"—the 6.9 was "a $50,000 exercise in going fast."

After the car's arrival, Tell phoned Perrier at his restaurant and asked him to go outside in fifteen minutes and stand on the sidewalk in front of his restaurant. "Just be there," were his last words before he hung up the phone.

Perrier went outside at the appointed time. He didn't have to wait long. Tell roared into view and pulled his sleek new Mercedes to the curb. He raced around to the passenger side and opened the back door. Out popped two gorgeous blondes. The pair wrapped themselves around Tell's shoulders, and one relit his Cuban cigar.

"Chef Perrier, I envy you," Tell grinned. "I have to travel all over the country to pay for these kinds of things—my car, these blondes, my Cubans."

Perrier was astounded, perhaps a bit envious, seeing Tell stand in front of him flaunting "the dream"—women, Cubans, money, a new car and, more importantly, the free time to enjoy them all.

"Tell, *mon ami,* I work like a dog too many hours in a day," he exclaimed as he hugged his friend, who hugged him back and looked at him with a big grin. Perrier continued, "But, of course, it's your style, your way."

Friends and fierce competitors alike, Tell and Perrier enjoyed the mixed feelings they each had for the other's lifestyle as only two fierce friends could.

The new decade of the 1980s marked the beginning of a productive era for America. Ronald Reagan took the White House by a landslide, and eight years of prosperity and consumer confidence began. The environment bode well for Tell to sell another cookbook.

32

THE DIRTY JOKE
BOOK DEAL

"Ein Ei, sagte zu den anderen . . ."
("One egg said to the other . . .")

—Chef Tell

ookbooks date back to the early Apicius of the fourth century. The major track followed through al-Warraq of Baghdad in the tenth century and Huou's work for Kublai Khan, *Kuchenmeysterey*—the first German cookbook. Next came, in the thirteenth century, *Le Viandier* by Guillaume Tirel and both *Le Guide Culinaire* by Escoffier and *Ma Gastronomie* by Point, for French cuisine led all the way up to the days of Beard and Child. It would be natural for Tell to want to add to the chain of influence by putting out his own recipe books.

With the help of Tell's publicist, Vanita, the people at *PM Magazine*, late in 1981 cobbled together a small production crew and produced a demo tape of several of his TV appearances plus a cooking demonstration that he made just for the reel. The package was combined with a formal book outline and proposal and mailed to several publishing houses. After the last taping, Tell rushed out the door. He never reviewed the tape's content. Weeks went by and then Warner Books offered the possibility of a book contract, if they could meet Tell in person in New York City.

Tell called a friend, vice president of Sichel Wines, the late John Rapp, and asked if he might persuade the owner of the highly regarded 21 Club to reserve Table 31 for his meeting with Warner—an almost impossible task unless you were really "somebody." Situated next to the water fountain where water splashes drowned conversations from nosey eavesdroppers, Table 31 was the perfect setting for a power business lunch. Rapp obliged and was able to pull off the coup.

The Warner publishing group arrived at 21 and was seated before Tell, just as he had strategically planned. Since word was out about 31, Warner was impressed.

At six-foot-three, Tell cut an imposing figure with his horseshoe moustache, open-chest silk shirt, and starched jeans over western boots when he strode across the dining room. He flashed his million-dollar smile and pumped the hand of each executive seated at Table 31.

"Don't get up. Sit down, please. Nice to meet you," Tell said as he circled the table—a tiger surveying his prey—before he sat down.

The Warner group was impressed alright, but their spokesperson straightaway asked Tell, "What was the dirty joke you told at the end of the demo tape you sent us?"

Tell had no clue there was a joke on the tape, but he didn't let on. He assumed when he told the joke to his camera crew that they had turned off the cameras and microphone. Thinking quickly back to the day of the taping, he remembered the joke and recounted it proudly to the Warner executives, using his best German enunciation for full effect before translating the joke into English: *"Es gibt zwei Eiern sitzen in einem Nest. Das einzige Ei, sagt derandere, "ich kann nicht schwer . . . Ich habe gerade gelegt."* ("There are two eggs sitting in a nest. The one egg says to the other one, 'I can't get hard, I just got laid.'")

The Warner crowd cracked up, and the ice was broken. Tell told more jokes and added a few kitchen stories, which kept the entire party happy and off guard. Before the meeting ended, Warner made a book offer that Tell liked, and a deal was struck. Perhaps it was the only time a cookbook deal with a chef had been sealed because of a dirty joke.

Power lunch at 21 . . . table 31? Indeed.

Warner would go on to package a number of guest appearances for Tell on nationally televised shows, which included *Dinah's Place* (Dinah

Shore), *The John Davidson Show*, and *The Mike Douglas Show*, among others.

The book deal led to other deals with companies as a spokesman for their products.

John Davidson Show appearance

33

A EUROPEAN KINSMAN

"Sie mögen diesen kochen ... Sie möchten, dass zu kochen."
("You cook like this ... you cook like that.")
—Chef Tell

L ike Dick Clark's *American Bandstand*, the hits just kept on coming for Chef Tell in 1982. *Evening Magazine* kept his name and image before his adoring public, which tuned in to his regular three-times-a-week segments. They loved his humor and the speed at which he cooked as he explained to them how to be irreverent with food and use unusual combinations of ingredients—he would later use plain ketchup as dressing on a sardine salad. Bookstores couldn't place enough books on their shelves fast enough for the demand.

"Chef Tell was the most popular TV chef in history," wrote Nordic Ware in its brochures. The company that invented Bundt cake ware had snared Chef Tell as its exclusive spokesman in 1980 for a signature line of Chef Tell brand cooking pots and pans.

The Warner book, *Chef Tell's Quick Cuisine—Gourmet Cooking Simple, Fast, and Delicious* by Tell Erhardt with Rosalyn T. Badalamenti, came out of the gate like a Kentucky Derby entry. At the finish line more than 230,000 copies were sold at $14.95 each, totaling more than $2,990,000 in sales. Tell was now a bestselling author. Further, the book was picked up by two Book of the Month clubs and enjoyed continued international appeal.

Tell's TV gravy train poured out a full thirteen seasons before the tureen emptied. In the same baker's-dozen years, he perfected his cooking style on small towned squares and in larger convention halls. He toured constantly, cooked everywhere, and appeared on-air in local segments, which spurred even more book and product sales.

Chef Tell's logo on his Nordic Ware line.

Chef Tell Nordic Ware

A series of Nordic Ware ads:

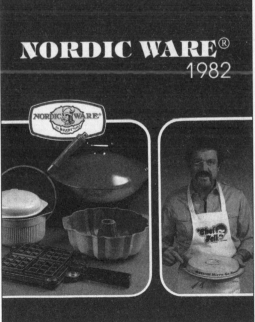

Nordic Ware Ad

Nordic Ware's innovative Micro-Go-Round was first touted by Tell, a marketing pioneer.

He was, in fact, on the road well over thirty weeks a year, and every bank deposit afforded him more silk ensembles.

"Silk, I'm vain when it comes to that," Tell told a reporter who quizzed him about a rumor that he liked to wear silk clothing.

Tell fulfilled more than his dreams when he toured and cooked to the delight of screaming ladies . . . and men. Mandatory touring was a common clause inserted into TV and book contracts back then. Shows sponsored by high-end magazines were a part of the deal and were conducted in affluent department stores like Bloomingdales in New York and I. Magnin in Los Angeles. In fact, the first Southern Women's Show featured among its celebrities Chef Tell in 1983. He also appeared with them in Charlotte, Raleigh, Birmingham, and Nashville and was regarded on his report card as "no less than the consummate showman."

In the I. Magnin store in Los Angeles, Tell—cruising for a date as he worked—risked a severe beating for his womanizing. He had spied a smart-looking reporter while doing a cooking demonstration sponsored by *PM Magazine* and Nordic Ware. Selecting the reporter out of the audience, he began a running monologue with her.

"You cook like this," he told the audience. "Miss Reporter, look over here. . . . You cook like that."

The reporter took notice as soon as she heard his German accent and she turned to face him.

"This is a nice piece of meat here," he said with a raised eyebrow, which brought titters from among the crowd watching him cook.

"Miss Reporter, if you're looking to cook, I can show you how right here," Tell remarked. (More laughter.)

The eyes of the audience turned to the reporter, who was listening to Tell and smiling.

Tell continued, "You should have dinner with me. I can cook." (Even more laughs.)

The woman turned him down, explaining, "I am already dating a European kinsman. Would you like to meet him?" She turned to see if her boyfriend was in the hall, and the audience looked in the same direction; so did Tell.

When her boyfriend walked—strutted—onto the convention floor with an entourage of he-men surrounding him, Tell was speechless. None other than Arnold Schwarzenegger—the "Austrian Oak," Mr. Universe, and seven-time Mr. Olympia—came out to the floor. He instantly commanded everyone's attention as he approached Maria Shriver, who would in 1986, become his wife.

Tell was big at six-foot-three, but Schwarzenegger was all-muscle. Tell turned his attention back to the crowd and continued both his cooking demonstration and his search for a dinner date without skipping a beat.

34

MORE PERKS . . . WHY NOT?

"Das ist die Art und Weise danke ich dem Haus."
("That's the way I thank the house.")

—Chef Tell

Since TV appearances did not pay well—the pay was union scale minimum—TV stars embraced the big money they could earn on appearance tours. If they connected well on television, well-paying publicity tour opportunities multiplied. Tell cooked in live shows for more than $1,000 a day, plus expenses; at times he took home $20,000. He met quite a few celebrities and scores of VIPs—the newly crowned Miss America, Vanessa Williams; Frank Perdue of Perdue Chicken; and country singer Jimmy Dean, among others, on the convention hall venue route.

He pitched his recipe books in fairs, malls, and convention centers—even cooking schools. On September 4, 1983, at Broughton Hall School of Cooking in Spartanburg, South Carolina, while cooking, he explained historical trivia. "It's rumored the shape of a champagne goblet comes from the breast size of Marie Antoinette, which shows you that women and food, for chefs, are not that far apart," which was one of the tidbits of data he had gleaned from the voluminous amount of reading he accomplished in his hotel rooms.

The money was nice, but Tell relished his opportunities to meet ordinary people from all walks of life. He often selected as stage partners volunteers who were more than willing to help him during his cooking sessions. Because of Tell's extraordinary showmanship and ability to work a crowd, he never failed to deliver a good show.

"Tell me, Mary, do you know when Italian meringue is blended enough?" he asked as she mixed the ingredients.

"I don't think so," Mary said. The audience tittering in the background.

Tell took the meringue bowl from Mary's hands, gave the mix a quick extra turn, and then flipped the stainless steel bowl upside down over her head. "It's when it doesn't fall out when I do this," he said. The appreciative crowds laughed and applauded right along with the surprised Mary. And then Tell would add the punch line, "Unless you're in Great Falls, Montana!"

No one else did that back then. Tell not only pioneered the concept, but he also got away with his antics. In fact, precisely because of his antics and personality, the public loved him. "Very simple, very easy, very nice," they would say with him, and they believed.

Under the fun was fact. Tell knew that *hot* sugar syrup prevented egg whites from weeping. Better meringue didn't fall from bowls.

Still, with Tell at the helm, audiences gladly went anywhere his humorous banter took them.

"My most important tip is this: always breathe through your mouth when cutting up onions. If you breathe through your nose, it activates sinuses, and I don't want anyone crying over all this," he told a volunteer slicing onions in Montana.

Though he cooked in a commercial kitchen most of the time, Tell understood his audience mostly cooked at home, so he had advice for them: "You can save lots of time at home if you take out all the ingredients you need first and lay them out in front of you. That way you won't suddenly realize you're out of sugar and have to go running all over the neighborhood with flour on your hands."

Tell's audiences ate it all up and laughed right along with him, because Tell was constantly teaching as he prepared foods. Tell was always about common sense.

After a time, the accoutrements of big money, women, posh hotel rooms and celebrity connections held nothing new for Tell. Living in a country far bigger and more populated than his homeland; loving people who lived and breathed freedom every single day—that interested him. For them, he was willing to share his basic philosophy of cooking.

"People think gourmet is expensive and extravagant and has to be French. It's not so. It is anything that is cooked properly and tastes good," he explained to an enthusiastic crowd of women at a Southern Women's Show in Charlotte, North Carolina, in October 1985.

* * *

For all the rewards of hard work and the serendipity that came his way, Tell never forgot his roots or the hard times he'd endured. He'd known that his father worked endlessly and had been popular within his business community. He'd watched his mother make ends meet in the kitchen. He knew how other women respected her volunteer work. In turn, he'd vowed to work hard to pay his own way and to honor the lessons of his parents, who taught him to never take what came to him for granted.

Helen Baum, recalling a trip with Tell to an Atlantic City casino said, "Tell laid $500 on the roulette table and played it up and down all night. When he'd had enough, he walked away from the $500 left on the table. I asked him, 'Don't you want the $500?' He answered right away, 'No. You see, that's the way I thank the house for the paid weekend they provide me as a celebrity.'"

(The anecdote begs the question: How many TV celebrity chefs would do that today?)

Tell enjoyed the perks and the freedoms that came with his fame. And why not? In the quiet moments when the audiences were away, the work of the day completed, Tell told himself he had to settle down. What he missed in his life was a real relationship with a woman he felt he could trust.

For all the bravado of the public persona that was Chef Tell, Friedemann Erhardt longed to find the right woman to complete him. He decided it was time for her to show up.

35

HER ONE AND ONLY
BLIND DATE

"Ich sage nicht, es wird ein Rosengarten werden,
aber Sie werden immer gut zu essen."
("I'm not saying it will be a rose garden,
but you will always eat well.")

—Chef Tell

Bunny Kule grew up in Bucks County, Pennsylvania. Tall and athletic, a swimmer and water ballet artist in the Junior Olympics, she clocked three years in the pool at Fordham University. At twenty-five, she worked as a wholesale wine representative for The Wine Merchant based within an hour's drive of Philadelphia. Her physical traits complemented those of her Chilean-Colombian mother's good looks, and she inherited a sturdy work ethic from her Polish-American father. He was a third-generation product of "good-stock" coal miners who, after emigrating from Poland, had settled into the hamlet of Glen Lyon, Pennsylvania.

Bunny also inherited a disposition which, if crossed, would grant you a second chance to make amends, if she liked you. If not, you were likely toast. In other words, she was like Tell.

Bunny lived in the apartment located upstairs at the Harrow Inne, a 1790 former carriage house and tavern in Ottsville, now a restaurant on the first floor. Owners Klaus and Marge Reinecke were happy to have her as a tenant.

In the spring of 1982, Bunny informed Marge Reinecke that she was open to dating, having broken up with a boyfriend. Marge knew Tell and she thought that he could be a prospect for Bunny. She approached him to arrange a blind date.

"I'll meet her on Thursday," Tell was quick to reply, forgetting that every Thursday night he had a "boys' night out" obligation to go out somewhere with a couple of his male friends to eat, drink, and smoke cigars.

When Tell called to inform her of his prior commitment, Bunny answered that she would be delivering bond documents to New York City on Thursday and she would only be able to see him in the evening, if at all. They decided to keep the date—her first and only blind date.

On the appointed day, a heavy rain caused Bunny to complete her task a couple of hours later than expected. Her return to the Harrow became a late-night proposition. She called from the road, but Tell told her he wanted to keep the date. Bunny then called her longtime girl-friend Sharon Dacey and asked her to accompany her. Upon Bunny's return, the two met in the Harrow parking lot and went upstairs to her apartment.

Dacey, wearing a conservative skirt and a loose-fitting blouse, walked downstairs alone. The men had already had more than a round or two of wine and champagne and one of them remarked, "Nice tits," upon seeing her enter the room. The over-the-top remark brought such a round of laughter that even Dacey had to join them.

Bunny, however, entered with fresh makeup, wearing a white silk blouse tucked into navy blue, skin-tight, Lycra jeans. Tell's jaw dropped. He was speechless. Turning to the others, he whispered, "I really like this woman."

"Tell almost fell out of his chair. He was mesmerized—could not take his eyes off her. He was enchanted," Dacey would later remark.

Tell made room for the women to sit together and offered a late-night dinner. Midway through the meal, he stood up, stretched his tight blue jeans, and walked in his blue clogs across the room to get another bottle of wine. Bunny watched him and then leaned over to Marge Reinecke, who had by now joined the group, and confided, "What are you trying to do to me?" She feared that her resolve to not get too involved with a man too soon might be slipping away, judging from her quickened heartbeats.

Max and Tell Erhardt, around the time Bunny first met Tell.

The party carried on into the early morning hours. At one point, Tell asked to see Bunny's apartment. She took him upstairs and guided him through the modest living space. On the way back down the winding stairwell, barely wide enough for one body at a time, Tell leaned close to Bunny and kissed her, saying, "I'm not guaranteeing it will be a rose garden, but you will always eat well."

(Quite the incisive proposal to a woman used to a lifestyle that included men with high-speed boats and racing cars.)

Then he escorted her outside to his, as he put it, "top-of-the-line, $50,000 high-performance, limited edition, 6.9, Mercedes luxury sedan."

Bunny, who had ogled his height, scarlet leather racing jacket, silk shirt, and tight-fitting jeans, however, was only marginally impressed with Tell's descriptive automotive pitch. She was decidedly unimpressed by the way Tell opened the car trunk, picked up a large planner book, and looked to see when he could fit her into his schedule. He found an open date three weeks out and penciled in their date.

Bunny leaned into him this time and whispered, "Call me when it gets closer." She started to walk back inside, but Tell stopped her. He explained what he did for a living—how his career was going and how his tightly scheduled itinerary worked.

"Oh, is that why you have all those cookbooks in your trunk?" Bunny jibed.

Trying to convince her of his legitimacy, he picked up one of his cookbooks and signed it, "I see you!" The phrase meant nothing to Bunny who thought, *'I see you!' Yeah, right! I'll never see this guy again.*

What Bunny couldn't know at the time was that back inside the restaurant, Tell had whispered to Dacey that he was hooked on Bunny, knowing his words would eventually lead back to her. "Tell said it, and I remember vividly, 'I am in love,'" said Dacey.

Tell was the luckiest man in the world that night, only he didn't know it yet. Bunny would become his wife one day, but she didn't see that in her future that evening either. For now, she was completely unsure she had any future at all with Tell, except for a nagging feeling inside that this could be something different.

Marge Reinecke kept tabs on her two friends and their progress. When Tell later didn't follow up on a date, she pushed for a mid-day rendezvous at the 1840 Blue Bell Inn the very next day.

Bunny arrived expecting a quiet lunch with a few friends and some fun but she was shocked. Six people accompanied Tell, who sat in the middle of them. Attorneys to his right discussed the Warner book deal; and to his left his publicist, Vanita, who appeared to be engaged in a more-than-professional relationship with Tell. Bunny felt under dressed in casual attire, compared to the business wear of the others present. However, Tell was even more impressed with what he saw.

By the summer of 1983, Tell and Bunny had gone out on several more dates spread out over months. His horrendous schedule prevented a predictable pattern of dates following their second meeting. Still, they talked on the phone a lot. Eventually, overnighters entered the mix.

Tell was living in a carriage house in Gwynedd when he met Bunny. He owned two cats, a Russian Blue he called Boris and an Abyssinian named Abby. Bunny owned an eighty-five-pound tan and white-footed, white-breasted Pit bull, Blue, who Tell fell in love with right away.

Overnight stays were logistical nightmares. When Bunny stayed with Tell more than a day, Blue was left at the Harrow Inne in her apartment. Either Bunny had to go home or Tell had to stay at her place, which, of course, created another problem: "Who feeds the cats?"

The Reineckes saw Bunny and Tell's difficulty differently six days of the week. No one was ever going to rob them with a Pit bull on the premises. They loved when Blue stayed at Bunny's place over the restaurant. They even volunteered to feed him, except on her home days when the restaurant was closed.

Somehow Tell and Bunny would have to come together or go bust. Bunny started to bring Blue over to his place after he agreed to cage the cats, which, of course, unsettled Boris and Abby.

Bunny could see that Blue was not going to get along with the cats. Tell, at first, did not agree, but in time they compromised. When Bunny visited Tell's house, the cats were restricted to one room in the carriage house out back, and Blue had the run of the apartment. That worked for a short time.

Tell insisted that they should try to put them together. The day of reckoning arrived when Bunny wasn't home and Tell attempted the merger. Blue chased Boris and Abby outside to the garden, up onto a tall fence, past the fence, and up an oak tree. Bunny arrived hours later and found Blue hanging by one arm on the low front branch of the oak, holding both cats hostage higher up the tree.

Tell promised not to try that again—until two days later.

Once again, Blue chased Boris outside. This time, both jumped the six-foot fence and then Blue held guard at the bottom of the tree, running back and forth, barking loudly for hours as Boris watched him from a high branch.

With great effort, Bunny coaxed Blue back into the house, but Boris stayed up the tree for three days. Bunny, Tell, and one of his friends, George, were unable to bring the cat down. Bunny and Tell, having to leave for work on the road, left George to deal with the cat situation. Not long after, Tell gave the cats away.

Blue, on the other hand, got a taste of Hollywood. He was televised with Bunny on *PM Magazine's* Valentine's Day Special, "Breakfast in Bed."

36

ENTREMETS

"Ich habe hart dafür arbeiten, was ich habe."
("I have to work hard for what I have.")

—Chef Tell

A Tell-hosted *Chaine* dinner was always a welcomed event. The parties were themed affairs with continental foods and liquors carefully selected and paired for the fortunate attendees. The other chefs of the *Chaine*, their spouses, and partners knew to come hungry to Tell's place on April 20, 1986—all hundred-plus attendees. The menu did not disappoint:

RECEPTION
Assorted Hors d'oeuvres
Mirassou Brut 1979
Meursault Boillot 1983

DINNER
Brioche Louis XIV, *Sauce Perigourdine*
Terrine *Fruit de Mer*
Gelee *"Façon du Chef"*

"Cadgery"
"Cochon au Lait" with Cabbage

Gewürztraminer Cuvee Theo – Domaine Weinbach 1983
Rüdesheimer Bischifsberg – Reisling Spatlese 1983
Chateau Vignelaure 1982.

Granité
Moose "St Hubertus" – Medley of Wild Mushrooms
Breast of Duck "Bangkok"
Pinot Noir 1981 Roudon Smith
German beer

Fromage (cheese)
(To clear the palate for dessert)

Sori Tildon – Gaja Barbaresco 1982
Schramsberg Cremante 1982

DESSERT

Pear *"Blanche et Noir"*
Coffee and tea
Digestif at the bar

As anyone can see, Chef Tell was not trained solely in his native German cuisine.
On that day his crew included:
Tell—Master Chef
Horst Herold—*Chef de Cuisine*
Patrick Byrne and Brian Platt—*Sous Chefs*
Melanie Melle and Frank Dugliese—*Chefs de Patisserie*
Joyce Fortunato—*Garde Manager*
Franklin Collins—*Commis de Cuisine.*

Russell Baum, *Baille* of the *Chaine* chapter, was the Dinner Chairman.

37

A NATURAL-BORN TV PERSONALITY

"Tell was a giant of a man, a great guest. He could cook and talk
at the same time. . . ."

—Regis Philbin

Television was a pioneer venture that worked out well for Chef
Tell and won him an Emmy. While other chefs felt better
working in their kitchens, safe within the confines of what
they knew, Tell stepped up to the camera from behind the
apron, put on a smile, and taught as he cooked. His animated, quick-
witted personality—well suited to the medium's lack of sophistication at
the time—"made love to the camera."

"Tell was a natural. He was charismatic and fun to watch," Chef
Staib remembered. "He was always on the news segments."

Being around people, talking with people, making them laugh and
feel good—that was Tell's game. Wherever he traveled, Tell was able
to—liable to, some would say—tell a joke. No matter the audience, Tell
told the jokes that he wanted to tell. He let the chips fall where they may.

In Tell's mind, there was no competition. He saw other chefs as comrades in arms. To Tell, these were people who by choice shared a love of cooking and kitchen battleground strategies. He expected other chefs to kiss, love, and respect each other like family members, not to compete like enemies. He set a friendly tone with his chefs and the others followed the example.

Of course, family members now and then fought, but if an outsider came between them—God help them.

Tell's contemporaries shared his ideals. They would miss Tell's presence when he was gone. Protégé Freddie Duerr recalled, "Tell made it all very different than the scene today. Today people are serious. They act like enemies at times. Back then, chefs were friendly in the city of Philadelphia. A large part of that was Tell's way of doing business—it was a family then. With Tell around, it was a different restaurant scene."

"He definitely added to our profession. No question about it," Chef Staib added.

"*D'accord!* One couldn't help but like the man," Chef Perrier concurred.

Scores of chefs agreed that Tell's greatest asset was his personality. He conquered people with this charm. He knew how to talk to the camera and he came across like a "people person." For a pioneer, nothing is a sure thing, and on a medium where judgment came quickly—ratings didn't lie; people watched you or watched someone else—Tell was a natural. He ventured where no chef had ever gone before in his local market. His timing couldn't have been better.

In reality, though, why Tell succeeded was not too difficult to grasp. He talked with people, not at them. Live or on television, he wore several hats with panache—cook, chef, teacher, friend, mentor, sideline encourager, and jokester. More than just "comfortable in his skin," he made audiences in their living rooms and their kitchens feel like they could at least try to cook the same foods.

TV talk show host Regis Philbin agreed: "Tell was a giant of a man, a great guest."

Three-time Emmy winner Chef Walter Staib grew up in the same neighborhood of western Germany as Chef Tell. He understood the backbone that gave him and Tell the stamina to continue in the face of adversity. Both were Swabian—occupants of the most successful economic state of modern Germany, Baden-Wurttemberg.

To be Swabian, at one time, was to be the butt of jokes—a sort of German "hillbilly." In the twentieth century, Swabian frugality and cleverness earned them a better reputation. A few illustrious, hard-working, entrepreneurial, and thoughtful Swabians come to mind: Albert Einstein, Bertoldt Brecht, Gottlieb Daimler, Karl Benz, Rudolph Diesel and, of course, Friedrich Schiller, playwright of Wilhelm Tell.

On the occasion of the fiftieth anniversary of the state's latest reorganization, Swabians boasted, "We can do everything, except speak 'Standard German.'" The show of humor worked as subtle commentary on the many language dialects in use throughout Germany.

Staib and Tell met by chance on the floor at a National Restaurant Association convention in Chicago in the mid-1970s. There Tell conducted food demonstrations, and Staib represented a large food concern. They spoke briefly about their common past.

"We were trained in the same military style—we worked eighteen hours a day. If the restaurants were slow, we worked in the fruit gardens, cultivating and harvesting the crops. We were told it was 'good for our character.'"

"Tell," Staib recalled, "said with a laugh, 'It did give us a good foundation.'"

Staib added, "Tell was a rising star in America when we met, but he was huge back in Germany. For the rest of us, he was a role model. He set the pace for those who followed."

Their paths would cross again in Philadelphia, and they would become fast friends.

Tell worked and advised people about food preparation because he knew his craft well. His generosity of spirit and cooperative attitude glued viewers to their TV sets and helped them spend more time in their home kitchens.

He was real, too. The man people saw on-air was the creation of that man off-camera. Organized, opinionated, funny, and engaging, he loved what his persona did. Using his talents in his unusual manner, he represented what is best about people, and viewers responded. They understood him when he not only cooked food, but also revealed every detail they needed to know and do to make the food they cooked taste good.

On one of his appearances on *LIVE! with Regis & Kathie Lee*, Tell de-boned a whole leg of lamb in minutes. After putting Regis to work pushing carrots and garlic into holes he made in the prepared meat, Tell

On the *LIVE!* set with Regis and Kathie Lee.

handled the leg, explaining as he went how to cut the bone away. Never missing a beat, he carried the conversation with Regis and instructed both his TV audience and his host, to the delight of the live studio audience. Such detail of instruction, action, and conversation would still be difficult to find on TV today. Tell was one of the earliest television multitaskers.

"Chef Tell was a man of great humor and incredible skills in the kitchen. He brought us love and laughter . . . humor and passion for food," wrote Iron Chef Cat Cora.

Through the course of his illustrious, though shortened, lifetime, Tell owned five successful restaurants. Like a champion thoroughbred not known for the long distances, he entered the gate, bolted strong at the gun, and won nearly every short race he entered. After succeeding in one location, he'd move on to greener pastures, eager to test his skills on a new challenge. His loyal fans followed him.

38

WANNABE JEALOUSIES

"Ich habe für das was ich habe Arbeit."
("I have to work for what I have.")

—Chef Tell

Tell's success on television suited his personality, because he worked on controlled sets which were, in effect, much the same as the controlled environment of kitchens where he ruled the roost. Out on the road, life was far different. There he mingled with people from all walks of life, including vendors who made their living out of suitcases, motel rooms, and pickup trucks hauling trailers of goods.

In the analog days of Tell's prime time, these road warriors were a hardy bunch, a close-knit clan of product-hawking gypsies. Chef Tell was the *pioneering* celebrity chef whose lot was to pick and choose his way around a veritable minefield of personalities, which surrounded him on the road.

These hard-working salespeople could grant that a chef, albeit one from Germany, worked hard once they saw him in action. But, whether they liked Tell or not, they just did not understand how television and book-sales success had apparently so easily come to him. After all, fame and fortune had not found them—*why the German guy that cooks?*

Tell had an answer for the question, if they were willing to hear it: "I'm not a comedian who can cook, as some people think. I'm a cook who is a comedian. I've always been able to ad-lib."

In some cases, jealous feelings and thoughts could not be hidden. Some envied Tell openly; some made less of him behind his back; others rode free on his coattails—partners in cooperative ventures they had persuaded Tell to join.

People either loved or hated Tell after they met him. Some of the road-show pitchmen, who hawked their products in the same venues, never appreciated the brash newcomer that women fawned over. To them, Tell was the loud-mouthed personality with the big moustache and the thick German accent, and they didn't like it. Of course: they couldn't be like him, nor could they be him.

We work these shows because our lives depend on it, not because we got some "cushy" book deal, was their way of thinking.

"Yeah, I worked with that Chef Tell guy," one road-lifer said to an inquiring journalist. "We did the same shows, talked a few times. Today, I have nothing good to say about him. My mother once told me, 'If you don't have anything good to say about someone, say nothing.'" And he hung up the phone.

The worst of the jealous ones never even made an effort to reach out and communicate with Tell. They never understood that their beef was not with him, but with his *symbolic* success. They had no way of knowing that Tell was just another man on the road, like them, working with his own set of skills and flaws—just another guy doing his job.

"He has a hundred-seat restaurant ('. . . with all fresh food depending on what's available, nothing's frozen') in a Philadelphia hotel where 25 percent of his clientele come because of his TV exposure . . . he runs a cooking school at which he conducts classes two days a week . . . spends one day a week taping television shows ('. . . always one take and ad-libbed; I don't want to be artificial.') and spends a couple of days a week appearing at department stores, food conventions, and cooking schools throughout the country," wrote the publication *PM Magazine* for Group W Productions of Westinghouse Broadcasting Company.

Jealousy snared the ones who got trapped by their own feelings of inadequacy. If they worried there were just so many dollars to go around they lived a lie, for that fixed idea was their own.

Tell didn't care if people loved or hated them; he loved them all, despite plenty of reasons not to, and he worked with those who gave him a fair shake. Having blazed the trail ahead of other road-show chefs, he also taught others in his profession what he had learned, so they could succeed in his footsteps.

So what if he made a lot of money? He earned it. One Chicago radio commentator with an agenda estimated on-air, right in the middle of an interview with Tell, Tell's income to be "$225,000 a year."

"More than that," said Tell.

Her answer didn't satisfy. She pushed for a clarification and, right on the air, got more than she bargained for "I have overhead—the offices, the printing, giveaways. I have a few cars. I have a blonde beside me. People say, 'Look at that guy.' They don't see you getting up at 5:00 a.m., flying to Chicago—cooking all day in different locations in the heat of summer, cleaning up, packing up, and flying home eighteen hours later. Day after day, month after month, I have to work for what I have."

With that, Tell stood up, placed the headphones on the table, and walked out of the radio station's studio.

The world of product-oriented ventures was a world of risk in Tell's time. Despite potential jealousies and the publicity-seeking motives of others, Tell partnered up on product ventures for the mutual benefit of his fellow participants. Some of these were very successful, some not so much.

Partnering with a chef on food-related ventures was uncharted territory, and Tell was the beacon lighting the way. In this arena, Tell was the vanguard who staked out the course for those who would run the same race today. When these product ventures ran their courses of time in the limelight, his partners had at least benefited by positioning themselves with the Chef Tell brand name and image. Co-venture partners and their families realized career advances and fortunes as a result.

For some that wasn't enough. They took advantage of their affiliations without Tell's authority, well beyond the scope of their contracts. Tell had no choice but to bring suit. Copyright and trademark law, then as now, required active protection and defense of the brand, under penalty of loss of those rights.

Offenders failed to remember that Tell agreed to their venture requests in the first place—he had not come to them. Blinded by *their* misguided emotions, they ignored relevant facts and lost their way. More than that, they lost a real friend, who in most cases was sensitive to the balance necessary to succeed in business and friendship.

The more successful venue associates, who looked past the rhetoric of the green-hearted noise-makers, saw and heard only a hard-working professional who cooked with a ready smile and a friendly manner.

Tell took it all in stride. He moved forward with his business and his life. His attention remained focused on the bigger prize of his mother's vindication, even as Alan W. Petrucelli of *US Magazine* on June 22, 1982, declared, "At thirty-nine, he's the most popular chef in television history, galloping past gourmets Graham Kerr and Julia Child."

39

COOKING FOR SUBLIME
ECSTASY

"Ich für das Vergnügen, kochen, wenn es alle zusammen."
("I cook for the pleasure of when it all comes together.")
—Chef Tell

rushing aside the convention hall venture partners, who took advantage of Tell's brand value, his peers back in kitchens in Philadelphia perceived his efforts and successes without rancor. Chefs at the top of their game, who knew him well, were already successful in their way, and they harbored no jealousy over Tell's successes. Hard-working premier chefs, they saw how hard he worked. They saw that his media prowess across the nation brought good news, and customers, back into their Philadelphia establishments.

To men or women inside the inner circle of the Philadelphia *Chaine* and other culinary associations to which Tell belonged, Tell was known for his generosity. They could not explain others not liking him, except out of jealousy or misunderstanding.

Upon learning how much money Tell earned at the height of his popularity, one of America's top chefs, who wished to remain anonymous, stated without reservation, "Tell made a lot of money! That was a lot of f***ing money! Much more than even me." In his next breath he added, "But, of course, he was special. I liked him very much. Good for him!"

Tell had earned and blown through two, million-dollar fortunes by the mid-1980s. Truth be told, Tell and his cronies cared little about the money. Those who shared his passions agreed that the true test of success was a simple one: *when your patron picked up a fork and knife, did they like your food?*

An unqualified "yes" was enough. The money followed.

Tell, blindfolded in his kitchen where he would know where his utensils and foods were located, could produce whatever dish or whole course that you wished, to perfection. Not unlike Michael Jordan with a Wilson basketball, Babe Ruth with a Louisville Slugger bat, and Steve Jobs with Apple computers, he was that good with cooking food.

The best chefs without fail are artists with extraordinary palates, who know their craft cold. The thought *How much better can I really get?* resonates in their hearts and is their private challenge. Tell's quest was for sublime ecstasy—a performance level beyond mere performance, the same awareness athletes call "the zone" and mere mortals call "rapture." Sublime ecstasy was elusive, ephemeral, valued—and priceless.

With nearly a combined century of cooking between them, Tell and Perrier could only count, on less than five fingers between them, the times they experienced such ecstasy. Despite the long odds, they continued to finesse their delicate performances, much like fly fishermen cast leader and fly, looking for that soft, timeless magic when all elements come together. Each plated presentation, each course or event congratulated, each award earned, did not satisfy the yearning that drove them the same way Picasso, Miles Davis, Dali, and their ilk were driven to transcend reality.

"Only three times in fifty-two years have I felt ecstasy: one was a dinner for the *Académie Culinaire de France*, which was fabulous. The way I was feeling that day—the sauce, the flavor, the presentations were pure ecstasy for me. I've only had that three times in fifty-two years of cooking," recalled Perrier.

"I eat too much food as it is, so I cook for the pleasure of when it all comes together. It doesn't happen much, but it is worth it when it does," said Tell.

Even the best of chefs, however, experienced days when they wished they did not have to cook. Perhaps the lowly commis learned to endure pots and pans thrown at him because the days would inevitably come when to shut off the alarm, pull up the covers, and roll over to sleep would beckon too strongly to ignore.

"It doesn't mean your food that night was going to taste bad, but it might," commented Susanna Foo with a Cheshire cat grin and a sparkle in her eyes.

At times unable to overcome his counter-emotional state, Tell knew who to call to rejuvenate his spirits. "Susanna, I'm thinking of Peking duck again," Chef Tell would say by phone to soothe Foo and elicit another elegant dish from his friend. No matter her mood, when Tell wanted more duck, she accommodated him.

"The best Peking duck I've ever tasted," Tell attested.

For those chefs who lived and breathed cooking, a wish to be some-place other than inside of a kitchen could be replaced instantly by a single phone call or unexpected visit from a good friend. With purpose rekindled, desire kicked back in. The challenge to please and inspire took over—the malaise replaced by a renewed drive to demonstrate excellence one more time.

Cooking was a crazy, exciting series of commercial events back in those days, but so were the other times—the holidays and days off—when the chefs of Philadelphia gathered to play together.

40

CHAINE LARGESSE

"Sie geben 10 Köche das gleiche Rezept, erhalten
Sie 10 verschiedene Gerichte."
("You give ten chefs the same recipe; you get ten different dishes.")
—Chef Tell

Philadelphia's *Chaine* picnics began in the summer of 1983. Well beyond the stereotypical American-family picnic of hamburgers, hot dogs, potato salad, soda pop, and ice cream, these were gourmet affairs. Top chefs and gourmands, who loved to dress up and dine indoors, liked to picnic outdoors dressed either in t-shirts and shorts or formal summer wear. *Chaine* picnics were favored opportunities for one hundred to two hundred revelers to let their hair down and party. Food, champagne, liquor, and beer flowed freely until the moon was higher in the evening sky than the picnickers.

Over the course of seventeen years, the favorite locale for the annual get-togethers was the estate of Bengt and Josephine Jansson in Ziglarville, Pennsylvania. Jansson, a Consul for Scandinavia, who ran a ship-handling business in Philadelphia, designed and built the multi-acre estate that included a large manor, an expansive lawn, a swimming pool, a fishing pond, walking paths, a separate guest house, and a working sauna.

Tell with Max and Liesel at a Chaine picnic.

Chef Tell's 1986 *Chaine* Member of the Year award was in part a recognition for his catered picnic, which was voted Event of the Year by the membership, but also for his "enormous contribution to the *Chaine*, since its inception in 1976," Russell Baum pointed out. Dressed in lederhosen shorts and faux suspenders printed on his white t-shirt, he labored from early morning throughout the day into the evening.

Arrivals found the Jansson estate transformed into a Swedish garden. They were straight away handed an aperitif consisting of a glass of dry champagne and Gravlax—a Nordic appetizer of thin-sliced, raw salmon cured in salt, sugar, and dill paired with a dill and mustard sauce, served on thin crackers or bread. Painted statues of gnomes "cavorted" among the trees and bushes. The Swedish sauna was hot and open, and picnickers in swimming attire ran out from its heat and plunged themselves under the cold fountain waters flowing into the pool.

While a motto of "Drink to the max!" might have ruled the day, in reality a better assessment for the activities was "Eat, drink, and be merry"—there was so much food to eat.

"Omigod, the food! The beautiful afternoon under the sun ... everybody was there, and there was such camaraderie," remembered Chef Patruno.

Bunny Kule recalled, "Those picnics were something else. People were just eating and drinking and dancing. There was so much food and great champagnes!"

Smoked trout, Westphalia ham, cheeses, and salads beckoned from appetizer tables. Hardy game meats like German boar sausages, venison, and brats were prepared a variety of ways. If you had a taste for wild boar, suckling pig, or smoked salmon, you didn't go hungry. Veal, ox, chicken, lamb, and goose roasted on the spit, enough for more than two hundred people, beckoned.

Meters of delectable desserts provided by Georges Perrier—*Chaine* Dessert Chef of the Decade—extended across tabletops also loaded with fresh fruit daiquiris, top wines, and liquors. Chef Tell provided even more desserts: fruit flans, pecan pies, mousses, sorbets, poached apples, cheesecakes, chocolate Black Forest cake, and Linzer and Sacher tortes.

In the evening, the cabins and trees, festooned with garlands and décor lighting, lit up the estate like Stockholm's waterfront. The bar was set high for every *Chaine* picnic to come.

The amazing thing was, the 1986 picnic came mere *days* after the annual *Chaine* dinner held in Atlantic City at the Sands Hotel—a wonder anyone had room left in their stomachs after that extravaganza.

* * *

Imagine if you will that you're dressed in black-tie formal attire. You and your partner walk to the entrance of the hundred-plus capacity dining room reserved for the *Chaine*, present your invitation, and then step inside a magical bubble of elegant guests and classical music.

You select from one of the roving servers a crystal glass of Meursault 1982 H. Germain, Brut or a 1982 Domaine au Ropiteau, Meursault. If you prefer a Riesling, you take a 1984 Chateau Ste. Michelle, Johannesburg Riesling. The two of you head toward the hors d'oeuvres where, between nibbles, you engage in conversation with friends until dinner is announced. Your formally set table is then peopled with new acquaintances.

Baby asparagus baked in warm herb and lemon, brioche baskets with purée of yellow peppers, and fried fennel greet your nostrils, eyes, and palate. Cold seafood and vegetable gazpacho with saffron crème fraiche refreshes your taste buds while they are further delighted by a 1983 Clos St. Landelin, Gewurztraminer or 1983 Simi Chardonnay.

Golden zucchini blossoms stuffed with smoked reindeer and fresh Oregon chanterelles dressed with New York State triple cream cheese and fresh-roasted tomato marmalade finish your first three courses. An intermezzo of a soothing-cold granité of watermelon with a pinch of sorrel follows.

A 1984 Beringer, Fume Blanc or, if you preferred, a 1982 Davis Bynum, Pinot Noir kicks off the second half of your meal and accompanies the fillet of sand shark grilled over apple wood and laid over a purée of sesame cucumber and fried ginger root. You taste the partridge breast and filet of ram, blackened over fruitwood and drizzled with Kentucky bourbon sauce, which is presented beside Napa cabbage and playful spaghetti squash splashed with orange-basil vinaigrette, and garnished with nasturtium and honeysuckle blossoms.

The welcome break before dessert provides the opportunity to acknowledge new levels of *Chaine* achievements and make recognitions of new inductees before dessert.

Then, a Sandeman, Royal Tawny Port goes well with your Angelo pear that is stuffed with caraway feta cheese, accompanied by toasted walnuts and pumpernickel crackers. If you chose differently, a tray filled with selected black and white truffles waters your palate. All of it finished with an international medley of coffees.

If you were Bunny and Tell, you ate and drank well into the night— in prelude to the Event of the Year picnic only five days later.

OOFDAH!

* * *

In the ensuing years, Tell would import a Caribbean-themed picnic from his new Cayman Island location. He would add not only the flavors he'd concocted from the Caribbean cuisine he'd mastered, but also a one-man band with steel drum island music. The Cayman bartender he brought with him, Mr. Paul—the hit of the picnic with his "Cayman Mama" drinks blended with three rums, grapefruit, pineapple and mango juices, coconut milk, and fresh pineapple, whipped up with ice—delivered his toast with every drink handed out, "Drink up, mon!" Again, Chef Tell won awards for the events.

Fostered cooperation among *Chaine* members recruited more restaurateurs into the Philadelphia fold. If accepted into membership, one had passed rigorous standards of qualification. The help and confidence of the very best chefs in the area were the reward. The result was a local chapter that guaranteed and measured the quality output of the local food industry, and, being part of an international society, ultimately raised gastronomic standards worldwide.

With the *Chaine* established and all palates covered by the diversity of cuisines, Baum and Rosenthal could take credit for having engineered a new world of Philadelphia cuisine with global cultural influences. Thanks to the *Chaine largesse* so generously shared among local chefs, Philadelphians, who had earlier endured long trips by train or car to Manhattan or DC, could now find the choices they preferred most right in their backyard.

Like icing on cake or fresh whipped cream atop chocolate mousse, Chef Tell's television presence assured, beyond the picnics and formal dinners, that Philly's chefs and restaurateurs not only operated in concert, but also stayed fresh in the minds of a national audience of home-makers/chefs whose desires to learn more about cooking were insatiable.

41

SELF-CREATED JUST DESSERTS

"Stand rund um das Feuer lange genug, erhalten Sie verbrannt."
("Stand around the fire long enough, you'll get burned.")
—Chef Tell

A basic datum of brand marketing is, "Whoever does it first, does it best." Hertz, though historically the second car rental company, marketed itself as Number One and thus gained and maintained a majority market share of the auto rental industry. Avis's 1962 campaign, "We're No. 2, We Try Harder" achieved another marketing "first"—no company had attempted that positioning before. Avis took significant market share away from Hertz, became profitable for the first time in thirteen years, and increased its growth from 10 percent to 35 percent annually.

Tell may have made branding a part of his bloodstream as early as 1953 when, only ten years old, he watched Clemens Wilmenrod cook on German television, wearing an apron illustrated with his mustachioed image.

In the 1980s, Tell, without an agent, using only his culinary knowledge, inimitable personality, and branding sensibilities, emblazoned his image across America and his restaurants. His staff uniforms and shirts were embroidered with either his distinctive curly-haired image or his scripted Chef Tell logo. He plastered the symbols on matchboxes, linens, polo shirts, stationery, menus, books, and aprons. While other chefs worked hard inside their kitchens, Tell marketed his image harder than any other chef of his time. As a result, his fan base grew and opportunities flowed toward him for decades.

On television, Tell was just being Tell, but this created genuine value for his Chef Tell brand. Spokesman endorsements for Nordic Ware, Southern Women's Shows, Ducane Gas Grills, and others inundated his bank account with checks.

Evening Magazine complained little when it came to Tell being one of their stars. His popularity pulled ratings that made happy campers of its advertisers. The only gripes at the production company were from mailroom employees, who struggled to push open the front door, as more and more mailbags with recipe requests blocked their way. At the peak, they handled more than fifteen thousand Chef Tell recipe requests weekly. Tell's on-air popularity drove his book sales through the roof. A third book, *Chef Tell's Menus in 30 Minutes or Less,* sold briskly in 110 cities.

The success of one medium led to publicity in other arenas. Robin Leach minted his TV show *Lifestyles of the Rich and Famous* in 1984. After his startup production became a hit, Leach produced a feature segment, aired on May 3, 1986, which featured Tell and his fiancée, Bunny. Tell was the first chef to appear on the new show.

Bunny and Tell got away for semi-annual vacations lasting a couple of weeks in late August and at the end of each year, when they might go up to Maine for Bar Harbor lobster. Shorter jaunts, when possible, included Montreal for wood-fired bagels and Jewish smoked meats, Lake Placid for Adirondack accommodations, and Quebec *tourtières* (meat pies) in the East. Going west, they visited Seattle for fresh Pacific salmon, the Oregon coast for steelhead trout, and Alberta, Canada, for the ski slopes of Banff.

Europe, where his reputation had gathered interest and altitude, treated Tell and Bunny like royalty. Chateau Moët, for instance, opened their gates and hospitality to the celebrity couple. The Chateau de Saran, situated amid the coveted grapes of its centuries-old vineyard, hosted twelve selected guests. From the veranda below the rustic suites with 1810 beds and bathtubs planted in the middle of their main rooms, Dom Perignon and hors d'oeuvres were served before dinner.

Precisely at 8:00 p.m. guests followed servers down a large carved-oak stairwell leading them into the private dining room. The six couples were broken up, seated at a long mahogany table, and encouraged to make new acquaintances.

Tell ended up with stuffy people, who snubbed his attempts to converse with them. Bunny, however, sat with vintner Paulo Villela, sommelier of the World Trade Center's *Windows of the World* restaurant and his travel mate, Robert Tishman, the (late) real estate magnate. The trio so enjoyed their discussion that later at a chance meeting in Bonn, Germany, Bunny and Tell were invited to an exclusive dinner with them at an old home in the country.

On this night, six courses commenced with chateau champagne; later, a pinot noir accompanied shrimp-mousse-stuffed baby eggplant. The next course: skate with a white wine and brown butter sauce with a white pinot. After an icy granité, medallions of tenderloin with bordelaise sauce came with a red pinot. Cheese platter selections were offered with brandy. And handmade mille-feuilles (Napoleans) completed the meal, accompanied by more champagne.

* * *

Tell's reputation crossed many industries and led to special event commissions and public relations opportunities. On November 13, 1984, Donald Duck's fiftieth birthday culminated with a parade at Walt Disney World in Orlando, Florida, an outdoor-screen film clip of Daisy Duck baking a cake for Donald, and a real birthday cake right on Main Street.

The two-tiered cake, designed and baked on exclusive commission by Chef Tell and his crew, weighed 550 pounds. Disney had provided a private jet to fly Tell and Bunny down to Orlando from his Pennsylvania restaurant to work with the Disney chefs.

After the event, Tell was asked what he was going to do next. He replied that he was going to Miami for three days off. He was then asked what he would do while there.

"I'm going to sit on the beach and drink mango daiquiris." The remark was part of an interview with a Miami TV station reporter who

Donald Duck's Fiftieth Birthday cake by Tell.

also reported ahead of his arrival that Tell would be taping a TV show segment there along with two radio shows, further illustrating not only Tell's humorous remark, but his work ethic, as well.

Saturday Night Live in its heyday aired parodies of Tell's TV image, which brought awareness of him to a new generation of potential fans and patrons.

In between the travel and the shows, the commissioned caterings, and more cakes—like the sixty-pound, eight-layer replica of the Philadelphia

Flyer's Stanley Cup complete with team signatures and "God Bless America!" inscription—Tell continued to teach cooking to younger aficionados and homemaker/chefs.

The *Boca Raton News* article that journalist Dorothy Sutton wrote on August 28, 1985, about the upcoming "Chef Tell 4-day, 5-star Cooking School" classes to be conducted by Chef Tell in the AAA 5-Diamond Boca Raton Hotel & Club reminded him that the self-created, just desserts of his lifestyle were a part of the legacy of his mother. Each time that he gave back to others what she had shared with him her presence was renewed in his heart.

Miami booth TV demo setup

42

EVERYBODY GETS THEIR PIECE

"Es ist alles für, wenn Sie sich anmelden bezahlt."
("It's all paid for, if you sign.")
—Chef Tell

Tell's latest showcase restaurant, Chef Tell's on Philadelphia's Main Line, opened for buisness in Wayne, in 1985. Shielded from any legal downside, one would think, by the inclusion of nineteen attorneys as partners, it appeared qualified for the record books as the most pro-legal-counsel restaurant in American history.

"Only Tell would have, well, mountain oysters large enough to open a restaurant with nineteen attorneys," noted Chef Freddie Duerr.

Customers didn't care who owned the establishment as long as Tell supervised the cooking. Area residents had heard about Tell's gift for creating outside the food box and, wanting to see and taste what was new, stormed the Wayne location on Strafford just north of Lancaster Avenue. Night after night, Tell didn't disappoint.

However, word of Tell's super-sized legal partnership also made waves among his closest peers, who warned that even a boiling-hot business could one day get blanched. Friends warned how easily infighting can bring down a business, a true fear with so many legal eagles on board.

Yankees owner George Steinbrenner and his nemesis team manager Billy Martin had nothing on what was going to go down in Wayne. The inevitable debacle sprang from a little company in Ohio. Like string beans cooked and tossed into ice water, it gave the attorney/partners pause. What happened was neither Tell's, nor the partnership's, fault. In fact, no one could have predicted its inception, let alone the outcome.

The unusual partnership's attraction to Chef Tell as an investment was not about Tell as a restaurateur. Tell was being courted by an Ohio food company to endorse and act as spokesperson for a new line of sauces they wished to roll out: Chef Tell's Pasta Pour-overs. A successful rollout would bring income to the company and would enrich the partnership with a return on investment that extended well beyond Tell's latest dream restaurant.

Tell's interest, in fact, stretched beyond the sauce deal. He wanted another restaurant but, to open it, he needed funds for an extensive kitchen refit, as well as a complete makeover of the two-hundred-year old, colonnaded, Georgian-style mansion he had located—hence, the arranged marriage of so many partners.

However, the investment funding opportunity went south when the food company deal soured. News of the change ran from Ohio through Philadelphia to Wayne. As a result, the line of sauces never saw shelf space in the marketplace. Without any means of recouping their funds from sales, the nineteen attorneys looked to other possible sources for a return. The restaurant made money, but these investors never wanted to be in the restaurant business. Instead, the attorneys turned their attention to the hefty advance they knew the ambitious company paid to Chef Tell. Now they thought they deserved a share of it, if they could get to it.

The attorneys' new target became Chef Tell's wallet. There was no basis for their claim, but try telling that to angry doctors of Jurisprudence. Wayne, Pennsylvania, as a location boiled over. Lawsuit briefs flew back and forth like confetti at a Manhattan parade.

Still, the restaurant made money, and the dining public was happy with the menu offerings. When blowback from the allegations tossed back and forth hit the local papers, however, it tarnished the restaurant and the restaurant's star. Tell was too distracted for his liking and fast getting to the point where he no longer wanted to be there. The turmoil affected his performance behind the line, which, in turn, affected his crew. He was under attack from all sides outside of the kitchen and, with that, he was more and more determined to find relief. Thoughts of a hiatus to the Cayman Islands came more frequently to mind. He had visited there before, even shared a small place with friends on Grand Cayman.

The dream of Tell's second restaurant was crumbling under heavy fire. One early casualty—a missing dessert chef—turned out to be a blessing in disguise when this setback lead to the discovery of one of the brightest stars to join Tell's team for more than a decade.

* * *

When Suladda Cronk (now Suladda May) first read Tell's classified ad for a pastry chef in the *Philadelphia Inquirer* she thought that he had to be looking for a better chef than she. Her initial reaction was that she might not measure up to his expectations. However, having been a daily fan of his TV shows in earlier years, and now a post-graduate student at nearby Temple University in North Philadelphia, she considered that it would be great to be able to work with him. Her passion and training included fine art, but she loved to create in the medium of food, specifically desserts. She mailed in her résumé.

A week later, Tell's secretary, Mandy Clark, phoned Suladda to say that Tell would like her to come in for an interview, if she would meet him at the Cooking School in Chestnut Hill near his restaurant. Suladda confirmed the appointment and was thrilled and excited to meet him.

Mother Nature dumped a heavy snow upon the city on the day of the interview, and Suladda, a new driver, got lost. She arrived late for the meeting. Inside her car parked at the school's lot, she primped and was lost in the rear-view mirror when a finger rapped her side window and startled her. A loud voice said, "Oh, you look good enough. Just come out and come inside." She turned to find her TV idol standing in the blowing storm in shirtsleeves with an apron wrapped around his considerable waist. His wide grin and humorous tone stifled her nerves.

Inside, the chill of the cold weather had worn off after Tell asked, and she answered, a dozen basic pastry questions. Suladda presented to Tell her extensive photo portfolio of desserts she had made. Halfway through, he stopped her.

"I've seen dozens of desserts that looked good but they had no taste; the ones that tasted good had no eye appeal."

"Well, my desserts have both quality of taste and they look good, too," she countered.

"Okay, you go home and make me some samples and then I will taste them," directed Tell.

A few days later, Suladda stood again in the Cooking School kitchen in front of Tell and waited as he tasted her Chocolate Praline Torte and Apple Walnut Pie.

"Suladda, you're hired," he said. Just like that.

"I was a little shocked but I was so happy!" Suladda remembered.

Bread Pudding by Suladda

In the next years in Wayne, Suladda developed daily dessert items. She concocted ice creams, sorbets, and mousses and she baked cakes and pies for the separate dessert menu she and Tell had planned out. The auspicious beginning for Suladda, after a brief hiatus, was to be repeated on Grand Cayman Island, where once again she would turn out delicate creations that satisfied customers and turned heads in her direction.

* * *

Scuba diving off Grand Cayman looked to Tell like a great way to forget Wayne and his ongoing health issues with kidney stones—it was the perfect place to get some peace of mind from all the hassles.

Tell and a group of old friends he'd known since 1982 had rented a house on Grand Cayman Island in the North Shore area known as Rum Point. The location was convenient for scuba excursions, and Tell was already a certified diver.

Soon enough, Tell tired of the bickering and attacks on his wallet in Wayne, threw in his apron, and boarded a flight to the Cayman Islands. Underwater peace and quiet would soothe his soul, and on dry land there was food and drink that he didn't have to cook.

Not before long, though, Tell was healed enough to itch for something more to do. The snail's pace of the islands was driving him nuts.

John Alliger, an old acquaintance, who happened to be down from Philadelphia, struck a conversation with Tell in which he broached the idea of opening a new restaurant on the island. Alliger and Tell drew up plans for a partnership right away, contingent upon Alliger's purchase of the island's most cherished plantation property—the historic Petra Plantation located right on the Iron Shore near Georgetown. A plantation-type wooden building on the southwestern shore of the Island, the structure was brought to the Island in pieces from its original location in Georgia in 1907 and then rebuilt. In those days, there were few restaurants with style and quality on Grand Cayman.

American citizens Robert and Jeanne Brenton, who owned the property at the time Tell was there, ran a quaint restaurant, which opened for business on April 15, 1970—a time when only thirteen thousand residents and few vacationers lived on the island. They had recruited attractive local young ladies, groomed them as waitresses, and dressed them in uniforms of blue gingham and mob caps. With a superb Austrian chef, a French maître d' cum sommelier, and the pantry and wine cellar filled, they commenced operation of what became an elegant, superbly-run, and successful restaurant mostly patronized by Caymanian locals and snowbird tourists.

Tell, Alliger, and friends recognized the potential of a restaurant venture and got busy with the acquisition, which turned out to be a simple affair. Since the property's current owners were American citizens, a complicated Caymanian law requiring joint-ventureship with a Caymanian citizen did not apply. Parties of the same nationality could make their own deals. The proposed arrangement was approved without a hitch.

Meanwhile, Tell stayed underwater as much as possible, cooling his fins, camera, scuba gear, and mind as the turmoil continued to swirl up in Wayne.

The Wayne partners wondered if Tell ever would return. After all, the Cayman Islands were a tax haven and point of refuge for European expatriates, notwith-standing the fact that Tell was now a naturalized U.S. citizen and hadn't done anything wrong.

Some partners accused him of cooking the books. One even got the IRS to look into Tell's tax situation and consider confisca-tion of his house on Grasshopper Lane. Anything was fair game to get Tell to return, but the plain truth was that he was, for the time being, unofficially on vacation.

The IRS audit found nothing

Grand Cayman Island suits Tell!

amiss. No fines or penalties were assessed or levied, and in the end he kept his house. Tell's fiscal practices were found to be routine, including his use of the advance from the food company. Tell, it was determined, had every right to use the advance as he wished. Much of it he used to aid his friend Horst Herold, who later became his replacement at the restaurant in Wayne. By the end of 1985, the Cayman Grand Old House restaurant opera-tion was in place.

Upon acquiring the restaurant, Tell added new items to the menu, ordered smart new uniforms for the staff, and ensured that his name was up on the signs for Chef Tell's Grand Old House.

The locals were pleased that many of their traditional favorites sur-vived the cuts of the menu, but they soon discovered the tourists knew more about this charming character, who had taken over their flagship dining spot, than they did. In their time, only a smattering of satellite TV dishes could be found on the island. None of the regular locals had them; they knew nothing of the chef with the large reputation on the mainland. They quickly found that they had to make reservations early: the tourists wanted to taste the food and get as close to the popular chef as possible to secure his signature.

Cold Appetizers

	C.I.$
Marinated Conch "Cayman"	4.95
Thin strips of conch, marinated and served the Cayman way.	
Carpaccio	6.95
Thinly sliced tenderloin with olive oil, parmesan, and capers.	
Pate Maison with Sauce Orientale	4.95
A country style home-made pate of veal, pork and fowl baked with pistachios and truffles, served with a tangy onion and raisin sauce.	
Swedish Gravlax with Mustard and Dill sauce	7.50
Salmon cured the Swedish way, served with a creamy mustard and dill sauce.	
Melon in Season with Proscuitto Ham	5.95
Seafood Cocktail "Chef Tell"	7.95
A sampler selection of our seafood appetizers.	

Hot Appetizers

Grouper "Beignets"	6.95
Marinated, lightly coated grouper, deep fried, and served with a minted yogurt and curry sauce.	
Escargot Bourguignonne	6.75
Escargot prepared the old fashioned way with lots of garlic.	
Conch Fritters	5.25
A Grand Old House specialty served with two sauces; hot and spicy cocktail and Sauce Remoulade.	
Fried Brie and Parsley	5.75
A wedge of brie, breaded then deep fried with a garnish of deep fried parsley.	
Spicy Fried Coconut Shrimp	6.95
With a light barbecue sauce	

Soups

East End Conch Chowder	4.50
A delicious soup like the Caymanians like it	
Cold Soup "du jour"	3.75
Hot Soup "du jour"	3.75
Ask your server for a description of today's hot and cold soups.	

Salads

Salad Du Jour	
Varies daily: with only the best and freshest ingredients. Priced daily.	
Danish Salad Composee	5.25
A selection of salads, each made individually then assembled to make an attractive and appetizing dish. This makes either a tempting appetizer or a healthy light entree.	
Caesar Salad	4.95
Fresh Romaine lettuce with home made croutons tossed in Chef Tell's creamy Caesar dressing.	
Greek Style Salad	4.95
Mixed greens in a cucumber garlic tetraziki dressing	

Menus from the Grand Old House

➤➤ Cayman Specialties ➤➤

ConchSteak   14.75
Thin strips of local conch, sauteed and served with a spicy Teriyaki Sauce.

Turtle Steak   15.75
Prime Turtle meat prepared the island way with peppers and onions When available.

Sauteed Snapper "Caprice"   16.75
Sauteed snapper finished with wine, bananas and our own chutney.

Ca Lji-Dschji (pronounced Car LEE Chee)   21.95
Local fresh seafood and lobster prepared in a Curry Sauce served with Mango Chutney

Caribbean Broiled Lobster Tail   26.00
With a sauce of sweet peppers, tomatoes, and onions

➤➤ Entrees ➤➤

Grouper "Grenoble"   19.95
Sauteed with Capers Lemon Julienne & Beurre blanc Sauce

Sauteed Red Snapper "Parisienne"   19.95
Fresh snapper sauteed, then finished with mushrooms & shallots presented with White Wine Buttersauce

Seafood Mix Grill   21.95
Local Fish grilled & sauteed to perfection Served with a light seasonal vinaigrette

Lobster Chefs Way"   26.00
Chunks of lobster meat dipped lightly in egg batter, sauteed with shallots and champignons and finished with beurre blanc

Baked Shrimp "Old House"   22.95
Large tender shrimp with garlic, spices, herbs & white wine presented in a ring of mousseline-potatoes

Roast Duck with Red Cabbage and Spätzle   19.75
Crispy tender duck served with red cabbage and spatzle. A specialty of Chef Tells.

Sauteed Wiener Schnitzel   19.75
Veal prepared the Austrian way. Requested so often, we had to put it on the menu

Medallions of Veal Chasseur   21.75
Served with chanterelles and mushroom reduced with White Wine & Demi Glace

Chicken Breast Milanese   16.75
A plump chicken breast coated in a light batter, served with fettucini.

Grilled Chicken Breast   16.75
Served on a red pepper coulis with vermicelli of vegetables

Schweinepfeffer   19.50
A delicate dish and a specialty of Chef Tell's. Thin strips of pork sauteed then finished with a cream and demi-glace sauce spiced with cracked black peppercorns.

Sauteed Pork Loin Hungarian Style   18.75
Boneless pork loin sauteed and served in a light paprika sauce

Tell, as usual, delivered with friendly welcomes, ribald repartee, and his trademark German accent. When the richness of the food or the tariff took a customer's breath away, Tell had a quick reply (in the words of his friend Ian "Boxie" Boxall), "Look Sir/Ma'am, you haf to understand, zis is a restaurant, not a Red Cross Station."

Friends and acquaintances endured the man—how could they not? Their palates and tummies had been satisfied beyond description. In reply to a cheeky comment from Boxie, he said, "Boxie, can you lip-read?" and without waiting for a reply, mouthed "F*** off."

Even partners in the syndicate, who purchased the property, were not spared. Naul Bodden, who also owned shares in a successful drug-store in Grand Cayman, complained that the dividends from the Grand Old House were not nearly as good as the ones from Cayman Drug. Tell, of course, was completely understanding, but in his own inimitable manner.

"Look, Naul, if you take a girlfriend for dinner to my restaurant, the likelihood is you're gonna get laid afterwards. You're not gonna get the same result by taking her to Cayman Drug and buying her a box of tampons, are you?"

Enough said, yes?

By its July 1986 grand opening, Tell had put significant parts of his earlier personal life behind him for good.

* * *

Six years of divorce proceedings against Nicoletti concluded with her signature on the dotted line in the same year. That lingering wound was closed by the simple expediency of buying her a brand-new Volvo sedan, which Tell purchased with cash. He drove it over to her place—the Swedesford apartment where she and Tell had lived together as a married couple—with the divorce papers inside a folder on the passenger seat. At her front door, he offered her the papers and a proposition, "See the Volvo there? These are the keys, and it's all paid for. It's yours if you sign the divorce papers now." The ink dried in minutes, and Tell took the cab he'd requested to the airport and flew back to Grand Cayman.

In the end of the drama in Wayne, each of the players received their just desserts. Nicoletti tooled around town in her new car, footloose and fancy free. The nineteen lawyers worked out a new arrangement with Chef Herold, compliments of Tell. The house on Grasshopper Lane remained in Tell's possession—Bunny lived there—and Tell had taken some needed time off.

The desk sign in Tell's small office at the Grand Old House read, THE FIRST THING WE DO, LET'S KILL ALL THE LAWYERS. It comforted and satisfied him as much as Shakespeare's *Henry VI* did for audiences on the banks of the Avon River.

Tell and Bunny would go on to live and work together in the Caribbean locale but not without surviving a controversy. And not without a nostalgic look back at what had gone right during the era of the restaurant in Wayne. After all, what had been eventful years for everyone involved with the restaurant and sauce venture, by no means soured the taste of all that took place at Chef Tell's in Wayne. There were positive and noteworthy events worth remembering.

43

A CHANGE OF SEASONS

"... America is a great nation today not because of what
government did for people but because of what people
did for themselves and for one another."
—Former U.S. President Richard M. Nixon

The scrumptious plates coming out of Tell's kitchen in Wayne pulled hundreds of lunch and dinner patrons, including a former U.S. President.

The day the president visited, the kitchen staff wore white polo shirts with the Chef Tell blue script logo emblazoned on them, baseball caps, and white aprons. The chefs wore black pants with traditional white stripes, and Tell wore a blue-logo, white polo shirt with blue jeans and blue clogs. A clean white apron was folded down around his waist. Luncheon servers wore black pants, white button-down shirts with ties, and white aprons.

Tell stood in the kitchen and watched as his sous chef discussed plating details with a commis.

"You need to arrange the plate like so, otherwise flavors mix and the palate is ruined."

"I understand, Chef," replied the commis.

"There needs to be balance on the plate—not just presentation, palate. Remember that."

"Thank you, Chef."

The luncheon hostess entered and informed Tell of the arrival of the anticipated VIP party. His eyes sparkled. Still monitoring the sous chef, he told her, "Tell the valet to inform our guests they have my approval to come in because my food is gonna taste good today."

Tell nodded toward his sous chef, who took note of the signal that they had arranged earlier for his take-over of the kitchen once this guest arrived. Tell had been notified several weeks earlier that the former president wished to dine at his restaurant. His reservation for a party of three was placed a week ago under an alias.

Tell entered the main dining hallway from the kitchen and walked into the twelve-seat, main-floor dining room to his right. Immediately across from the winding, wide-planked oak stairwell, which led to three other larger dining rooms and a small bar upstairs, Tell stood and surveyed the room and its occupants. His presence lent assurance to them, but they knew something was up. A RESERVED sign had been placed on one of the three tables in the room. While there wasn't a spoken buzz about it, the diners took note and wondered who would sit there. The extra activity around the table now charged the atmosphere and heightened everyone's anticipation.

Tell returned to the kitchen.

The long black limousine idled in front of the multi-pillared 1800s mansion packed with 210 lunch patrons. Without fanfare, the valet opened the back door and three passengers alit from the vehicle. David and Julie Nixon Eisenhower preceded former President Richard M. Nixon unaccompanied by former First Lady Patricia Ryan Nixon who, three years earlier in 1983, had suffered the second of two strokes.

Once inside, the luncheon party was greeted, taken to the small room's reserved table, and seated without commotion. The maître d', Joseph ("Seph"), presented the food and wine menus.

Kitchen staff members wrangled over what Tell should do and how he should address President Nixon. Most wanted him to display a two-fingered "peace/victory" sign, the way Nixon had before boarding the Marine One helicopter that took him to Andrews Air Force Base for his final trip to California after he resigned the presidency. Some wanted him to say, "I am not a crook," just as Nixon had.

Tell said nothing. Again he signaled the sous chef and left the kitchen in his hands.

I'm just going to please this party like anyone else, Tell thought as he entered the dining room. He extended his hand with a flourish and addressed Nixon, "Mr. President, I just became a Republican."

Tell had once cooked for Nixon, but he had not met him in person.

"Great. Do you plan to vote?" the President replied.

"Unfortunately, I'm not an American citizen yet."

Nixon's patented wry smile crossed his face, and he said, "It doesn't matter. They have aliens voting in Chicago all the time."

Anyone within earshot of Nixon's remark couldn't help but laugh. His humor blurred the political lines.

The assigned waiter then informed the party of available luncheon specials, took their orders, and left for the kitchen.

Nixon asked, "May I ask you, Chef Tell, would you want to become a citizen?"

Looking Nixon straight in the eyes, Tell replied, "Actually, Mr. President, I've been trying for years."

Nixon's wide-eyed response came with no words, but the Eisenhowers remarked how such an omission didn't seem right.

Tell covered the ensuing pregnant silence with wine choices that would complement their meal.

Nixon deferred his choice to his daughter, "Julie, have you a preference?"

"Perhaps we should let Chef Tell choose our wine for us, Dad." She looked up at Tell.

Tell made recommendations to his sommelier, who left to retrieve the wine. Upon his return, under Tell's watchful eye, he presented the bottle and cork along with the traditional first sip to Nixon, who again deferred to David Eisenhower, declaring, "Better you than me," with a playful smirk.

With the wine poured, Tell congratulated David Eisenhower on the completion of his book, *Eisenhower: At War, 1943–1945*, a volume depicting his grandfather's Allied leadership during World War II. Tell wished him luck on his book and departed just as the early course arrived—a ragout fin with apple truffle.

The rest of the luncheon progressed smoothly—roast duck with fresh asparagus and desserts of chocolate decadence cake—a chocolate cake with dark-chocolate icing and a raspberry middle filling—and crème brulee.

The VIP party departed after a short tour of the kitchen guided by Tell, who introduced his crew one by one to them. Nixon promised a return and did, in fact, fulfill his promise at least three or four times.

The next day Tell received a phone call from Washington, DC. He was informed that Nixon had personally sponsored him for U.S. citizenship. He was as dumbfounded and delighted as a child opening an unexpected Christmas gift.

"My lawyer's not gonna be happy about this. President Nixon just screwed him out of filing fees he was gonna charge me," Tell laughed.

Another surprise came a month later when Tell was asked to deliver the induction ceremony speech. The finishing touch was the flag that flew over the Capitol that day—the one that Pennsylvania State Senator Arlen Specter packaged up with its letter of authenticity and mailed to Tell.

The day the package arrived, Tell opened it in front of his crew. His reaction was immediate—he wept. It was the only time his staff would ever see him cry.

The flame of freedom at times burns more intensely for naturalized citizens than for natural citizens born in America. For one German chef, born merely four decades earlier under the threat of Allied payloads, becoming a naturalized American citizen was one of the sweetest moments of his entire life.

44

QUESTIONING THE HONOR

"The finest steel has to go through the hottest fire."
—Former U.S. President Richard M. Nixon

What had moved former President Nixon to sponsor Tell Erhardt for citizenship? Nixon's early life was so marked by hardship and similar to Tell's. President Dwight Eisenhower's words about boyhood, "We were poor, but the glory of it was, we didn't know it" so applied to both men that Nixon might have considered Tell a kindred spirit.

Nixon was noted for his love of history, a passion also shared by Tell. He championed America and family over personal interests all of his life, like Tell. He accepted naval duty when called and, though raised as a Quaker, a sect known for pacifism, he achieved the rank of Lieutenant Commander during WWII.

Perhaps Nixon had done homework on Tell before they met and knew that Tell had been a military scuba specialist with the German Kampfschwimmers—Germany's equivalent to the U.S. Navy SEALs— during mandatory service to his country.

Nixon, like Tell, doggedly pursued his goals until he attained them. He chose public service over a lucrative private law practice; became first a California congressman, then senator, and later vice president of the country. After losing a bid for the White House in 1960, and a campaign for the California Governorship in 1962, he won the presidency in 1968, which he resigned from in 1974. Still, on a personal note, he looked upon his role as protector of his family to be his most important.

Nixon would have understood Tell whose reputation spread out ahead of him the way the Mississippi widens at the Louisiana delta. Not even Tell could know how far his influence had expanded until he crossed paths with Nixon years before they met in Wayne.

Nixon had requested Tell's services for a dinner he was hosting in New York City. Tell was unsure how Nixon had heard of him. He thought it might have been from the time he worked for Marriott up and down the Northeast Corridor, which included Washington, DC.

Whatever, Tell stepped up to the Secret Service guards posted at Nixon's hotel and showed them the contents of his custom briefcase. One look inside the case at the complete set of knives, and they drew weapons. Déjà vu snapped into place for Tell. They wanted to confiscate his knives, but this time he stood his ground.

"You want to take my knives? I'm the f***ing *chef!* I'm not going to cut the president with them. I'm going to cut his f***ing food!"

The direct approach worked. He was allowed into the suite's kitchen where he cooked for Nixon's party and then left without incident.

Almost.

When Tell returned to the hotel garage under the watchful eyes and care of the Secret Service detail, he noticed the mileage gauge of his beloved 6.9 Mercedes read 424 kilometers (264 miles) higher than when he entered the garage. Someone had retaliated. The distance, he determined after a little calculation, matched a trip to Atlantic City casinos on the Jersey shore and back—the only nearby attraction worthy of the effort of such a drive. Tell was incensed. He could not complain to Nixon, but wanted retribution from someone. He wrote a letter to the Department of Justice asking for compensation. It worked. While never receiving an explanation for the actual mileage usage, even though he pointed out in his letter exactly what his calculations suggested, he did receive an official government check, which he cashed with a smile on his face.

Tell's prized Mercedes was no ordinary sports car; this sedan happened to be one of the last 6.9 models ever to come off the line in Stuttgart. Anyone watching it pass them on the New Jersey Turnpike or U.S. 1 might have noticed the sticker Tell had plastered on the rear license plate, "Chef Tell—I see you!" Now that's branding.

Considering the comparison of their life facts, the answer to why former President Nixon sponsored Chef Tell's naturalization as a U.S. citizen is clear. If ambition, aggressiveness, and impatience for perfection in politics and in food service were prerequisites for top-flight success— and Nixon and Tell had aimed for the top and won—Nixon's act was a professional courtesy from one "survivor" toward another.

Apart from the restaurant and invited opportunities, Tell searched for and found new ways to keep his brand relevant, just as he had done in 1980 with Nordic Ware. From Wayne, he launched a signature line of German stainless steel knives made in Solingen, Germany, the "City of Blades" known for keen-edged weaponry dating back to the Medieval Age. Each blade bore the etched Chef Tell logo on the right side—the side where TV cameras zooming in would pick up the logo front and center. He added a set of kitchen gadgets to the knives—zesters, slicers, ballers, and the like—and branded them all with his logo.

45

RUN FOR THE ROSES

"... All good things in all good time."
—Jerry Garcia

Concierges and taxi drivers never lost touch with Tell as he opened restaurants further out in the suburbs. For them, he was a "sure thing." Tell could be counted on to satisfy the guests they sent his way. Musicians, actors, celebrities of every kind, sooner or later wanted a party caterer for a nosh. And there were those in need of full-blown meals outside of the spotlight of the press, often at odd hours. Given enough notice, Tell came through when satisfying hunger was needed.

One such music group preferred to conduct its business meetings with its attorneys late at night. The Wayne restaurant's proximity to Center City was an ideal location for them, yet was outside the regular domain of the paparazzi. Since the band had earlier used Tell's catering services, they knew they would like the food.

The small crew Tell and Bunny handpicked were sworn to strict secrecy on the several occasions of the band's visits. They didn't mind— they were all fans. This particular band, dressed in uncharacteristic suits and ties to avoid recognition, met for months of late-night soirees without the pressure of fans and paparazzi. In a relaxed atmosphere, attended by the pre-selected servers, they ordered anything they wished from the kitchen. Tell cooked their orders, aided by the one chef he now counted on most, Freddie Duerr.

Because he was a long-time fan, the sous chef, Patrick Byrne, arranged for a bouquet of fresh roses to be placed on the table where the band would sit. Roses long had been the symbolic flower associated with the leader of this band. The band and their entourage took notice and showed their appreciation with signed photos and album covers.

The roses, of course, were homage for Jerry Garcia and The Grateful Dead, who, like Tell, delivered, and then kept their publics wanting for more. Ironically, Garcia's signature, *Run for the Roses* lyrics made for an excellent description of the Wayne debacle:

> *"Run, run, run for the roses*
> *Quicker it opens, the sooner it closes . . . "*

The Dead of San Francisco saw their reputation blossom like wild spring flowers from coast to coast. In the late 1960's they performed free concerts in the Lower East Side of Manhattan, just because they could. Their loyal fan base preceded the big money and fame. While both came their way, neither was the goal of their game. They simply made the music they liked, played the best way they could, and took the journey as far as it would go—a lot like Chef Tell. Garcia's lyrics also eerily, albeit unintentionally, foreshadowed Tell's forthcoming future events.

* * *

When not dealing with the lawyers in Wayne, working inside of the kitchen, or making TV appearances, Tell enjoyed exploring other aspects of the restaurant and wine business. He would often heed the call for his services, provided the price was right, at most any venue. One such place was the Monterey Food & Wine Festival.

After thirty-six years, the festival is Monterey's longest-running food and wine event. In 1987, Tell participated as one of the invited celebrity-chef wine tasters during its tenth anniversary celebration. Bunny accompanied him. Along with celebrity chef Jacques Pépin, the food editor for *Bon Appetit* magazine, and their entourage, they celebrated wine and dined on the food offerings of local restaurants in nearby Carmel.

The party after the workday wine-tasting was in full swing in the evening. Pépin had taken center stage at the table and had the entire circle of friends and acquaintances dressed to the nines in formalwear attempting to balance *food on their noses* while standing on their chairs amid the giggling, music, and flowing wine and bubbly being consumed. Into the nasal/culinary festivities walked none other than actor Clint Eastwood and his girlfriend at the time, actress Sondra Locke. The whole place went wild, among them Tell and Bunny. People yelled repeatedly, "Make my day!" at the star. Star-struck celebrities lined up with glassed-over eyes and waited their turn for a hello or an autograph written on any loose piece of paper they could expropriate from the table tops. Eastwood took it all in stride, graciously signing his name, and flashing his trademark smirk until the party had settled down. For the revelers, it was a Kodak moment for sure; for Tell and Bunny, a weekend to remember.

46

GRAVITY PULL

"An invoice here and there . . . who's going to notice?"
—Anonymous

I n mid-December of 1986, with new restaurant plans on Grand Cayman coming together, Tell finally received closure on the financial problems surrounding Wayne. The IRS had cleared and confirmed that neither he or the restaurant owed back taxes. Chef Herold was now free to carry forward traditions left by his predecessor, though the namesake chef no longer worked there.

Herold did the right thing, which was not to change a thing. He turned out the same menu offerings that Chef Tell had—mostly French classics among a few German dishes.

Sauces of balance and beauty graced carefully constructed presentations. Elegant signature desserts like white chocolate mousse finished with white chocolate crumbles over drizzles of red raspberry sauce sparkled at night.

A peek at the menu discovered appetizers of angel hair pasta tossed with jumbo shrimp in lobster sauce, dusted with parsley flakes and fragrant white peppercorns. *Escargots Forestiere*—tender snails nestled on wild mushrooms under pine nut sprinklings set adrift in a rich garlic-butter sauce—was a favorite.

Heavy cream soups loaded with chopped shrimp and bold, dill-accented potatoes, and New England clam chowders bursting with tender chopped clams were mainstays in case anyone wished a soup course.

Salad of the day was a portrait plate constructed with rows of tangerine segments on bright red radicchio leaves and shredded beets, accompanied by sautéed pears on a bed of mâche leaves (lamb's lettuce) splashed with a contrasting herbed-sherry vinaigrette.

Sauté of veal medallions Alfredo under prociutto or mushroom and tomato *concasse* over spaetzle in a rich cheese cream sauce might be ordered as the Special of the Night.

For his part, Herold never second-guessed Tell. Loyal friendship and honesty outranked commercial considerations. The two friends had helped each other and even provided for the attorney/partners, who over time would see a return on their investments.

Shakespeare wrote, "All the world's a stage, and all the men and women merely players." In the act that was Wayne, Tell could stand tall like the gentlemen he was, because he had played his part with honor. He had made the situation right before he exited that stage and assumed his new role.

Still, like a professional actor yearning for a role on the Great White Way, Tell was not satisfied with the fame and fortunes of his charmed "Hollywood" life. He wanted the hot lights of Broadway. Chef Tell's "Broadway" was a running TV show with his name on the marquee. He would not rest until he reached this goal.

* * *

The problem with TV shows as stages, or restaurants for that matter, is that, like theater productions, they are more than a little risky. The final curtain can fall anytime. When the padlocks are placed on the doors, the lucky ones get out with only the tools of their trade in their hands—their knowledge and their knives.

But when the curtains go up, the hot lights paint the night brightly. When the audiences stand and demand encores amid shouts of "Bravo, Bravo!" exhilaration reigns. For the chef, when all of the plates come back empty, and no one has complained . . . he soars.

"Tell had the same motivation as me—as precious few other top chefs. He fed on that warmth of the people who made him work harder, better, and use all of his talent the best he could," said Georges Perrier.

Flying high emotionally, the mode of transport must equal the task. There are no non-essential parts miles up without a net. If we are all "players," there must be substance to the play and a well-organized group to back up the production. For the chef, there must be his food and his crew.

While Tell flew high, there were times he crash-landed hard. In time, the inevitability of gravity brings us all back to earth.

The catch-all phrase of the restaurant criminal, "An invoice here or there—who's going to notice?" is the bane of any restaurateur. Tell's crashes, at times, reflected betrayals from within his business organizations. He was robbed blind by bartenders, who stashed small amounts of cash, here and there, out of the till into their pockets. Over-padded food and wine orders diverted to people on the line, rather than Tell's pocket at the end of the line, where the money belonged. The fruits of his hard work, which he generously shared with his personnel—opportunities to learn the culinary craft and then go out and work to succeed on one's own—were ignored by a few employees for whom the temptation to steal cash was too easy an alternative. The consequences of their acts, however, affected the honest majority. For Tell, unsuspected losses mounted until it was too late to avoid the inevitable harvest of too many bills in the face of cash shortages.

There would be no winners if a Chef Tell restaurant folded due to financial losses stemming from internal crimes. Loyal patrons, who enjoyed his cooking and camaraderie, would lose their favorite son. Tell and his crews would be forced to find work elsewhere.

"The restaurant business is a cash business. It's too easy for the restaurateur to lose the cash, which is there daily. Or to use it and not realize there are bills to pay at the end of the month," Bunny noted. "Lost income from criminals was not so easily detected."

Tell's front-room clientele paid good money for his performances and the food on their plates. They asked for encores and followed Tell to new venues. Yet for Tell and other restaurateurs, the threat of the curtain coming down for good, for the stage going dark because not all of the money reached their pockets, was constant and real.

Continual vigilance alone didn't guarantee viability. Gravity pulled hard. Divorce was imminent. Tell was grounded after conflicts mounted in Wayne, but he was free at last to be more of a father to his son. He moved on and eventually rose again as the celebrated chef heralded by a different crowd in the wild Caribbean frontier of Grand Cayman Island.

47

FRUITS OF THE SEA: SCUBA

"Ich mache eine obszöne [weiß]Schokoladenmousse."
("I make an obscene [white] chocolate mousse.")

—Chef Tell

Christopher Columbus in 1503 landed on the spits of land known today as the Cayman Islands. The grouping comprises three main islands with a total area of approximately one hundred square miles, located about five hundred miles west of Jamaica, south of Cuba. Because of the numerous turtles that inhabited the islands, they were named "Las Tortugas" and were a godsend for seafaring ship crews short of meat. Later, when the turtle population was cut short, the islands were renamed, "Caymanas," after seagoing alligators.

The Caymanian motto was "Endless Possibilities," but in the 1980s of Chef Tell's time, the Coat of Arms shield added the slogan "He hath founded it upon the seas" from Psalm 24.

During his mandatory German military service, Tell discovered an affinity for the ocean and its abundant sea life. So now, the sea surrounding the Cayman Islands was a safe haven for him. Grand Cayman Island became a platform for more money, fun, and fame than he'd had to date.

* * *

Torsten was a young man, who had just finished college by Christmas time in 1987, with an Economics degree and A-plus grade scores. He was ready to build something with his famous father when he stepped out of the 727 fuselage into the humidity and natural beauty of Grand Cayman. Up to this point, his relations with his father had been a series of timed connections slipped between Tell's work obligations and the logistics of international travel. He had spent six-week vacations with Tell in Pennsylvania and gone on trips together to Universal Studios in Burbank, California, and to Kennedy Space Center in Titusville, Florida, where they watched a spectacular shuttle launch.

The direct and bright Cayman sunlight made Torsten adjust his dark sunglasses and squint in the direction of a small reception group of onlookers as he tried to find Tell. He waved but never spotted him. Instead, Tell's designated driver took his bags and led him to a waiting car. There would be no grand welcome from his father, who might have craned his neck upward at his son, who was now six-foot-nine and weighed 240 pounds. However, he might have had to duck: Torsten was pissed that his father had not met him at the airport.

"Before his son arrived, Tell had counted the days. He kept calling and asking me, 'Are you sure the boat will be available when he's here?'" said Lenny Mattioli—TV's "Crazy Lenny"—who was a boat owner and friend that Tell had met on the island.

Long before Torsten arrived, Tell earned his certification as a Dive Master in America. In fact, the reason for his first-ever visit to the islands was a group trip with his dive class. After diving in caves and large ponds stateside, the divers were able to experience the deep and vast waters and world-famous reef flora and fauna of Grand Cayman. He knew that Torsten was a snorkel enthusiast and remembered that he had already spent hours in the water around Grand Cayman once before.

Torsten grew up in water. Swimming began at eleven months, and when he was fifteen years old, he performed lifeguard duties on weekends at the local public pool. Still, he feared scuba and going deeper underwater using compressed air. Sensing this and needing to make better use of his time at the restaurant, which would enable more scuba trips with his son, Tell arranged for the young man to go out first with a third party closer to his age. Torsten would go out with Jeff Kingstad, a dive instructor who was engaged to Tell's secretary, Janelle.

Kingstad was a former Olympian from Munich's 1972 Games. In 1974, he won the Big Ten championship in the pole vault and spent part of the following three years traveling and competing across Europe. In 1978, he dropped the sport cold and moved to Grand Cayman where he settled in with a local diving school.

Kingstad took Torsten on his twenty-foot Zodiac out to a place one could not reach by swimming—certainly nowhere the young man had ever been before. The water covering the sandbar nicknamed Stingray City was about ten feet deep. Kingstad suggested tanks for convenience. The idea was to sit on the bottom and watch the stingrays.

Torsten was up for the trial. He sat underwater next to Kingstad and let scuba capture his heart. His two-day dive certification training followed without delay and on January 15, 1988, he certified.

"I am sure it was a strategy as he was aware how much I was fascinated about the ocean," wrote Torsten about his father's ruse.

Tell accompanied Kingstad and Torsten on the next day trip out to the North Wall, which was a favored dive spot for divers from all over the world. When the dive ended, Tell climbed onto the boat and realized he had lost his heavy gold chain necklace, which had been a Christmas gift from Bunny. In an attempt to recover the lost jewelry, Kingstad dove over the side and retraced their dive. "Voila! It was hanging on a sea fan perched over a mile-deep drop-off called The Cayman Wall," recalled Kingstad.

Kingstad kept the necklace out of sight as he swam back to the boat. Before he climbed aboard, he announced he'd had no luck. Tell looked crestfallen and stared at the boat's deck. Kingstad climbed into the vessel with the necklace around his neck. Tell looked up.

"His eyes lit up. He laughed aloud and cursed up a storm with spicy German words I didn't understand. He sure was funny!" Kingstad remembered.

Thereafter, when Tell could take the time off, father and son dove twice daily, usually at six in the morning and right after lunch. However, these dives were usually in the company of other people, not strictly father-son occasions. If both dives were in the afternoon, after the last dive Tell repaired to whatever was the closest local watering hole for Jamaican Red Stripe beers and fish and chips on the North Sound side of the island. And if not that, the Rum Punches made with equal parts of orange, grapefruit, and pineapple juices mixed with liberal amounts of grenadine, coconut, and white and dark rums blended with ice worked.

Torsten couldn't get enough of his father. "Times when we were together, man by man, nobody could influence or interfere with us."

Tell and Torsten scuba

He confided to Tell's friend Mattioli that he still wanted more time with his father. And who could blame him? What he could not know at the time was that his father had mutual feelings.

"Tell let his guard down around kids. One time, during Pirate's Week, Tell hired a troupe to 'attack' his restaurant when my two young boys were there (four and two years old). When these 'pirates' attacked and demanded that all the women and children go with them, Tell provided dull swords to my two surprised youngsters to fight off the bad guys in a mock battle. He convinced my kids that they had saved all of us from the invading pirates," recalled Mattioli, who continued, "and then he confided to me that he wished that he could have done those things with his son; wished that he had been able to do more hunting and fishing with his boy. There was a sensitive side to Chef Tell, which not too many people knew."

Mattioli empathized with Tell. Knowing the words could not do justice to the feelings his friend felt, he told him, "All you can do is love them."

Since the entire island was only nine miles by twenty-one miles, Tell and Torsten couldn't get lost, except in their laughter. When the two tall, German-speaking men—one in a Speedo swim suit, the younger in Adidas—arrived . . . of course, no one dared to interfere with Tell's jokes.

"Why does the new German Navy have glass-bottom boats? So they can see the old German Navy."

"Two ethnic guys were going bear hunting. They had all their gear ready and they drove to the forest. There they saw a sign, 'Bear left.' So, they went home."

Once the laughs subsided, a relaxed Tell, happy to have his son at last by his side, looked with at him with pride—wordlessly and full of love—in a way only a father can.

But it was only a temporary respite.

Within a few short weeks, although Torsten had planned to scuba and work with his father for years to come—he even was willing to learn the restaurant trade and work with him for a year or two to stay by his side—Tell was not able to either show his true emotions or balance his business persona with his love for his son: he ended up bidding Torsten good-bye.

Father and son at Grand Old House

Since both father and son did not understand what was happening at the time, it is easy to imagine that the pull of their father-and-son love simply never bridged the gaps left by all of the prior years away from each other. Tell's mistress, the business, demanded his attention every day for almost more hours than there are in a day.

Rightly or wrongly, Tell assumed as he watched Torsten's plane take off that he had done what was best for his son. He had learned long ago in the kitchens of his training days and nights that when emotions try to rule judgment, a man should heed his disciplines to see him through his path in life.

Shortly after, Chef Herold back in Wayne reported to Tell that his protégé, Chef Duerr, was floundering without Tell's personal guidance. Though the news weighed heavily on him, Tell already had a surprise planned for the young chef.

48

FROM THE ASHES: REDEMPTION

"Nous les cuisiniers sont tous les hommes spéciaux.
Nous sommes des artistes."
("We chefs are all special men. We are artists.")

—Chef Perrier

Tell's sudden departure from Wayne in 1986 had left Freddie Duerr demoralized. At the urging of friends, Duerr took time off in the Caribbean where he hoped to work out his frustrations. His friends had told him that surfing, drinking piña coladas, and listening to Rupert Holmes sing about the drink and lost love were the perfect potions for what ailed him.

Drinks in Aruba did bring cold relief. Whenever Duerr got hungry, he ate burgers accompanied by Jimmy Buffet's "Cheeseburger in Paradise," and he spent time with tanned, hot, and willing women. But now Duerr's drinking money had run out. On a Cayman Air flight northbound for Philadelphia, he resigned to return to his sous chef position under Chef Herold.

In the ensuing weeks, his tan, which had been as deep as it was ever going to get, paled as much as his attitude. He didn't know what else to do other than work in Herold's kitchen. He missed Tell. *Even the sound of Tell's voice would be welcome relief from my doldrums,* he told himself.

Then the unbelievable happened.

"Would you be willing to come down to Grand Cayman and help me out?" Tell asked on the taped phone message Duerr discovered one morning.

Duerr played that message so many times the tape broke, but from the first second he had made up his mind. For a college-aged, young man, who had just tasted island life for the first time, the offer from his mentor was a no-brainer.

"I discovered that Tell had moved permanently to Cayman," said Duerr, a broad grin stretching across his face. "It didn't take me long to tell him I was ready to work on Grand Cayman. I already knew all the Caribbean women that I'd meet had great tans!"

Having returned Tell's call, Duerr waited for the FedEx man to deliver the air ticket that Tell had promised was on the way.

Duerr boarded a June 1988 flight to Grand Cayman within hours of the ticket's arrival. Tell met him at Owen Roberts Airport and spirited him to the Grand Old House bar. There he handed him a tall glass of champagne. Tell's partner Alliger looked on as both chefs threw back their entire champagnes in one gulp. Duerr hadn't realized it, but Tell had decided to elevate Duerr's status and responsibilities. He knew the young man was ready—the moment for which he had groomed the lad to work side-by-side with him was at hand.

"Freddie, here's another champagne," Tell said as he poured. "You've been with me through one restaurant now—gotten quite an education— so now it's time to put that training to the test."

Tell raised his glass. Alliger moved closer and raised his, too. As their glasses touched Tell toasted, "To Chef Freddie, our new assistant executive chef at the Grand Old House!"

Are you kidding me? Freddie couldn't think anything else as he stood up and looked from face to face at the two partners, who were grinning like Cheshire cats.

"Oh, man! You've got to be kidding."

"Say yes, Duerr. You can change your mind later," said Tell.

"Of course, I accept! Yes!" Duerr jumped, whooped, and spun around, a wide grin across his twenty-year-old face. "When do we get started?" *The next four years are going to be like college with fringe benefits galore,* he told himself.

"Tomorrow morning, 5:00 a.m. sharp," Tell replied.

* * *

A large orange sun emerged from the eastern horizon as Tell discussed with Freddie the nuances of operating an island restaurant. Ordering ahead for food supplies, he explained, would be a difficult task that Freddie would have to master.

"Working with purveyors and vendors, your main goal is to obtain consistency of product quality," he heard Tell say. "It's always about the freshest-possible quality first."

The protégé took notes as he listened. His only option was to order supplies two to four weeks in advance, because items arrived by boat, at times infrequently. Relations with purveyors depended on trust—by necessity, all the meat came in frozen, sight-unseen. With delay a part of the routine, island restaurateurs helped each other get through lean pantries—traded goods were later replaced in kind.

Unlike other restaurateurs, Tell instructed Duerr that he didn't want to pay the lowest prices. His thinking was that *quid pro quo* demanded more of a give-and-take approach, where you gave a better payment on some items to surprise and satisfy a vendor, and you expected better quality in return, when it counted most.

Tell spared no details teaching Duerr, but there was more to running the place than just the food. There was managing personnel.

A newspaper columnist, who had replaced Tait in Philadelphia, once wrote, "Working for Chef Tell is like working for a U-boat captain in the German navy." The writer's opinion, masqueraded as fact, went unchallenged. However, most personnel who worked for Tell at the time, including Duerr, felt the author of the piece had interviewed a fired, disgruntled employee.

True enough, in the heat of acrimonious exchanges, Tell's preferred salutation—notably, "dumb ass"—popped out of his mouth toward anyone, male or female, more often than not. But he was willing in turn to tolerate whatever moniker his staff hung on him, including The

Nazi. If the food leaving the kitchen was up to his expected standards of appearance and taste, and those plates were served and welcomed by his paying customers, Tell never minded whatever name the staff wished to call him.

"All comments or name-calling is just a part of the game, Freddie. The tone you set with your crew determines how high-spirited their work will be. Teams will only work as hard, play as hard, and cover each other's backs as much as they agree on the purpose and tone that you set. Please the customer, Freddie. Please the customer and you will be all set," Tell instructed.

And then he added, "No matter what anyone tells you about me or whatever you read about me, remember this: You have two eyes and two ears and a brain in your head. Use what you have."

In other words, go with what's in your pantry.

Though vendors and employees that he knew were professionals, on a personal level Tell disliked people who did not like him. However, he always set aside his feelings in matters of professional judgment. If an employee got testy with him, he first evaluated their actual work. If the work was up to par, but a dispute had become personal, his policy was to permit, even encourage, a problem's resolution by direct communication. Of course, not all words expressed were fit for print in the heat of the battle.

Tell discerned the important from the unimportant when it came to his employees. He rarely handled a staff problem within the confines of his office. Direct confrontation in front of the eyes and ears of other people gained more agreement and production from the person called out. There were no secrets in a Chef Tell kitchen. This open approach led to a strong group ethic, which pretty much policed itself. An argument that opened with "You dumb ass!" was often ended by a joke from Tell. This method often worked to keep the peace between Tell and employees, but there were always customers who tried to spark disagreements between the two.

49

PERSONNELITIES

"Tell broke them down just to build them up, never to be mean."

—Chef Duerr

Barbie Murphy was serving a conservative, newlywed couple from Washington DC and their guests from the nearby Hyatt Regency Resort when the husband noticed a cobweb strung across the lights and commented on it inside the five-table gazebo where each table had its own chandelier.

"Is that what I think it is?" he asked Barbie.

Barbie looked up at the web and remarked, "Guess that's why it's called the Grand Old House." (She knew that Chef Tell, Duerr, and rest of the crew worked diligently to keep a tight ship when it came to such details.)

Her remark didn't sit well with the gentleman that night. After two or three weeks, a letter arrived from DC addressed to Tell, who read it. He called Barbie to the table where he sat between service hours.

"Barbie, please read this letter," he said, handing the paper over to her. She read it but said nothing.

"What do you think about it?" Tell asked.

Barbie, who by that time had several years in the food service industry, yet few negative reports in her file, replied, "I remember that the man was a complete ass, Chef."

Tell stuck his hand out, gesturing for the letter to be handed to him. Without saying a word he crumbled and tossed it into the wastebasket.

"Get back to work, Barbie."

One of the other servers asked her what happened.

"Oh, nothing, but I just found out that Chef listens to us."

If Tell found he was in the wrong, he would own up and make amends to any person he had offended. Rank didn't matter. He would not hold grudges against any of his employees. But if their work didn't cut it, Tell fired offenders on the spot, handed them a pink slip and a final paycheck, and moved on without looking back.

His crews preferred the tough standards and no-nonsense atmosphere he set. They felt this gave them room to do good work in an environment where only real producers survived. No one was immune, not even Bunny, who, at times in the Wayne establishment, had given back as much as Tell dished out, much to the amusement (afterward) of the staff.

No walls were thick enough to prevent the decibel levels from carrying throughout the entire building the day Bunny and Tell argued in the kitchen, and right in the middle of a busy lunch. Guests and staff listened to a mind-numbing row, which lasted twenty minutes.

When a happy ending appeared hopeless, and whispered prayers from staff and customers alike seemed all for naught, Bunny and Tell found something on which they could agree and laughed. They walked out of the kitchen together and greeted customers and staff with big smiles as though the incident never happened. Shocked faces melted. Everybody moved on. Most chalked it up to the weariness of a couple who worked together every day.

What was the argument about? Seating arrangements.

Bunny laughed. "We rarely argued, unless over seating arrangements. Even then I would yield to his wishes, wait awhile, and when what he wanted was found unworkable, we'd arrange the seating to my original idea, which was found to work better."

Chef Duerr, an innocent bystander, learned how to handle personnel by observation. Tell also explained to him that he had to pick his battles.

"In the heat of our work, conflicts will come, always. The next day, it's over. Everything is professional, not personal. Be good at delegating responsibility. Motivate your people to use their best skills. Never hold grudges," he told Duerr.

Every once in a while someone earned a full dressing down in front of the staff. Even if deserved, the calling out was never personal. The offender stood their ground with shaking knees. They ducked or stepped aside from a thrown pot or pan, knowing the objects were aimed for effect, not at them.

"Tell broke them down just to build them up; never to be mean," observed Duerr.

Outside of work, Tell let his crews make fun of him. An unshakeable esprit de corps developed in its wake. The camaraderie was a definite plus over time, especially living on an island, catering to wealthy tourists.

One day a group of forty cruise-ship tourists booked a lunch at the Grand Old House. They enjoyed the food and service and, after, were invited by Tell into his kitchen for a quick tour. There he posed with them for photos—the way he had hundreds of times before. Behind Tell, personnel made goofy faces and added "rabbit ears" over his head. Cameras, including staff cameras, clicked and flashed, and then the tourists waved and returned to their boat.

When the developed photos were processed, a server picked them up at the local shop. She ran in and splayed them across one of the dining room tables. The staff gathered around her, and the laughter began. The photos developed back in the States by the tourists were going to get a lot of surprised looks when the tourists discovered their shenanigans. Tell and Duerr laughed just as hard as the crew.

Kodak moments, for sure.

* * *

When Tell opened the Grand Old House, he hired Janelle Backlund (later, Janelle Kingstad, wife of dive guide Jeff Kingstad) as his operations administrative assistant responsible for telephone reservations, daily cash reconciliation, group bookings and foreign employee work permits, as well as acting as Tell's personal assistant. From a close-quarters office above the restaurant, she had an eagle's view of what transpired at the restaurant and in Tell's personal life.

"I got the dream job with a great man."

Backlund's days began between 8 and 9 a.m. By the time she bid Tell "guten morgen" he would be hard at work food-prepping in the kitchen or directing chores with a maintenance staff member.

"He worked continuously until after the lunch hour completed at 2:00 p.m. A short break followed until 4 p.m. After, he would be back down until the restaurant closed for the night," she recalled.

The Grand Old House operated seven days a week. Tell set the standard and led by example daily. He followed this hard schedule without fail and extended it with stateside television appearances and contracted cooking demonstrations. Backlund observed the master chef at work every day.

"I was so amazed by this man, his work ethic, and his personality. Always a joker, he was the best joke teller. But, sometimes when the restaurant was 'in the swamps,' Tell would walk around like nothing was amiss. He would stop tableside and chat with his customers, then be back in the kitchen, making sure the food came out right, which it always did."

* * *

Tell's personality obviously went a long way to smooth out bumps that would come up from time to time in the restaurant. The bumps by anyone else's standards could have developed into hills or mountains, but that wouldn't happen in one of his restaurants.

Case in point, "Silly Coffee"—best described by Tell's friend, Ian Boxall.

"In the early days, a favorite tipple to end a meal was a drink we called Silly Coffee . . . like an Irish Coffee but made with one or more West Indian liqueurs.

"The proper way to assemble one was to mix the liqueur with demerara brown sugar (less molasses) and hot coffee and top it with thick cream floated on the top. Then you drink the coffee mixture through the cream. Delicious," said Boxall.

Unfortunately, the staff at the Grand Cayman locale squirted canned cream on the top, which disappeared into a nasty-looking sludge by the time it reached the table.

Boxall continued, ". . . At the end of a lunch I was hosting, Tell announced that he had fresh cream available for Silly Coffees. Most of us ordered, but one sniff of the drink told us the cream had soured. Tell, taking a turn at the cash register, shrugged and said, 'Boxie, sh** happens in the restaurant business. Last night the governor came for dinner and his chair collapsed. You just gotta get over it.'"

For all the bravado of that statement, Tell underneath was a softie for his friends. Not long after that episode, he made sure that Boxall and his friends were not left with their jaws on the floor and their tails between their legs after leaving the restaurant. Tell was full of surprises for his friends.

In 1987, Boxall remarried and his wife, Mary, and he lived close by in a house on the same road as the restaurant. After the wedding at the house, Tell catered a fairly small party, which the newlyweds planned to follow a month later with a black-tie, drinks-only party for 280 people. That is, until Tell decided he had a better idea.

Tell, instead, closed his entire restaurant for the evening of the affair; hired The Tradewinds, a top local band; and cooked and served a complete, multi-course dinner accompanied by industrial quantities of Bollinger Champagne and a full bar.

Boxall's take on the event?

Tell shows off at Ian Boxall's place

"This is how you do it," 1987

Wedding night with the Boxall's.

Three a.m. at Boxie's wedding 1987

"It was a marvelous, moonlit evening. We ate, drank, and danced our way through the evening until we bid farewell to the last guests at 2:30 a.m. The bill was *eye-watering*, but friends still talk about that party as Mary and I celebrate our silver wedding anniversary."

* * *

Backlund doubled in the evenings as cashier and cocktail waitress, when required. The international makeup of the staff, which came from all over the world to work for "the famous chef in his Grand Cayman location," was fun for her. Mostly hired from the Culinary Institute of America, they included personnel from Thailand, India, Germany, Ireland, Jamaica, Grand Cayman, and, of course, the U.S. mainland.

Having diversity within his personnel's ethnic backgrounds was a smart move by Tell and easy enough to come by, since an employment advertisement in the local newspaper usually brought candidates who were visitors with work permits, looking for work or seeking to switch restaurants. Additionally, when he took over the restaurant, he also inherited at least two diverse Caymanian families—employees that he kept on the roll, which also positioned him on the better side of Cayman public relations opinion.

Tell drew from the diverse taste predilections nuances of spicing that broadened the palate offerings of his menu. Such diverse backgrounds also brought him myriad conversations with people for whom newsworthy issues varied. Having a strong, ongoing interest in world affairs and history, this kind of repartee was good for Tell—a chicken soup for his soul.

Backlund continued, "He was so giving to all his staff. Although some may not think so, I saw in Tell a chef who provided staff meals to all employees prior to their working shifts. On weekends, he often cooked for the smaller weekend staff—food that was unbelievable!"

Tell was never above giving more to others than he might have received.

"I never met anyone like him—so giving. Now in my work today, when I ask a restaurant to give for a charitable, good cause, and they decline, I realize how truly generous Chef Tell was," offered Backlund.

More than just generous, Tell was also a friend with desires to cook and to party with his crews on Sundays. He got along extremely well with just about anyone *he liked*.

People from all walks of life commented to Backlund, "My relationship with Tell is like a marriage, except that he has a wife, and as anyone married knows, 'anything goes' in married life." Backlund compared the 1988 atmosphere to a bestselling novel, "If you've ever read the book, *Don't Stop the Carnival* (Herman Wouk, 1965), that was about as crazy as life with Tell was at the Grand Old House."

Aside from fun and games, Tell never neglected to encourage other island chefs and restaurateurs to make the success of one of them be the success of all of them—the same way it had gone in Philadelphia. Once he obtained enough agreement from the others on the island, he brought the *Chaine des Rôtisseurs* to Grand Cayman Island.

50

GRAND CAYMAN INDUCTION

"I would do anything for him in return . . . and now, to return."
—Chef Duerr

When Tell decided to create a *Chaine Baillage* on Cayman, he knew the best move he could make was to seek out and obtain Russell Baum's advice and assistance. He made his plea, and the Baums flew to the island from Philadelphia. They were put up at Tell and Bunny's home on Rum Point. The first planning meetings ran smoothly, and legal rudiments were in place in no time. The *Baillage's* inaugural reception and dinner was scheduled and invitations to chosen restaurateurs and their guests mailed out. Judging from the replies, the event would be a smash hit.

Tell was the first *Bailli* (leader) of the Cayman Island chapter. Inaugural protocol called for him to host the event. Cooking the dinner while hosting would be an impossible task, so he asked Duerr to assume the role of chef de cuisine and prepare the dinner. Duerr assembled his event staff from the crew and got plans started right away, even though it was several weeks out from the important date.

On the appointed date, arriving guests—would-be *Chaine* inductees and Island dignitaries—expected nothing less than the best food and service. Aromatic wafts from the kitchen whet their appetites as introductions progressed on the veranda, accompanied by samosas (fried pockets of potato and spices over a spread of green and tamarind chutneys) and fresh tuna tartare appetizers (wontons of fresh tuna, avocado, lime juice with spices, and wasabi) served with Red Stripe and Guinness beer, and *Moët & Chandon* champagne.

Duerr's sous chef, Chef Anthony, hailed from India and he was responsible for the samosas. Tell and Duerr had known that Caymanians had a fondness for Indian cuisine when planning their menu. Suladda, the pastry chef with roots in Thailand, would make interesting desserts.

Appropriate wines were presented with entrées of roast duckling, filet mignon, and chateaubriand. After an entremets of flavored shave-ice, a salmon *en croute* continued the dinner, followed by a course of selected cheeses. Of course, Suladda's fine desserts—fluffy, white chocolate cheesecake with raspberry sauce and a dense, chocolate-raspberry cake with raspberry *grenache* between layers, accompanied by the "Bismarck" of Tell's desserts, moist apple-sour cream torte derived from his German grandmother's recipe—admirably finished off the repast. After-dinner liqueurs and Cubans out on the veranda followed the sweet delicacies.

In a smart public relations move, Caymanian real estate investor and Grand Old House Caymanian partner Naul Bodden described Tell as, "a man of great stature with the ability to entertain and, importantly, to make local residents feel especially welcome."

Island restaurateur and long-time friend Brian "Buzz" Murphy (Barbie's husband) called Tell, "a warm and caring, huggable kind of a guy with an unstoppable repertoire of jokes, who always makes you feel welcome."

Tell brought Chef Duerr out and introduced him to the guests. "He [Tell] gave me the credit for the night. He was always good for that. He brought me out and introduced me. He built me up to make me go the extra mile, and I would do anything for him in return," said Duerr.

Duerr, in turn, introduced Chefs Anthony and Suladda and extended his credits to them. The guests lauded the chefs for presentation and taste, and hailed their work as "divinity!" Later in the evening, Duerr and Tell sat with Helen and Russell Baum and capped the rewarding night with cognac and cigars.

The successful launch of the *Baillage* benefited the best restaurants on the island and established the same culture that enabled Philadelphia's culinary renaissance. An added benefit was the door opening wide for scores of top-notch, mainland restaurateurs and chefs to come down and cook at some of the *Chaine* dinners on the island.

Non-chef Chaine honoree

Chaine honoree and guest, Bunny and Tell Erhardt

Tell and the Baums created a stable foundation for the Cayman *Chaine* chapter to flourish. Due to their success, in November 1991, at the annual induction dinner grand master and co-founder of the *Chaine des Rôtisseurs International* Jean Valby personally inducted new members as the local *Bailli*, Chef Tell, watched with great pride.

51

A RESPITE WELL DESERVED

"He earned every bit of it."

—Helen Baum

Before the Baums returned stateside they marveled at Tell's mellowed outlook and the lifestyle he achieved at this point in his life. And in a way they never would have dreamed.

Helen Baum was asleep in one of the Rum Point bedrooms when, without warning—as loud as could be—the first four notes of Beethoven's Symphony No. 5 in C Minor seared through her brain:

TA, DA-DA-DAH!

She awoke in a confused state, dazed, disoriented, and not knowing what she had just heard. She sat up in bed, shaking. In seconds, the second set of the same four notes repeated.

TA, DA-DA-DAH!

Throwing on her robe and slippers, she ran from the darkened room, in search of the source of the incomprehensible notes as her mind awoke.

TA, DA-DA-DAH ... TA, DA-DA-DAH ... TA, DA-DA-DAH!

She stepped outside onto the porch and faced the calming, blue-teal waters of the Caribbean just as the music shifted to its first chords of the symphonic melody performed on piccolo flutes, brass horns, flutes, and bassoons. Now she knew what her ears heard but not why.

With her hand over her brow to shield from the daybreak streaming onto her bleary eyes, she focused on a lone figure seated half-submerged fifty yards offshore.

Out on a kaibo (sandbar) in ankle-deep water, on a comfortable folding lounge chair facing the shoreline and house, Tell sat, wearing no more than a blue-white patterned Speedo swimsuit and a straw hat. In his right hand, he held a full glass of champagne, a lit Cuban cigar in his left. To his right, a small table supported an ice bucket encasing an unmistakable bottle of *Dom Perignon*.

Unmoving, except to sip more champagne and draw from his cigar, goose bumps on his arms, eyes closed, Tell let Beethoven's notes and chords wash over him. As his deeply tanned body absorbed the early sunlight, Tell finally had found a sublime ecstasy outside of the kitchen.

With Russell's arm around her shoulders, Helen Baum wiped away a tear. She was happy for Tell. She and Russell had watched from the sidelines of his playing field for years. They had stood by his side in times of unexpected success and happiness, and in moments of horrible sorrows. They knew him as well as if they were his parents.

For the Baums, the image of Tell at ease was like viewing a Picasso.

Friedemann Paul Erhardt had become that dream promised in the ad that he kept folded in his boyhood pockets. With a strong will and persistent drive over decades, he had arrived at this respite, having earned every minute of it. Every counter-emotion, every counter-effort that had ever attempted to defeat him, was held at bay by the solitude of this morning. For a brief time in eternity, Tell was a man *temporarily* at peace.

52

YOU GET WHAT YOU PAY FOR

"He's been kind to me so far."
—Bunny (Kule) Erhardt

Meanwhile, Bunny back in Pennsylvania continued to hold a candle for Tell as they dated. She lived in the Grasshopper Lane house and worked out of Bryn Mawr, a Philadelphia suburb. One day, with Tell not yet returned from Grand Cayman—he was commuting back and forth to the mainland for his TV appearances and live show demonstrations—Tell's ex-wife, Nicoletti, stood on Bunny's doorstep. Bunny, home for the day due to illness, asked how she might help the woman standing in front of her.

"You don't know me, but I am married to Tell. Do you live here?"

"No, not yet," Bunny said.

"Is he in? May I come in?" inquired Nicoletti.

Curious because she knew about Nicoletti from Tell, Bunny let her enter the house and attempted a conversation with her. She ended up doing most of the listening.

"You do know that he's a pathological liar, don't you?" Nicolletti said as she roamed the house upstairs and down with Bunny in tow, looking here and there for items she might claim. (Years later, Bunny would find items in Nicoletti's place, which she knew had been Tell's. For now, she was charged with the chore of unpacking the house for Tell, since he was too busy and was out of town.)

"Tell and I, are pretty new. He's been kind to me so far," offered Bunny.

"Well, you'll learn differently over time." Nicoletti kept moving non-stop as she looked for valuables until she had exhausted all areas of the house. Not finding anything worthwhile, she retraced her steps down-stairs. She hesitated on her way toward the front door but she never said another word to Bunny before she left. One can only wonder if she had decided that she should step away for good, for they never met again.

Seven years later, Tell received news that Nicoletti had met her death in the Swedesford apartment, an apparent "victim" of a psychiatric drug overdose. On hearing the news from Tell, Bunny whispered a small prayer for Janet's soul.

Connecting the dots between such mind-altering, prescription drugs and terrible acts of suicide was not yet in practice.

53

SCORCHING HEAT AND FLAMES

*"Love is . . . a madness most discreet, a choking gall
and a preserving sweet."*
—William Shakespeare *(Romeo & Juliet)*

Generally speaking, a chef's first marriage commitment is to his kitchen. That relationship lasts forever. Away from the kitchen, chefs' spouses stay, on average, only so long as more money arrives than can be spent. By the time chefs hit forty-five they're either on their third marriage, engaged to a waitress, with whom they've been having an affair for months or years, or consorting with paying customers as time and opportunity permit.

Even the best of chefs understand they are like soup—fine when fresh and hot, but as a cold leftover, not so much. They know they are *chef du jour*. When the young, fresh stock takes center stage in the kitchen and bedroom, they'll no longer be the life of the party. The insecurity of aging hangs like a sword of Damocles over their heads and makes them feel vulnerable.

"Tell at times seems afraid that I will leave him, even when there is no reason to think that way," said Bunny to a friend.

Long before Tell's upcoming trip down to Grand Cayman, and well ahead of his next scheduled Texas tour, Tell and Bunny had tied their futures together with promises and words of love. Yet, the house they built together would soon tremble like a structure made of playing cards. Though their relationship had been a passionate one, they were about to go through a trial that would test their faith and the depth of that love. Tell moved at an extreme pace, feeling his constant need, and the expectations of others, to bring on financial success and to reach his TV show goal; this took a toll on his physical and moral defenses, wearing them down. In this vulnerable condition, a woman did brush up against him, leaving a discreet note on the table in his presence, which swayed him toward her seductive charms.

Inhaling the scent of his favored cologne, she made other casual advances toward him. With too much wine circulating in his veins, the tired chef acted like a large-mouthed bass in front of a gold-feathered Stanley Wedge jiggle lure—tantalized and itching to take the bait.

Jeannette, the vivacious female who pasted her eyes on his physique, leaned toward him more than a few times. The soft floral scent of her *Eau de Givenchy Women* cologne—*his favorite*—intoxicated him and left his head spinning, his body warmed.

If the public noticed any visible reaction from Tell, it had the potential to tarnish his public image. Would he risk the damage to break bread with this vixen? And possibly break Bunny's heart? Would he, indeed, tempt the gods of Fate by dawn's early light in San Francisco—as Jeannette had suggested in her note?

Tell, the acceptable charmer by day, became Tell the beguiled by midnight. Tired and thirsty, he mimicked butter melting in a saucepan, soon to burn.

Even before Ulysses, sirens have tempted men with song. This California siren was irresistible. Tell might have hoped that Bunny would come along and rescue him. When she didn't, he remained rooted where he stood. Instead, the temptress's sly winks beckoned. Her well-timed smiles spread her ruby, red lips and nailed him even after she stood up and departed.

Tell sat down at the table, awash in a flashflood of conflicting urges. From the closest waiter, he ordered a coffee and a cognac. He had some serious thinking to do.

An hour passed. Tell took Jeannette's phone call, knowing that he should let it ring. She wanted to talk, but small talk led to discussion of his trade shows and soon Dallas—where his next live show would take place— came up. The phone call ended with plans for an overnight tryst in foggy San Francisco, with fresh-cooked crabs and plenty of champagne from the room-service menu, for the night following his upcoming Texas show.

The cagey angler would soon land her trophy fish, but at the high cost of a broken heart back in Philadelphia.

The Dallas cooking show and demonstration progressed well. *Smooth as silk,* Tell thought as his mind wandered over imagined images of the evening ahead of him—late-night room service, musky overtones of *Givenchy,* and silk lingerie strewn across the floor, and perhaps, a ser-enade of foghorns from freighters anchored in the bay.

Dismayed gasps filled Tell's ears and brought him back to Dallas and to the food cooking in front of him on the convention floor. With a sweep of one hand in the air, he flipped the nearly burned food high above and back into the hot pan with a quick snap of the wrist and a German-accented quip, "That's what I do to see if you're paying attention!"

Later, the applause of the relieved fans, who had almost witnessed the unthinkable—Tell's food burning—faded from Tell's reverie as he pushed back into his first class seat on the jet headed northwest toward San Francisco. One can imagine the plumes of steam rising from behind his forehead. How hard it must have been to push thoughts of Bunny to the back of his mind, at least for the next twenty-four hours.

Tell was mid-flight when Jeannette in San Francisco realized she was running late and would not arrive at the Fairmount Hotel on time. Leading up to the 1987 clandestine affair, easily toted cell phones and texting services were non-existent, and voicemail messages hummed only through land-line devices. In her haste, amid thoughts of taking his big German frame in her arms that night, she dialed Tell's home number to leave a message.

Bunny was tired by the time she pulled into her driveway. She expended her day on a series of scheduled meetings with clients over potential wholesale wine deals. As she entered her home, she noticed that the red light on the answering machine flashed intermittently in the darkened room.

Perhaps Tell is leaving me a message, she thought as she ran across the room, switched on a lamp, and picked up the receiver.

"Tell?" She caught half of the message being left, ". . . running a bit late, so just meet me at the hotel bar. I won't be too late," the female voice said.

Bunny was stunned but she asked, "Who is this?"

"This is Jeannette. I was leaving a message for Tell."

"Well, Jeannette, this is Bunny. Tell's fiancée."

"Oh, I'm sorry." The phone line went dead.

Seconds later, Bunny's numbness rose to unexpressed resentment and then blossomed into full-fledged fury as the car keys, which had been in her right hand, left a noticeable mark on the living room wall where she threw them. She had no way to vent her anger at her intended target. She knew he would probably commit perjury on the good book of love and faithful promises when she saw him. Looking into the mirror, she saw, under the harsh light of reality, tears streaked with mascara running down her cheeks and she felt the heat of her rage on her flushed cheeks.

Like Pick-Up Sticks, Tell's mind became a mass of conflicting vectors as he sipped wine and waited for his paramour's arrival at the Fairmount Hotel's lobby bar. A formerly married man on the rebound, newly engaged to Bunny, he knew he had cornered himself into a Pandora's Box filled with lustful sensations, unwanted emotions, and impending conflict. With the power of one phone call and one tempered decision, he could have called off the meeting, but this ephemeral line of thinking abruptly ended the moment Jeannette walked into the lobby. When he stood up, the promise of his heart to Bunny was still intact, though fading to black. As he walked across the lobby toward Jeannette, he wondered only about how it would feel to stand in the Fairmount's elevator with this woman wrapped around him.

Any man, even a TV chef, can get away with lust in darkened alcoves in unannounced places, but sooner or later such things get found out. Tell didn't know it, but he was better off cracking crab legs, sipping champagne, and overlooking the bay. He was safer sitting across from the fresh face that glowed from the candlelight, because the unsuspecting moth that he was had already moved too close to the flame. Tell's secret was out, uncovered at home, and he didn't even suspect it.

In the cab the following evening, heading south toward San Francisco International, Tell still didn't know his treasonous cover had been blown. He boarded an American Airlines red-eye flight headed east for Philadelphia, unaware that Bunny called in sick earlier and would take the next two days off from work.

Tell alit from the cab on Grasshopper Lane and paid the driver. He put his key in his front door and turned it without considering what he might find on the other side.

Inside, Bunny inhaled a deep breath and exhaled slowly.

Tell at first denied everything. In his mind nothing had happened, because he chose tired, old pejoratives—"it was just sex; it wasn't love"— to justify his actions. *She (Bunny) wasn't there for me; we're not married, yet; she's better off not knowing,* and all the other cowardly justifications ran through his brain. He denied there was another woman, denied he'd ever gone to San Francisco.

But Bunny wasn't crying. She was waiting. She waited for the man that had gotten under her skin and invaded her heart to run out of the lies he had to tell her. She waited for her turn and waited for Tell to have nothing more to say.

In the silent aftermath of his justifications, Bunny hit "play" on the answering machine. She watched as he reacted to the dialogue she'd had with Jeannette. She watched Tell sit down. She listened when he confessed his lies. But she listened in vain for any apology.

"I want you out of this house. Better yet, I'm leaving," were the first words out of her mouth. No tears. No joy. Nothing.

She had nothing left.

Tell wasn't up to the responsibility. Instead, in a selfish act of making himself right and her wrong, once Bunny moved out, he phoned Jeannette and told her that she and her young daughter should come and live with him on Grasshopper Lane. Months later, he moved them down to Grand Cayman and put them up in his Rum Point house.

There was almost nothing idyllic about the arrangement. Grand Cayman offered only one local radio station and a few satellite dish TV channels. The beaches were wide and sandy white, but Tell lived in the Grand Old House apartment above the kitchen on weekdays and worked daybreak to midnight, six days a week.

In Bunny's words, "Cayman, at that time, was, if you weren't working or visiting friends, *boring!* [Nothing but] a series of long, hot days."

If you were a water sportsman, your days were filled with snorkeling, scuba diving, and hours and hours of either reef- or deep-sea fishing.

At Cayman Kia, if you were over-age and so inclined, you could drink and tell stories with the regulars in the Kaibo or the Rum Point Club. If you weren't grilling, swimming, or cooking fish, periwinkle, cracked corn, or lobster, you swam in the ocean, searched for shells, caught a tan, or walked the beaches under romantic moonlight.

Jeannette and her daughter just waited.

Tell with Naul Bodden

54

THE GRAND CAYMAN
EXPERIMENT

"A meal without wine and without friends is like
a heart without love."
—William Sonstein, illustrator and friend of Chef Tell

The Grand Old House overlooked the South Sound shoreline of Grand Cayman. From the start, the place brought in good revenue under Tell's guidance assisted by Chef Duerr. Its legendary location played a definite part in the venture's success.

Bostonian William Henry Law constructed the landmark on the island in 1908. Frederic N. Lambert conceived and commissioned the structure. He designed the home's foundation to be able to withstand the island's fickle and, at times, voracious weather. Its main support beams—136 pilings of locally grown ironwood, one of the hardest woods in the world—fixed directly into the underlying Iron Shore rock bed. Even the toughest of storms would not blow the sturdy building away.

Lambert allowed local resident Miss Olive Hinds to oversee the house for several years. Though the surrounding Petra (Greek and Arabic, "Rock") Plantation where the house was situated saw coconut

The Grand Old House the way Tell discovered it

as its first commercial venture, in the Lambert's time their hosting of frequent extravagant balls, elegant parties, and banquets made up the main focus of activity.

The Lamberts left Grand Cayman for Jamaica in 1925. The family housekeeper continued to care for the house, and Mr. Law never returned. The structure survived the horrendous October hurricane of 1932 unscathed, although more than one hundred island residents lost their lives. Later, the place morphed into a temporary Sunday School for local children, a hospital for soldiers wounded in World War II, and a worthy storm and hurricane shelter for island residents. It also experienced a stint as a beauty parlor of note for a few years in the late Forties.

In the 1950s, retired U.S. Army Colonel Bruce Pirnie from Boston bought the place for $15,000. He founded the Rotary Club of Grand Cayman and conducted meetings there until Bob and Jeanne Brenton came with partners and purchased the property in 1969. A rutted track of a road led to the entrance, and oil-lamp illumination in the dining rooms defined its ambience without air conditioning. The Brentons renovated and upgraded the upstairs apartment. They lived there and ran the business on the main floor.

The site where Chef Tell would make his mark offered an even richer patina. In October 1917, the real Lawrence of Arabia recruited Bedouin women to defend Petra from marauding Turkish and German forces. They crushed the Hessians. The *German*, Chef Tell, ended up with the last laugh, though, when he took up residence on the island and created an iconic oasis on the site, serving Caribbean-influenced *German* and French foods to locals and tourists alike.

The gable-roofed main building with the million-dollar view offered a perfect setting for a brunch, business luncheon, seaside dinner, or wedding. Patrons walked up the steps to the screened-in porch and traversed the wide veranda to the hostess dais where they were greeted. The split-level veranda allowed for plantation-style dining, and a seaside deck placed diners right at the water's edge. An added walkway deck doubled the original one-hundred-seat capacity and extended over the water. At night, spotlights attracted silver tarpons for diners' visual pleasure.

A five-table, screened-in gazebo reserved for private parties, with seashells adorning the porch pillars and live Caribbean musicians, complimented and completed the outside ambience.

The inside dining room displayed whitewashed walls painted a pastel light yellow and festooned with upbeat island art. Rounded archways dressed in contrasting Grecian blue added panache to the resort ambience. Large overhead fans hung from sixteen-foot ceilings lessened the heat all year round, especially in the dog-day months of July, August, and September.

With almost nil humidity and temperatures seldom dipping below 80–90 degrees on the islands, winter offered the idyllic vacation time for Caribbean travelers. Given pleasant weather and a high-season crowd, the Grand Old House was the place to go for good food or, if you were staff, good tips.

The lure of the islands made Tell's place an easy recruitment "carrot" during the high-season months. Mainland employees welcomed the break from inclement weather. For the seasoned servers and chefs, who transferred from other locales, living and working on the island brought unexpected consequences.

Staff accommodations varied and were assigned by rank or seniority. The choicest apartments were closest to the ocean, because these offered inland breezes, which helped make nights bearable. Living off the ocean by two or three blocks meant hot, humid, and often sleepless nights, which new recruits discovered the hard way. Upon arrival, newcomers developed heat rashes, which disappeared after a week or two. For those whose rashes continued or who found the heat too unbearable, job swaps were available with other hopefuls on the waiting list, ready to join Tell's Cayman crew.

Tell paid employees 20 percent above what most other restaurateurs paid. Coupled with the islands' tax-free income advantage and gorgeous settings, working for Tell was an irresistible option that involved a 60–80 hours per week workload. Assistant executive chefs earned $1,200 per week; a sous chef $800 per week; a chef de partie $600 per week; and a commis about $300 per week. Bartenders and waitresses worked for minimum wages and shared tips, which could be lucrative. Of course, meals and accommodations rounded out the employee compensation package.

The Cayman crew was "family."

Tell's largesse with payroll came with strings. He expected staff members to give 120 percent effort in service and loyalty to the professional standards he demanded. "Work hard; keep it ethical whatever you do. Use what's been proven to work well. Keep your wits about you and heed the guy next to you, who might need a helping hand. Always remember, the customer's experience is most important on our list of priorities," were the basic rules.

No one complained behind the line if they wanted to keep their job in the kitchen, which was far noisier than stateside kitchens. A nine-by nine-foot swamp boat propeller fan that hung at one end of the room noisily sucked the heat out through a wall opening. Interesting hand signals among the crew facilitated communications and plating. Without the whirring blades, the room would have been unbearable for anyone.

Although Tell owned a house in Rum Point on the North Shore and the actual mileage from home to restaurant was not a great distance, the remoteness and pavement condition of the only road prevented an easy, daily commute back and forth. Of necessity, the apartment above the kitchen sufficed as his living quarters 90 percent of the time.

The cramped conditions did not agitate Tell as much as a Grand Court appearance he once endured. Cayman Grand Court issued a speeding ticket summons to Tell. He was busy on the appointed day and he showed up wearing his white Chef Tell jacket and loose-fitting chef pants. The judge, the Honorable Kipling Douglas—a.k.a. Crippling Kipling—reprimanded him in public for not dressing "appropriately and disrespecting the Court."

Tell was quick to correct the judge and explained that he considered his uniform, ". . . something I have worked very hard to acquire. This uniform brings to me, and to the islands, money, fame, and success."

The atmosphere was tense as Douglas considered Tell's words for some minutes. He looked up and apologized to Tell. Then, in the next breath, he hit Tell with a $500 Grand Cayman charge, which Tell paid.

The apology was small consolation to Tell, who was now hours behind in his food preparation that day, but he kept his cool. "Judge Douglas, you must stop by the Grand Old House and dine on my food some time."

The good judge, indeed, dined there. Tell, seeing the judge dining in his restaurant, asked, "Why did you charge me so much money, Your Honor?" Douglas answered, "We have to make you an example, so the fee was high." Later, upon receiving his dinner bill, the good judge saw that Tell had not overcharged him. They were quick "friends" after that.

Tell and Judge Kipling Douglas, 1989

55

MAKING FRIENDS CAYMAN-STYLE

"Two out of three ain't bad."

—Meat Loaf

Barbra and Buzz Murphy married in 1978 and they lived at the former Galleon Beach Hotel on 7-Mile beach. They later ran The Kaibo, a small eatery catering the lunch crowd of local snorkelers and tourists where a "fresh catch of the day"—whatever was brought in from Stingray City reefs—was offered alongside cheeseburgers and dolphin sandwiches. A handmade sign posted the dress code, No SHIRTS, NO SHOES, AND NO SANDALS. Aromas of coconut oil intermingled with fish fry and burger oils, and the sound of snorkeling lingo cascaded into the background music of reggae and rock tunes.

Because the Murphys operated a gasoline pump on the adjacent dock, business remained steady almost twenty-four hours daily. Their place, a good bet for local grub, gas, and gossip, brought Tell in on a regular basis for gas for his motorized eight-foot runabout.

Buzz was the first of the Murphys to meet Tell. He'd gone over to the main Georgetown dock landings to pick up his order of meat, fresh vegetables, fruits, and milk (which came in frozen and had be set out to thaw) from boats just arrived from Cuba, Jamaica, and the Honduras. From his loaded flatbed truck, he spied Tell and Duerr hitchhiking for the fun of it. He pulled over and picked up the duo. Tell sat in front with Buzz and traded anecdotes and jokes with him. Duerr rode in the back with the vegetables.

When Buzz pulled up to the hotel, Barbie was there. Buzz introduced her to both men. Barbie recognized Tell, as she had seen him on TV years earlier. Island-friendly like most residents, she right away invited Tell to accompany her on the Hobie-cat sailboat she was about to take out for a fifth practice lesson in a series of ten. That morning she needed to practice tipping over and recovering the craft and she was anxious to put herself to the test for real on the sea.

Tell asked, in reply to her invitation, "Well, do you know what you're doing?"

Barbie replied, "Of course, do you want to come or not?"

"Okay, I'll come, but wait a second. I want to get something." He turned and walked into the bar and in a few minutes came out with a bottle of Grand Marnier tucked under his arm.

"This will help with the lesson."

Barbie and Buzz laughed. They loved his style and his German accent, although neither was too keen on his Speedo swimsuit—it seemed all the Germans on the islands wore Speedos and not the baggy snorkeling shorts in vogue.

Once they had cleared the port area, Tell point-blank asked Barbie, "Where are your tits?" Though she considered it rude and not the type of question she, or any of her friends, would ever use, Barbie ignored the question about her petite breasts. As she worked the Hobie, she tried to think of a way to retaliate at the right moment.

After traversing a few tack lines and sharing some drinks, Barbie tipped over the boat unexpectedly. All three precious cargoes fell overboard—Barbie, Tell, and the Grand Marnier. Two recovered, and one was lost—buried forever under years of shifting sand and tides. Barbie knew the mishap was accidental, but as she pulled herself back aboard the craft, she did feel that Karma was alive and well. And that she and Tell were now even.

Meanwhile, back at the bar, Meat Loaf's smash hit, "Two Out of Three Ain't Bad" warbled on the radio, even as on the sailboat Tell joked with Barbie during the return to port.

"Did you know, Barbie, that every one of my ex-wives was a great housekeeper? They kept every house I've ever had."

She laughed. *This guy is really different,* she thought, *maybe that outrageous remark about my bosom was nothing.*

Barbra, Buzz, and Tell got along from there on, and the lost bottle was never brought up.

Barbie recalled, "I felt badly that his bottle had gone overboard, but Tell never mentioned it. I learned in time that he wasn't a materialistic person at all. In fact, he was one of the most generous persons I've ever met."

Questions like the one that he shot at Barbra were mere window-dressings: an empty store stood behind them—Tell had meant no malice, but it took getting to know him to understand that about the man. Contrary to most adult thinking, those who do not take life too seriously more often than not win the top prize. Tell's approach to life began and ended with an open heart and an almost child-like curiosity for the people he met and the things that surrounded him. He ended up achieving success with most of the endeavors he attempted, including the loyalty of worthy friends.

A chiropractor friend, Tell, Bunny, and Buzz, Barbie, and Falynne Murphy

56

L'ESCOFFIER SALADS
FOR THREE

"Man kann sehen mich, ich werde Sie sicher erinnern."
("You can look me up; I'll remember you for sure.")

—Chef Tell

Barbra Murphy was working as a hostess at the Grand Old House when her sister, Theresa Badmann, visited her from the States in 1987. One of the trusted few Tell counted on for the lowdown on day-to-day island living, fishing tides, and assorted gossip tidbits, Barbra secured Tell's permission to spend the first day with her sister at his Rum Point house.

The sisters thought the bright, open floor plan in Tell's place created a relaxed mood. They noticed that the wall of windows captured ocean breezes as well as the North Shore vista.

Theresa felt honored, if also a little intimidated, to be visiting a real celebrity's house. However, the Rum Punches and Piña Coladas that Barbie concocted in the spacious kitchen where pots and pans hung over the cooking island softened her nervousness. She looked around at the paintings of vegetables and peppers, which decorated the walls, and thought it odd that Tell would choose art depicting food for his home kitchen. She had to agree with Barbie that the vibrant colors of the paintings popped against the pastel-shaded walls.

The sisters walked outside onto the patio, which was arranged with several cushioned beach chairs that overlooked the surf. They were engaged in conversation when Tell walked into the house, intending to make lunch for the women.

He went straight to the kitchen. He took from the refrigerator cooked roast beef slices, which he julienned along with onion and green pepper. He then diced tomatoes and dill pickles and placed the pieces in a stainless steel bowl along with some ketchup, Dijon mustard, Tabasco sauce, Worcestershire sauce, and sprinkled salt and pepper. The Escoffier Salad came to life as he talked across the house with the women.

"Barbie, I didn't know you had a sister."

"Well, she and I don't get to talk much."

Tell covered the salad and set it aside in the fridge to let the mixed flavors infuse.

"I wish I had a sister. I only have one brother," Tell offered as he joined them on the porch.

"Hey, how come you never mentioned a brother?" Barbie asked as she poured and handed him a drink.

"That's because Uli and I don't talk at all."

"Why not?" Theresa asked.

"You don't really want to know," answered Tell, who walked back to the kitchen and returned with three plated salads, forks, and napkins.

Just the mention of his brother in such informal circumstances reminded Tell of the love he had for his brother and the deep hurt that stood between them. Only someone with a sibling could fully understand the turmoil he felt when he could no longer include his brother in his storied life: the depth of a well of ill feelings can only be as deep as the pool of love that preceded it.

Conversation and drinks mixed well with the fresh salad. The wide range of topics the trio covered included the possibility that Theresa might one day work for Tell back in Pennsylvania, should he return and open another restaurant there.

* * *

Theresa Badmann's visit to the island was by no means Tell's only notable event in Cayman. In fact, the winter morning a white, square-rigged, four-masted ship appeared in Georgetown harbor, showing a German flag and a dark blue flag with a golden crown—the colors of the House of Thurn und Taxis—was a momentous occasion for the Islanders. That night its passengers, who dined in the Grand Old House, were none other than the Count Johannes von Thurn und Taxis and his wife, Gloria, Princess of Thurn und Taxis (dubbed "Princess TNT, the dynamite socialite" by *Vanity Fair's* special correspondent Bob Colacello) and their entourage, proving the adage "the celebrity's celebrity is his chef."

57

LOW SEASON DUPPY MAGIC

"We got lucky that day . . . had it blown we'd be unemployed."
—Chef "Freddie Flintstone" Duerr

Tell mentored Duerr on a daily basis. He explained that making do within the pantry's limits was of paramount importance when operating from an island. Working with large quantities of fresh and frozen food, enough to feed up to 300 patrons nightly for weeks at a time, was an awesome task.

Consider that just one night of 300 dinners consisting of at least one appetizer; an entrée consisting of a meat, vegetables, and a starch; plus a dessert and a glass of wine or another beverage, involved at least 18 different items to offer three choices on the menu—5,400 potential pantry food items and 300 bottled beverages *for one night*. Because of the need to order supplies three to four weeks in advance, this quantity soared to 24 nights monthly, or 129,600 pantry foods, and 7,200 beverages, not including the plates, cups, glasses, and silverware required to be washed and cleaned and/or replaced due to breakage or theft.

Duerr found that the magnitude of the responsibility demanded a real understanding of pantry and cash flow management.

Tell orders food at the Grand Old House 1987

But the food pantry was only a portion of an executive chef's responsibility. "Behind the line" (kitchen) and "front of the line" (dining room) personnel rosters had to be assigned and managed through squall lines of volatile angers and tear bursts that blew in, at times, in the middle of high-season, service hours. These firefights, of course, needed to be squelched as close to instantly as possible.

Duerr needed just as much mentoring from Tell to learn the nuances of low-season (slow-season) work. Fewer food sorties arrived in the summer months, and this fact led to harsh circumstances that required imaginative solutions to keep enough food on hand in the pantry.

Sometimes a little island magic lent a helping hand in the summer doldrums. If idle hands are the work of the devil, the "duppies" did the devil's work in Cayman in the slow season. Island lore had it that ghosts known as "duppies" visited the Grand Old House on a regular basis, perhaps even resided there. Native inhabitants spoke of those among them capable of actually seeing these duppies. Stories abounded that a Petra Plantation "lady in waiting" showed up, from time to time, dressed in formal Victorian garb and joined a handsome "gentleman" for a dance or two in the evening.

The legend of the duppies, most agreed, began after a previous Petra owner lost the love of a woman. His sorrowful, subsequent binge involved several bottles of cognac and visions of the duppy pair. True or not as to origin, other duppy sightings have been recorded in several island locations over several decades.

Real or not, duppy mischief was thought to have taken hold of one of Tell's crews the slow, summer afternoon they allegedly manufactured their own brand of "high-class" cognac. By mixing spices with honey and making a reduction, which they then allegedly added to the cheap stuff, they extended the dwindling supply of the more-expensive brand. Then again, stretched thin in the pantry, chickens marinated overnight in red wine allegedly became "French pheasant" on the menu, and shark meat morphed into "scallops" or "swordfish" (*wink-wink*). Given slow-season circumstances, conjuring up duppy "magic" from inside the kitchen could make sense. For sure, *something* influenced an alleged bake-in of "weed spice" (marijuana) into the appetizers on the night the Grand Old House recorded the highest decibels of conversation and food and drink totals than any previous night in its history.

For the record, the alleged incidents lacked Chef Tell's presence, since he was on the mainland, making television appearances at the time.

Alas, Mateys! Factual accounts of the alleged events shall remain in Davey Jones's locker forever.

* * *

Although food know-how might have been misused by idle hands manipulated by summer devils, in the face of Mother Nature's fall hurricane season, the duppies lay low.

Caribbean storm patterns were marginally predictable in the 1980s. A hard blow could be counted upon to appear from time to time in the fall months. The severity of the storms, on the other hand, was far less predictable. One such storm altered the course of a season for everyone at the Grand Old House. The week of September 12, 1988, Chef Duerr and the rest of the staff weren't sure they would survive the fury of Hurricane Gilbert.

Gilbert formed off the African Coast on the 3rd of September and made landfall over Jamaica by the 11th. He packed winds that measured, in the days of far-less sophistication and prediction of weather patterns and hurricanes, at *156 miles per hour* in Grand Cayman. Gilbert was the seventh named hurricane of the season and Duerr's first.

"My apartment was about a mile up the road on the same side as the restaurant. One morning we woke up to the ringing of fire alarms. A bad storm was upon us. On the way over to the Old House we watched a wave pitch a propane tank thirty feet in the air. The tank landed on the well pump adjacent to the restaurant. Propane fumes, with the aid of the wind's direction, leaked *away* from the sparking pump—the only reason a fireworks display of major proportions was avoided. Had it blown, we would all be unemployed without a restaurant. And Tell, who was on the mainland at the time, would have been pissed," recalled Duerr.

That same morning Barbie and Buzz Murphy were on the island, back in charge of their own resort after a brief hiatus to the States to welcome a daughter to their family. They followed the "nor'wester" from a boat with an on-board weather tracker, anchored in port. They could see this unusual storm was aimed at the south side of the island—right at Georgetown and the Grand Old House.

Barbie looked up at the sky in amazement. The sun shone through most of it, but ominous, dark clouds approached eastward. She and Buzz watched the surf change from a soft roll of azure water into tall, white-foamed breakers. They decided to drive to Tell's restaurant, a seven to ten minute drive. There they joined Duerr and the rest of the staff members at the bar.

"We ran to the other side of the restaurant and poured some Absolut vodka, cranberry, and orange juice—one of Tell's favorite mixes. A bunch of us pulled up the lawn chairs still left on the deck and sat and watched with mixed emotions as the new dock washed away piece by piece under the onslaught of the wind and each succeeding wave," said Duerr.

Barbie remembered, "The surf waves were breaking too high and too close together for any of the dock to remain; even the gazebo out there was swept away."

True to its foundations, the Grand Old House survived Gilbert intact. When it was safe to inspect the side of the restaurant and the now-empty propane tank, Duerr discovered that with another two feet in the air the propane tank would have landed inside of the kitchen. "We got lucky that day. The propane tank ran out of combustible content first without blowing us all to bits."

Most of the crew never realized the impact of Duerr's discovery because so much alcohol swirled inside them the sobering thought never registered.

Tell returned from the States after the storm passed. He supervised a rebuild and expansion of the old deck. The restaurant's renovations worked out better than before the storm. The Grand Old House now could accommodate over three hundred January-to-April patrons every night. For most of 1989, the restaurant was packed with diners every night, reservations only.

Heavy publicity from press releases and storm coverage helped the Cayman Islands gain prominence among the affluent crowd. Cruise liner tourists from a wider circle of influence visited. More first-timers booked vacations to Grand Cayman than ever before and most of them ended up at Tell's place. The "busy season" at the Grand Old House became a twelve-month *tour de force*.

Perhaps duppy magic *was* real and working in Tell's favor. The reappearance of an old friend made it seem so.

* * *

A newly divorced Suladda once again caught up with Tell in Pennsylvania. She asked if he had room for a good dessert chef in the islands. On the spot, Tell responded with the money for a plane ticket to Grand Cayman. Suladda joined his crew and played a major role in its successful expansion from that point forward. Her desserts were so good that patrons asked Tell how he found her, and he always related how they met in the snow. And then he would add another anecdote about the day he stood in the kitchen and savored one of her creations:

"Suladda, I have traveled around the world and eaten gourmet food in five-star restaurants all the time," he told her, ". . . I must say that your desserts are still the best I've eaten."

"She asked me, 'Do you really mean that, Chef?'"

"I told her, 'Von der wahrheit meines herzens' ('From the truth of my heart'). And then the kitchen crew stopped cooking and applauded. Suladda grinned from ear to ear."

Tell's listeners loved the story he told. They ordered more desserts, too.

"That statement is still worth more than anything else in my professional pastry chef career," remembered Suladda.

While business continued to boom for the island and at the Grand Old House, unfinished business between Tell and Bunny lingered in each of their hearts.

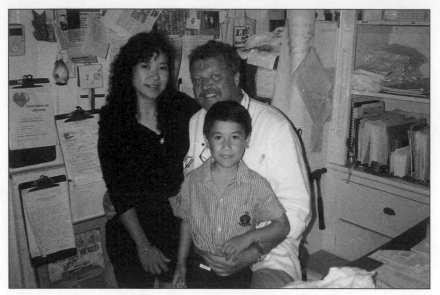
Suladda May, Jason Cronk, and Tell

58

DECIDE WHO YOUR
FRIENDS ARE

"If you can't be with the one you love, love the one you're with ..."
—"Love the One You're With," songwriters, Clifton George
Bailey and Stephen A. Stills

Steven Stills heard his friend Billy Preston say the phrase and, with his permission, he wrote the line into a song, which became a signature hit. Preston's advice was good in 1970 and still applied in 1989.

Bunny had moved out after Tell's affair with Jeannette. She moved into a small house near Gwynedd, took in a housemate nicknamed Charley, and tried the best she could to throw her attention back into her work. She dated some, but she was still in love with Tell.

Believing all along that Jeannette was a gold digger whose motives sooner than later would destroy her new relationship with Tell, Bunny decided not to give up. She managed a timely phone call or two to Jeannette and dropped a few not-so-subtle hints.

"Would you like to know who Tell visits when he comes up here? Are you sure you know who really has his heart? I'll bet I spend more quality time with him than you do."

Bunny understood this war that she was in, and that *Sun Tzu's Art of War* rules applied: "If you are far from the enemy, make him believe you are near." And this: "You have to believe in yourself."

Bunny was available when the predicted fall out arrived. Jeannette and her daughter winged back to California empty-handed, save the memories of lonely sandy beaches. The ennui of hours, weeks, and months of waiting for Tell, while tucked away in the middle of the Caribbean, flashed like neon signs and eventually faded for them.

For the first time in years, Tell would have to make do on his own. He needed to make time to figure what kind of future he wanted to have with Bunny. For sure, he would have to start with admitting that she had been right—about Jeannette, and that she knew him better than he knew himself. The sooner that he would come to realize that—the faster he would win her back.

Bunny would not make it easy for Tell to get her back into his life. This time she wanted to be sure he was as committed to her as she knew her heart was to him. She had fought for him, now she would watch and see if he would fight for her.

Tell came on like a short-order cook under pressure. Once he got his head straight, he wasted no time boarding a plane headed for Philadelphia with only Bunny on his mind. By the time his airliner landed at Philadelphia International, he was feeling his oats. He even thought he'd let the familiar customs official see the Monte Cristo Cuban cigars in his bag, since he had traveled back and forth through this terminal many times. This time, however, an unfamiliar agent was on duty.

"Are those what I think they are, honey?" the officer asked.

"Sure they are. I smoke them in Cayman where I have my restaurant."

"Well, I'm going to have to confiscate them, you understand."

The customs officer by now had garnered the attention of several of her fellow officers, who approached.

"Well, if you have to confiscate them, let me do one thing," said Tell as he leaned over the bag and fist-stomped every single one of the cigars to shreds—no doubt remembering the time his 6.9 Mercedes was abused by Nixon's secret service unit and the earlier night when he'd arrived in America for the first time.

"Dear, I could have you arrested for doing that."

"If I can't keep them and smoke them, nobody else will smoke them." With that, Tell took a step back, pushed up his opened palms into the air, and stared at the customs agent and the group of officers behind her, which stared at the ruined Cubans.

After a tense moment, the official stamped Tell's passport and waved him through without further incident. Tell was pissed, but he let it be. He had one thing on his mind far more important to him—how could he woo Bunny back into his life?

Tell pursued her relentlessly. He showed up at her house and at her office. Speaking with her on the phone, he invented excuses to see her. Sometimes he threw in a grand gesture or two—an over-the-top dinner in a special location or an impromptu vacation, first-class all the way for good measure. More than once, a sparkling "big gift" landed on her wrist or around her neck. Like one of his mastiff dogs, Tell latched on and he wasn't letting go until she agreed to take him back.

Truth be told, Tell had not wanted to leave Bunny for the other woman. He had committed one premarital, adulterous affair with the woman and then, out of spite, had parked her on the island near him. Behind the scenes, both Bunny and Tell kept communications going on a regular basis, even if only by long distance.

Bunny, for her part, never considered Tell out of her life.

"It cuts both ways," Best Female Latin Artist of the Year Gloria Estafan sang at the top of the charts at the time. Tell had his work cut out for him. He tried and tried and tried to win Bunny's heart, never knowing that she still had a soft spot for only him.

Bunny wanted amends for the damage done to her trust. Tell would remain a liability to her if he could not be trusted. His serenades and well-crafted words would no longer be enough for her to once again give her heart to Tell if she could not see for herself that the man she knew he really could be—the only man she could love completely—had returned.

"When he turned on his masculine charms, he always turned me on," she confided to a friend. "But, if he really wants to get married— which is his idea mostly—it's going to have to happen before I move down to Cayman with him."

Tell, for his part, had really come to realize that he had a weakness, a sort of ethical "blind spot." He was confused about it. The hurt of losing his mother so inexplicably, which had guided and sustained him, was at odds in his mind with his desire to love someone faithfully. What had attracted him to Nicoletti was her likeness to his mother, which he only understood in hindsight. This time he was looking for someone who could make him feel understood, with whom he could say anything— someone with whom he could feel safe and accepted for his flawed love in return. Without that, he doubted himself, made mistakes, and caused damage to others.

Time alone healed Tell's earlier wound enough for him to realize that he wanted to love only Bunny. In his pursuit of her this time, he realized that she was his friend; that Bunny didn't try to make sense of what was illogical about his behavior, only that she loved him without question.

For her part, Bunny allowed him back only after she felt that Tell, by his actions, had done more than what she normally would have expected. She told him she would leave Pennsylvania and fly to Grand Cayman with him for the Christmas Holidays on one condition: if they agreed to get married *forever* right after New Year's Day.

"When the chimes finish, begin. . . " the words from *High Noon* drifted back into Tell's head. It had taken his getting a taste of real blood in his mouth—the loss of the woman he really did care for—to accept that he would never find happiness in love and marriage unless he cared more for his woman than for himself.

There was, however, the matter of Bunny's one ground rule: there would be no relationship without marriage and no marriage without "until death do us part." This time, Tell really did have to confront his demons, move on from the void left by his mother, and understand that this time he was getting married forever.

Tell and Bunny boarded the Cayman Air flight to Grand Cayman on December 23, 1988. They worked the Christmas holidays together at the Grand Old House and then flew American Airlines to Nevada on January 1, 1989—right into the middle of one of the most brutal snow-storms in Lake Tahoe's history.

59

BACHELOR PARTY DREAMS

"Überraschen Sie uns. Geben Sie uns Ihrebesten."
("Surprise us. Give us your best.")

—Chef Tell

Through his friend Herbert Pleissnig, general manager of the Hyatt Regency Grand Cayman Resort, Tell arranged for accommodations in Tahoe. Pleissnig secured two VIP rooms at the Hyatt Regency Lake Tahoe Resort nestled in the Sierra Mountain Range of Nevada—one for the wedding couple and one for Bunny's sister and her husband, Alicia and Dan DeGowin, who would witness the ceremony and help them celebrate their new beginning.

It is fair to say that the foursome knew each other as long as they had known themselves as couples. Although Bunny had two other sisters, Ali was closest at the time, ever since she and Bunny shared a Jersey Shore house. A lot of water passed under the bridge between the two couples, including an incident, which had occurred years earlier, now vivid in Tell's mind as he closed his eyes and pushed back his first-class seat. He watched images of what could easily pass for a bachelor party. A smile drew across his face.

Tell and Bunny had flown out to southern California for one of his appearances on Gary Collins's *Hour Magazine* television show. Since the DeGowins lived near LAX airport, Bunny and Tell stayed at their place after the Friday show went off without a hitch.

The weekend forecast called for more sun. Saturday morning, the foursome rode in Dan's Peugeot sedan, north on Pacific Coast Highway to a spot just beyond Malibu Beach right at Corral Canyon. Dan drove into the parking lot of the Mediterranean restaurant, Beau Rivage, owned by Chef Daniel Forge and his opera singer wife Luciana.

Bunny and Ali opted for a stroll on the beach for sister talk. They figured to be gone for quite a while. Tell and Dan stepped inside the bar. Under a slanted wood-beam roof and surrounded by glass-paned walls, which afforded them an uninterrupted view of the Pacific Ocean, Tell scanned the bar shelves. He spied a dusty cognac bottle at the top, a Louis XIII by its baccarat crystal construction. If he were right about the brand, there would be at least a shot of the original distillation inside of the bottle. Connoisseurs considered Louis XIII the best cognac in the world for at least that reason alone.

Tell asked the youngest bartender he could find to reach up and let him see the bottle closer. The young man, who paid more attention to a buxom server walking by than the cognac, dusted off the bottle and handed it to Tell. On closer inspection, Tell saw that it was, indeed, a Louis XIII—about $1,500 per bottle with content of only fifteen shots when full.

"I'd be curious to know how much you charge for a shot of this cognac," asked Tell of the unsuspecting acolyte.

"I guess $30 a shot, sir," the young man replied, still ogling the waitress. He never saw the sly look Tell gave Dan, who had only heard of the drink but never tasted it.

"Pour me two of them, and charge me $70 per shot," Tell requested of the hapless bartender. The tender shrugged, poured the shots, and took the $140 Tell placed on the bar. He dropped the bills into the register and walked in the direction of the flirtatious server.

Tell turned and lifted his glass against Dan's. "Dan, my brother, you are drinking history here—at a great price." That said, the gentlemen tipped their glasses.

Dan had traveled the world as a fashion model, and drank some very expensive cognacs, but he never expected the smooth strength of his first taste of Louis XIII. He almost coughed. Every sip thereafter turned out to be by far the smoothest cognac he had ever sipped anywhere in the States or on the continent. Tell not only knew and expected both the flavor and bouquet of the rare drink, but he also watched Dan's reactions. He enjoyed how Dan learned to savor its seductiveness.

They swaggered right through the entire bottle.

Tell spied two more bottles on the shelf and remarked to his drinking partner, "This guy might get fired before we leave."

Dan tipped another shot past his numbed and grateful lips and saluted, "Thank you, Louie XIII. No pain, Tell."

"It's not about the alcohol, Dan. It's about the history," Tell avowed before swallowing another round down his throat.

When Bunny and Ali returned, they did not find the boys at the bar. They discovered the two "brothers" slumped on a bench outside on the wooden deck, mesmerized by the blue of the Pacific Ocean. Each wore a strange, beatific smile plastered across his face from ear to ear, and they were unable to stand up without assistance.

Bunny inquired, "Tell, what have you guys done while we were gone?"

"I would have charged $150 per shot in my restaurant . . ." said Tell before he passed out in the back seat of the Peugeot, right on Dan's shoulder.

Tell listed over onto Bunny's shoulder on the flight to Nevada, so she nudged him out of his reverie. The captain announced the beginning of their descent into the Tahoe area. Tell straightened, nodded, and then went back to dreamland, this time to 1984.

60

GETTING TO THE WEDDING

"Es gibt zwei Leidenschaften mit Lebensmitteln:
die erste ist, gerne essen und genießen es, die zweite ist,
um Nahrung fürandere zu kochen."
("There are two passions with food; the first is to enjoy eating
and savoring it, the second is to cook food for others.")

—Chef Tell

T
ell and Bunny opted to fly to Tahoe for their nuptials because after a tough, hot holiday season of long hours in the kitchen and serving thousands of guests, the cold climate of the High Sierras seemed deliciously inviting. Good skiing was on tap, which Bunny loved, and Tell could relax in the cooler environment.

Bunny's closest sister got wind of the impromptu wedding and called Bunny before they left, "Bunny, if you two get married without inviting us, I'll never speak to you again." Bunny knew that Ali meant it, so she invited the DeGowins to join them. "Besides, who are you going to ski with on the slopes, Bunny?" she added.

When Dan got on the phone, he reminisced with Bunny about his and Alicia's own pre-wedding dinner.

Dan DeGowin and Alicia Kule were already living together in California when they planned for their wedding on the East Coast where most family members lived. The Pennsylvania parish priests, however, refused to marry them on grounds of a church doctrine that Catholic women must marry only within the local parish where they reside. To date, the confrontation had come to a draw and was heading toward stalemate.

Tell wouldn't stand for the situation. He bypassed both sides, went straight to the highest church official in Philadelphia, His Eminence Archbishop Cardinal John Krol, whom he happened to know, and asked him for assistance.

Cardinal Krol had worked as a meat department manager of an Ohio Kroger Foods store at the age of eighteen. On later occasions, he sampled Tell's cooking. He also harbored a not-so-secret passion for fine cigars, since he had operated a cigar outlet during his days in the Ohio seminary where he studied to become a priest.

Cardinal Krol's office arranged for a special dispensation to allow the local priests to marry the DeGowins in their chosen parish. Tell had offered to cater one charity cooking event in exchange for the favor and had promised, if allowed, a box of fine cigars for His Eminence.

The rehearsal dinner for twenty-five was held in Lansdale, Pennsylvania, in the restaurant of a good friend of Tell's. Like some of the other guests, Dan's mother had put away a few drinks by the time she was served one of Tell's dishes. Unfortunately, she requested a shaker of salt within Tell's earshot. Tell turned to the woman and inquired, "Madam, do you ask for a paint brush every time you see a Picasso?"

"No," she answered.

"Have you even tasted my food, madam?"

She had not.

"I think then, madam, that you should taste my food first before you ask for salt or pepper, because that food is my Picasso."

A pall hung in the silent room. The bride-to-be stood and said, "Today, Tell, it's not about your food; it's about my wedding. Give her the god-damned salt, if she wants it."

With that said, everyone moved on. When Ali sat down and continued her dinner forgiveness reigned. It appeared to be a family trait, even at a wedding rehearsal dinner.

When the letter fax from the office of His Eminence Cardinal Krol informed the priests they could perform the DeGowins' wedding in their church, they were not happy. One of them lodged a verbal protest with Ali's mother. He wondered aloud how she could let her daughters live "in sin" and still consider herself a good Catholic mother, since she was aware that Ali and Dan lived together, as well as Tell and Bunny, who were not married. The priest had underestimated the intelligence and conviction of the devout Catholic mother.

"Who are you to pass judgment on me or my children, Father? My faith tells me that only Christ and God have that right," she said. "Is it not my duty as their mother to be there for my children, whether they are doing right or not? That is my role here, Father. I am my children's mother."

Bravo, Mom!

The priest was stunned and silenced by the logic of her faith. He had to admire the strength and brilliance of her words.

Tell awakened at the pilot's announcement of their imminent landing on the snowplowed runway at Lake Tahoe Airport. They landed as smoothly as the DeGowin wedding, which went off without a hitch inside the East Coast church.

The airport terminal was located less than fifteen minutes from Heavenly Ski Resort, state-line casinos, and the Hyatt.

61

FINALLY ... WEDDING DAY

"...The snow matched my colors, silver and white."
—Bunny Erhardt

Thirty-one inches of snow fell in the Sierra and Tahoe region in December 1988. Another fifty-five inches would accumulate in January. At mid-morning of January 2, 1989, snow continued to fall as it had all of the day before, all night and all morning.

The DeGowin/Erhardt party of four rented an SUV for the thirty-mile drive to Carson City to obtain a marriage license for Tell and Bunny. After, the foursome returned to the Hyatt resort, Tell and Bunny waited with anticipation for their wedding day to arrive.

"We awoke early. It was still snowing heavily, and the snow matched my colors, silver and white. By the time we got to the chapel, another foot of fresh powder covered the ground. Everything was white," Bunny remembered.

The climate change from Grand Cayman to the ski trails of Tahoe was what she had hoped for, but the storm delayed their ceremony at least an hour while the Universal Christian chaplain attempted to drive to the chapel through the snow storm.

"The chaplain was late from a morning wedding. We opened the bottle of champagne we had brought with us and drank while we waited," laughed Bunny.

The bride wore high-heeled white leather boots and a tailored white wool suit with a silk beaded camisole. Her long blonde hair pulled back on one side was interwoven with a few sprigs of baby's breath. She held a small bouquet of white roses. Tell wore a white rose boutonnière on the lapel of his gray pinstriped suit, and on his feet, gray lizard-skin cowboy boots.

Cupid brought Tell and Bunny together in Ottsville. They lived in Pennsylvania and on Grand Cayman Island. And they married in a tiny Elvis chapel located in Reno, Nevada, with a ceremony officiated by a Universal Christian minister—Tell the Lutheran; Bunny, Alicia, and Dan the Catholics from Marina del Rey, California.

When the ceremony ended, the wedding party was drunk on love and champagne. They were also famished. They piled into the SUV and headed slowly through the drifting snow to *Le Petit Pier*, a French bistro. Overlooking the lake that never freezes from the North Shore near King's Beach, the place was cozy. It had less than fifty tables, set with white linen and formal silver tableware, stretched across three intimate dining rooms. The award-winning *auberge* was considered the finest in the area.

The hostess seated the party at a premier table next to a window with a wide view of the snow-christened hills and pine trees surrounding the blue lake.

"*Bonjour.* Welcome to *Le Petit Pier*. Are you here for a special occasion?" asked headwaiter, Steve Marks, noting their attire.

Tell answered for the group, "Our wedding day."

"Congratulations. Is there anything special I may get for you?"

"I would like to speak with your chef. Tell him Chef Tell is here."

Marks took the message back to the kitchen. In seconds owner and restaurateur Chef Jean DuFau presented a bottle of *Prestige Cuvée Louis Roederer Cristal*, saying, "Chef Tell, what a pleasure to meet you! Congratulations on your wedding! What would you like me to cook for you?"

"You are the chef today. Surprise us—give us your best."

Chef DuFau prepared and served five courses. Included were pâté foie gras, soup, salmon, a cheese course, and dessert soufflés and pastries.

"The chef just went nuts as soon as he found out it really was Chef Tell," recalled Dan. "The wine, though, cost more than the dinner."

Tell knew what Bunny liked to drink. He sprang for a Jeroboam (three-liter bottle) of Bunny's favorite *Grand Vin de Chateau Latour*— 70 percent Cabernet Sauvignon, 30 percent Merlot—priced at about $1,700 a bottle (today about $10,000). Chef DuFau decanted the bottle for his guests and, at Tell's invitation, sipped with them and lingered to hear Tell share a few jokes, which were as ribald as ever.

Tell was in rare form. His party laughed through all five courses, except Bunny, who was up and down with family phone calls, since there were no convenient cell phones in those days.

Chef DuFau returned to the table toward the end of the repast and asked for Tell's assessment. Unknown to the others, and confirmed years later by Marks, DuFau had prepared several of the dishes with the same blueberry sauce base, a definite haute cuisine no-no.

"Chef Tell, how did you like my dinner for your party today?"

"That was the best dinner I've had today," Tell said as he simmered.

DuFau had not fooled the palate and training of the master chef. DuFau, Bunny, the DeGowins, and Marks all knew what he meant.

"What I remember most was that I was happy, and Tell was happy that day," Bunny preferred to recall.

Once again, in the words of Chef Perrier, "Tell had married a saint."

The next day, on the other side of the lake, Bunny skied with Ali and Dan for a few hours. Tell stayed in the ski lodge for what he called, "Black Diamond après ski activity"—hefty drinking. The auto accident in 1969 near Calw, Germany, cut short his skiing days when his left hip had to be replaced. He had been an avid skier before that, yet he would never be able to ski with his bride.

Ali and Dan departed late the following day after snow-mobiling in the morning and hot toddies at the chalet. The honeymoon for Bunny and Tell continued for a solid week after a change of hotels from the Hyatt casino resort in Nevada to the non-casino Four Seasons Resort on the California side of the lake.

Though skiing was out—just as well since temperatures dipped as low as a record −19 degrees Fahrenheit by January 8—cross-country snow-mobiling was not. An incident when Tell fall off his machine and ended up waist-deep in a drift of the white stuff, from which he had to be pulled by another machine, was a highlight. A relaxing sauna and drinks at the lodge followed.

The newlyweds flew back to the Grasshopper Lane house where they had lived together—this time only to engage with the real estate agent, who would sell it for them as part of the final divorce settlement with Nicoletti.

Once the house sold, the Erhardts gathered one hundred friends there for a high cuisine, black-tie affair. Festive balloons and jazz music performed by the trio and piano player they'd had at the Wayne restaurant helped their guests bid *"Auf weidersein!"* The celebration was the couple's send off to Grand Cayman Island living.

62

HIGHS AND LOWS

"Man kann nicht hart genug daran."
("You can't work hard enough at it.")

—Chef Tell

T he Grand Old House had by 1989 survived the earlier tribu-
lations of weather and relationship patterns. Local residents
long attracted to the location for years were grateful for its
ongoing good fortune. Ever-growing legions of tourists and
top-name celebrities discovered its charms, and the steady stream of
business expanded because of Tell's TV appearances, which helped spur
tourism for all of Cayman. Here again he was ahead of his time as his
sphere of influence spread from cooperative marketing ventures and
Chef Tell articles in *Cayman Airways* magazine issues. The more word of
mouth spread, the more travelers' appetites clamored for Grand Cayman
and Tell's Grand Old House.

On *LIVE! with Regis & Kathie Lee*, Tell promoted the islands and
his restaurant with every appearance from as early as 1988. Regis and his
wife, Joy, flew down to Grand Cayman and dined at Tell's place, part of
a friendship with Regis that began with their early days on road tours.
Regis got his start on TV in Los Angeles where Tell made many TV

Cayman Airways features Chef Tell.

appearances for his book-selling campaigns. Their paths crossed, and they became friends and, as entertainers, they shared similar turning points in their respective careers. That friendship would include, in the coming years, Christmas dinner on Grand Cayman and an invitation for Tell to cater Regis's nephew's bar mitzvah, which he did cater and would years later explain his menu choices during an appearance on *Donny & Marie*.

Like clockwork, Tell was on-air somewhere promoting the Cayman Islands. A tireless workhorse, his influence took effect on a larger scale as his TV appearances accumulated from 1988 for another six years.

* * *

The Grand Old House's early years saw a sprinkling of celebrities show up among the regular dining public. Three Dog Night's lead singer Danny Hutton; comedian Don Rickles; film director Sydney Pollack; and writers Michael Hausman and John Grisham enjoyed the food. (Grisham preferred to sit near the dais on the veranda, and the same table was reserved for him every time he visited—a writer's vantage point from where he could observe other guests with discretion.)

Scores more came later, including supermodels, the cast and film crew of *The Firm*, and Senator John McCain from Arizona. Don Knotts, fresh off a reunion with Andy Griffith in the 1986 made-for-television movie *Return to Mayberry*, came down to the island for lunch and joked around with Tell in a round-by-round laugh fest.

Tourists who had never seen Tell on-air found his place through local ads and articles, that touted his celebrity. His popular books, *Chef Tell Tells All* and *Cayman Islands Recipes* (with sketches by Tell's longtime friend, William Sonstein), moved people to visit and taste his incredible food.

Perhaps drawn by the publicity—*Wine Spectator* magazine gave its Award of Excellence to the Grand Old House every year beginning in 1990 (a run which through 2011 has never been broken)—Willie Nelson, who was one of Tell's music idols, found the Grand Old House in the early 1990s. After performing an open-air concert on the island,

Tell meets 1989/1990 Mrs. Florida, Marianne Carson

Nelson's band and entourage—a group of sixteen without their leader—showed up late at night and dined inside. At 6 a.m., the dinner party was still going strong outside. Nelson's lead guitarist, Ira Nelson, stood on the end of the deck as he shot photos of his new bride. Other band members and roadies sprawled along the long deck and watched the sun rise. Suddenly, two hungry people, Willie and his sister, Bobbie, walked in through the open back door of the kitchen and called out for Chef Tell. They kept calling as they walked out to the front room.

Tell turned and saw Nelson standing there, and a sheepish grin crawled across his face. He shook Willie's hand like a child meeting a hero. Tell was a solid fan of the singer and loved his music. Nelson appreciated the gesture and was about to tell the chef that he was hungry when Bunny walked onto the veranda.

"Mr. Country Singer, Mr. Nelson, this is my wife, Bunny."

Tell talks movies with director Sydney Pollack.

"Well, I'm very pleased to meet you, ma'am." Nelson took her hand, bent forward, and kissed it. She was impressed. "While Tell introduced me, Willie held and kissed my hand like a real southern gentleman. After Tell cooked and served breakfast, we all went to the bar. Tell offered up drinks, and he and Willie joked about Tell's recent encounters with his attorney-partners and the IRS up in Wayne."

Tell and Honorable McKeever Bush, (former) Premier of
Grand Cayman Islands

(Less than twenty-four months later, Nelson would have his own public troubles with the IRS, a situation he would settle for millions of dollars.)

"The rest of the band stayed on for breakfast and then they all thanked Tell for the hospitality and left," Bunny remembered. "Tell was as excited as he'd ever been, having just met and talked with Willie."

Not that Tell was only a country-music aficionado. In fact, his musical taste was wide-ranging and included Julio Iglesias and ABBA. Of course, Beethoven's Symphony No. 5 in C Minor was his classical favorite.

Tell, Liesel, and Max at the GOH.

* * *

Twenty-something Sacha Alexis Lichine—his father Alexis Lichine was the acknowledged "Pope of Wine" for his taste and for his ability to write about the subject—possessed an insouciant personality and a knack for success at an early age that fit right in with Tell's dossier.

As a teenager, Lichine toured wealthy Americans throughout France, taking them to two three-star restaurants a day on custom tours that he arranged. "I'd call up and say, 'Mr. Lichine is coming with a group,' and the restaurant people would go bananas, thinking it was my father. They'd be a little sore when I walked in, but so what? My money was good."

He fit right in with the Erhardts: "After we'd met him at the Grand Old House, Sacha was out to our home at Rum Point on at least two occasions when we invited him for lunch and drinks. We sat around, relaxed, and drank *Vueve Clicquot* champagne on Sundays away from the restaurant," recalled Bunny.

Politicians from all over the world also found their way to Tell's tables. The Bush family, Secret Service agents in tow, came from Texas and visited several times. Senators and Representatives from both sides of the aisle in the American Congress sat on the veranda and marveled at the shoreline and ocean breezes. Some say one Congressman, Tip O'Neill, Fifty-fifth Speaker of the House of Representatives, even sent Tell an official House of Representatives glass paperweight etched with his name.

A high-ranking German official arrived with his wife and entourage for lunch one day, looking like the ancient Egyptian King Tutankhamun. Dripping with gold and gemstones, they alit from a motorized dinghy that brought them from a fifty-foot yacht anchored offshore to the restaurant's dock.

On another occasion, Alan James Scott, Cayman Islands Governor appointed by the Queen of England, attended a catered luncheon at the Erhardt's Rum Point house with his wife and entourage. For the occasion, Tell laid out a sumptuous royal buffet that spread across the lawn. Champagne flowed before the guests sat down, but the governor's favorite South African wine, Rust en Vrede Estate Red Wine Stellenbosch, was poured during the meal. The outing earned the Erhardt's an invitation to dine at the governor's palatial home.

The governor's house, a large ranch with five bedrooms situated right on 7-Mile Beach, overlooked the water. Dinner was set up on the patio where invited guests, including Cayman dignitaries, lawyers, judges, business executives, bankers—a Who's Who on Grand Cayman—and Bunny and Tell, mingled. After champagne and hors d'oeuvres, they drank the governor's favorite Stellenbosch and ate entrées of conch fritters and tenderloin roast with a side of goat cheese salad. Hundred-year-old family recipe Tortuga Rum Cake, made right on the Islands, finished the meal. Coffee and liqueur accompanied Cuban cigars, and conversation among the guests continued well into the night. For Bunny and Tell, the occasion marked further acceptance into the culture of the island and recognition for his promotional activities, which placed Grand Cayman squarely on cruise and airline maps.

* * *

Cayman life hummed along for the Erhardts, but obstacles popped up at odd times. In a week when Tell was responsible for Blue—Bunny worked in the States that week—he let his house neighbor put his face near Blue's for a kiss. Blue bit the neighbor. The man ended up in the local hospital. Three stitches closed the gash on his face, but a local reporter hanging in the ER got wind of the incident and head-lined his over-the-top story, "Pit Bull Attacks Man at Rum Point."

All hell broke loose. Brown bags of money allegedly were left behind the restaurant to make the incident go away and to save Blue from being put down.

Bunny was angry when she heard the news, but not over the head-line. She had told Tell not to let anyone near Blue while she was gone. She knew the dog had not yet settled in Cayman, and that you don't go telling neighbors to stick their mugs right in front of a Pit bull's face. The accident cost Tell one round-trip air ticket for his neighbor, who told him his vacation was ruined, plus $500 hush money. It could have cost a whole lot more. Had the neighbor been a Caymanian and pressed charges, Tell's business license might have been revoked, possibly by Judge "Crippling" Kipling Douglas.

Island legislators did get involved. They banned all Pit bulls, and other Mastiff breeds, from Cayman after another dog-bite incident involved a different neighbor and dog. Blue, however, was "grand-fathered" beyond the law. Though he had to stay on the island, or lose his privilege to return, he was allowed to live out the rest of his seventeen-year lifetime with Bunny and Tell.

The day Bunny and Tell had to put Blue down because of his aged condition was the first day Bunny ever saw Tell cry. She had not been in the Wayne restaurant the day he received the American flag from Senator Specter.

Bunny's sister, Terry Anne, smuggled a young puppy named Jade, a gray Presa Canario, onto the island to help the couple. Jade looked like another Pit bull, albeit with green eyes.

63

UNDER THE FAÇADE, DEEP THOUGHTS

"Ich weiß nicht, warum sie es den Civil War nennen. Es ist
ein Widerspruch in sich." ("I don't know why they call it
the Civil War. It's an oxymoron.")

—Chef Tell

Tell threw Sunday parties at Rum Point that were wild times to remember. Bombay Sapphire Gin, Cayman Mamas, Mud Slides, and Rum Runner Punches quenched thirsts. "Shoot the whipped cream," a game involving tipsy, open-mouthed servers who swallowed aerosol-driven toppings as fast as possible, was the game of choice.

"Tell was a wild man. He worked and played hard," said Chef Duerr.

Binge drinking, swallowing dollops of cream, and whatever else happened at those parties gave reason to expect a little understanding for tardiness the next morning in the kitchen. Tell did forgive Monday-morning lateness, now and then, when, after all, he partied right at their sides the day before, but always with his drink of choice, not what the others were drinking. If he harbored resentments for single-handing in the kitchen when Duerr was late, he never revealed them. He preferred to set a good example, if only for Duerr, by doing the work that had to be done, regardless of whether he had anyone to help him. The man at the top of the organizing board bore the responsibility, and dining patrons with hungry palates had to be satisfied.

In short order, Duerr got the message, as did the other chefs on the crew, and the kitchen the day after parties hummed early in the morning with high morale from getting the work done.

Hands-down, Tell bested everyone with non-stop jokes that kept the kitchen tone light. He was an equal-opportunity offender like Don Rickles, another of Tell's Cayman patrons, who wrote to Tell, "I enjoyed your charming restaurant; the delicious food and your terrific charm . . . hope to see you along the way."

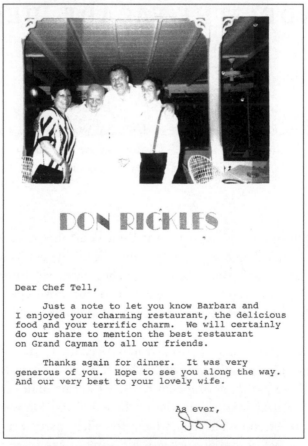

l. to r., Barbara and Don Rickles, Tell and Robert, a waiter

Tell whipped up series of jokes aimed at any ethnicity or occupation faster than a pat of butter could melt in a preheated sauté pan. He'd just as soon tell a rabbi an irreligious Jewish joke, and a group of old ladies an off-color joke, than not say anything at all. The audience didn't matter—that he had someone to talk to mattered. In most instances, the audience ate it up (awful pun intended.)

Tell lived to have people around him not because he loved the limelight, but because he liked and needed people. His memories of Nicoletti's depressed condition, which her family denied for the most part, were sufficient to serve Tell with a heaping plate of Karma. He'd left losses for Helga, the mother of his only child, and spent time away from fiancées and spouses, not to mention his son.

Having people around him with whom he could talk, lessened the impact of his memories of friends who had died young and hungry after the war. Constant communication reduced the unwanted emotions connected with the loss of his mother and made him forget that his brother wasn't speaking to him or that an uncle had died in a mountain fall.

As long as Tell moved forward with a good heart and tried to take responsibility for his mistakes and omissions by working harder and better, his private life had balance and meaning. The evidence, as the cliché goes, was in the pudding. Tell's life continued to be charmed, yet he never felt sure that he was doing enough—rarely felt the peace and quiet that he sought.

Tell hid the bulk of the burdens he carried by making people laugh. Everybody laughed along with him but, unless they looked into his eyes with enough care to see all of what was there, they would never see the dead-calm seriousness. When the comic stood up, few saw the real Tell—the powerful professional who towered in the kitchen, possessed an intellect gifted with insight, and expressed interest in others more than his self—qualities that made him all the more interesting.

In truth, though, his fans were not obligated to look any deeper.

"Two ethnic guys were walking down the road and came upon a sign that said TACO BELL," Tell joked, "One remarked to the other, 'Look, Mexicans have been here only a few years, and they already have their own phone company.'"

"What three facts prove that Jesus Christ was Jewish? His mother thought he walked on water, he never moved out of the house until he was thirty, and he took over his father's business."

"I like to make easy recipes using eight to ten different ingredients at the most. Other cookbooks, they give you a whole list—five you never heard of and ten you can't get in the United States."

If you laughed, you understand Tell could be funny, but there was more to the man than jokes and laughter.

"Tell was talking with us at the bar, telling us about history, his passions, the woman that he loved, the reading that he preferred, and his general thoughts. But as soon as he had to go over to a table to work a party, he leaned in to us and said, 'Watch me work. This is all show,'" said a confidante not there to be entertained. She and her husband were people of substance who saw in Tell an intelligent, complicated man.

One Memorial Day at an outdoor event appearance, Tell told an audience, "I don't know why they call it the Civil War. It's an oxymoron." Not a joke or a jocular anecdote, these remarks made people think. This was Tell the historian, the intellectual speaking his mind and his heart— the same man who cooked for people from locations chosen because they had a historical place in America's revolutionary struggle for freedom.

Tell's strategic career decisions, looked at collectively, reveal a complex thinker and intellectual.

Regis Philbin once told him on-camera on national television, "You sure have some kind of crazy humor, Tell." Tell retorted without hesitation, as he continued to cook, "I'm not crazy, Regis; it's just humor." The passing remark, which lasted a split-second, bore substance in its meaning: Tell knew *exactly* what he was doing and the effect he was creating when he spoke or acted while on TV. One wonders what he was thinking a few minutes later as he handed over to Regis and Kathie Lee Gifford a white chocolate cheesecake with fresh raspberry sauce drizzled on top, which he had prepared in minutes.

* * *

Tell was born where free people (the Jews) struggled against an enemy (Hitler's Nazis) that desired to snuff them out, and where the air power of other free men (Allied forces) threatened annihilation, because Stuttgart built advanced fighter planes. Yet, confronted by the *will* of all free men, the dictatorship lost the war—a lesson impressed deeply into Tell's outlook on living. He spent hours devouring historical accounts of World War II and Germany's role in that theater. And then he arrived, of all places, in Philadelphia, the center for America's struggle for self-determined freedom. He opened his first restaurant in a building in Chestnut Hill, which had housed volunteer troops—valiant fighters against the suppression of the Crown. On Grand Cayman, his Grand Old House symbolized the Islanders' resistance against evil forces—Hessians, Mother Nature, and duppies.

In his next two restaurants, similar threads of historical struggles for emancipation were documented. Prima facie evidence labels Chef Tell a funny man and a masterful cook with a lucky rabbit's foot in his pocket. A second look reveals a man of sturdy backbone and character, a genuine intellectual with a first-rate knowledge of significant American historical facts and events.

Tell and Chef Walter Staib talked beyond the kitchen. They discussed history, their own and America's. Staib and Tell, both Swabian Germans, both chefs, both graduates of the same apprenticeship gauntlet, and both students of American revolutionary times and culture, desired to give more than they ever took from the "Land of the Free."

Staib has continued a plan, derived from discussions with Tell about America's heritage, to show to American TV audiences and the rest of the world how foods of the era of the American forefathers were prepared and cooked from a heritage rooted in southwestern Germany.

Beneath his exterior, Chef Tell was a Renaissance man, one concludes. Still, his humorous antics were indelible parts of the child-like texture that was woven into his fabric.

64

LIVE! WITH CHEF TELL

"Ich schneide mich nur einmal im Fernsehen,
und es war jetzt nicht mehr."
("I only cut myself once on TV, and it wasn't now.")

—Chef Tell

"Ouch!" Tell yelled, looking straight into the lens of the TV camera. When the effect had worked its way in, he said, "Just kidding. I only cut myself once on TV, and it wasn't now."

Tell's playful attitude on-camera also educated. He explained what other chefs would not—little things like how to press your knife against your knuckles when chopping foods, and to move your knuckles for speed, not the knife—the difference determined the thickness of food slices as well as finger preservation. He set the bar high.

The producers for *LIVE! with Regis & Kathie Lee*—coincidentally, eleven years later, the same Art Moore Tell knew at *Dialing for Dollars* and *AM/Philadelphia* was now executive in charge of production for *LIVE!*—were never prepared for what Tell might say on-set, but they could tell you that once it was time to work for real, every single time Tell nailed his on-air performance and prepared food dishes that tasted good.

Moore commented, "Tell could adapt quickly and be entertaining and informative. A scheduled seven-minute appearance might get cut down to three and a half minutes, because he was often the final segment on the show, but he could adapt his message to the time left. On live television, the clocks were constantly ticking."

Tell was popular with the off-camera crew members who fought for food shares once the on-air cooking segments were complete. They elbowed one another out of the way not only for the food, but for the best morsels of banter—the latest joke or anecdote that he might share.

"Tell's food was always remarkably good, no matter what he cooked," said Moore.

"They loved his food; they couldn't get enough of it. As soon as the cameras went off, you had to fight your way to the set to get a piece. That never happened with the other chefs' food," said Victoria Lang, who was Tell's personal liaison for many of his appearances, perhaps never realizing that Tell would on purpose prepare more food than required for his TV segment so that the staff could enjoy his cooking.

Lang's mother had watched Tell's *Dialing for Dollars* TV segments and his appearances on *The Mike Douglas Show* airing out of Philadelphia. That was Lang's first exposure to the chef. Later, when she worked with theater shows on and off Broadway, she walked by the WABC Studios where *LIVE!* was produced in Manhattan. Hearing that Regis might be going national, Lang "rigorously watched show after show for weeks" because she had decided she deserved to work as a producer there. She had good reason to think so.

Lang did her homework and then showed up among five hundred other applicants for the open producer position on *LIVE! with Regis & Kathie Lee*. Asked by show executives why she should be hired, even though her résumé was thinner in some places than others, Lang said, "My lack of experience works in your favor. Because I don't know better, I will do whatever you want."

That remark led to an interview with Regis himself, who said to her, "But you don't seem to have much experience at this sort of thing. Why should we hire you?"

"Regis, you know those concerts that you and Kathie Lee are doing together, making you so much money? They were my idea."

Apart from their TV show, Regis and Kathie Lee had been performing in live concerts. Regis worked stand-up comedy. Kathie Lee sang. They appeared at the Westbury Music Fair on Long Island in New

York and the Valley Forge Music Fair in Pennsylvania, which happened to be booked by a company for which Lang was a talent coordinator. In a position to watch both Regis and Kathie Lee perform separately, Lang came up with a novel idea, which she pitched to her employer, "Put both talents on the same bill as a show, because they complement each other. Together, they might be a better draw."

The company liked the concept and pitched it to the William Morris Talent Agency, which represented the artists. The first three-thousand-seat offering sold out in one hour. A second and a third sold out just as fast.

Regis was stunned.

Lang, the diminutive woman of less experience but with bright ideas and chutzpah, got the job.

She was a producer on the show when, weeks later, a show executive at a morning staff meeting asked for a volunteer to produce Chef Tell because his producer had moved on to another show. Lang raised her hand when no one else did. She said she felt it was like asking to help an old friend.

Lang knew Tell was funny and thought he could cook, but she didn't know that "he was such a character in real life. He had a great heart and spirit. His humor was dry and ribald—a real 'Oscar Madison–type.'"

Tell and Lang hit it off right away, but oddly. The first thing out of Tell's mouth when they met was peppered with his German accent, "So, you're my produsah?" The question echoed as though he was looking down a canyon or an empty beer stein. Lang, five-foot-three, short, and Tell, six-foot-three, tall, looked a bit like Bud Fisher's cartoon strip characters, *Mutt & Jeff*—the first successful American daily comic strip in print.

Tell liked to test people with whom he had to work. He wanted to see if he could trust them and to find the limits that he could go with them. Lang's test was brief.

"I met Maria Shriver once, and she was a produsah. Probably the only produsah I didn't sleep with."

Lang shot back, "Well, then I'll be the second."

Tell looked over and down at her and laughed, "So, you're like a queen?"

"Yeah, I'm your queen on this set. I'll be telling you what to do," quipped Lang. "You're going to do like this, do like that." It was a parody of a phrase that Tell used often when he cooked on TV.

Tell never tested Lang again. She thought, *This is gonna be fun!*

"Tell was a real professional. He did things that most of the other celebrities didn't," she said.

Tell arrived before most studio executives and producers. He entered the NBC Studio building through the same entrance door that his audience would use. He preferred the anonymity. To him, cooking shows were about the food and the fans.

Other chefs submitted their food orders through staff members days before a show and they used on-air whatever had been selected for them. Tell, on the other hand, visited the markets before dawn on show days and handpicked his fresh ingredients. He always arrived with his cooler filled to the brim and the food in the freshest condition.

Tell often completed food preparations far ahead of the show's actual on-air time, allowing him time to talk with the stage hands. He asked meaningful questions about them, their families, and their jobs. He listened to their answers. Other "celebrity" guests rarely spoke with the crews.

When Lang entered the studio, she followed the noise of animated conversation and laughter and found Tell in the middle of it every time.

"Never put more items on your menu than you have chairs in your restaurant. You can't make any profits that way, and at least people know you can cook a few things well," she overheard, followed by laughter.

After one of his earliest appearances on the show in 1988, Tell invited Lang to lunch in TriBeCa at Bouley—Chef David Bouley's flagship restaurant. She accepted because she would be part of a larger group of people. Lang was dating her future husband, Tony Baarda, at the time and invited him along because, when Zagat asked seven thousand subscription diners, "Where would you want to eat the last meal of your life?" New York resident respondents overwhelmingly chose Bouley.

When Chef Bouley discovered that Tell was dining in his restaurant, he came to the table and took his order in person. TV and film stars, including Bill Cosby, were seated in his restaurant, but Bouley made Tell the center of his attention. He didn't just greet Tell, he treated him like royalty and even cooked for his party. Large bottles of wine and champagne were opened and emptied as plate after plate arrived from the kitchen.

Tell encouraged everyone to taste everything. He told them to pass their plates to their left so that others could sample each dish. Lang sat in amazement and watched Tell direct his one-man show.

Bouley's *piece de resistance* on the day was a bright green spun-sugar apple—a signature dessert which, when tapped, spilled out a white-chocolate apple mousse set on top of raspberry purée.

On other dining occasions, Lang discovered that Tell preferred to sample foods all the time in the manner she had observed. Like a youngster in a candy shop, he wanted to try everything. *The prophetic advice of his mother, "If you become a chef, you will never go hungry," she thought, must never be far behind.*

* * *

Tell lived as large as his circumstances permitted, and his style was contagious. But when it was time for work, he was all business. The expected thing to do was at least one rehearsal before going on-air at *LIVE!* However, Lang had her hands full getting Tell to rehearse the show.

"Tell, I need you to stand over here," she would say, pulling or pushing him over to the spot.

"You're telling me?" he'd ask.

"Yes. You need to stand here for the cameraman so he can block his shots." Then she pulled him in another direction, saying, "and one for the director, too."

Tell toyed with her. He gave her what she wanted when, in desperation, she pleaded, "Don't screw this up!"

Still, the fun part was when the cameras rolled and the on-air action began, according to Lang, "Tell and Regis got along like a house on fire and would simply depart from the script set up on the cue cards. They loved their repartee, had fun with the audience and each other and, somehow, always came back to the scripted cards on time at the end."

Regis and Tell were alike. They projected brusque exteriors, yet had hearts of gold. Regis grew up in The Bronx section of New York City in the Depression Era, and Tell, of course, in war-torn Germany. They came from "no money" and worked their way up their respective ladders to fame and fortunes. Self-made men with similar work ethics, they shared one attitude: a love for life and people.

Philbin wrote, "Chef Tell was the first, big-time chef we had on our *LIVE!* show years ago. He was a giant of a man, a great guest, could cook and talk at the same time. He started all this television madness about chefs. His delivery was fun. He had a slight German accent that was charming. He did our show many times and developed quite a following. He had a number of restaurants, one in Pennsylvania, another in Grand Cayman Island where Joy and I were guests. They were always run beautifully, with precision and efficiency. We got along so well, on-camera and off. Just a great guy."

Regis and Joy Philbin agreed. "Tell was one of the most fascinating people we've met. His was always the best food."

For his "produsah," Tell always made sure to put on a really good show.

65

THE PRODUSAH'S
WEDDING DAY

"Who do we know with a beach?"
—Victoria Lang and Tony Baarda

When Lang and her fiancé tested a chef's food in his home environment for possible inclusion on *LIVE!*, Tell accompanied them as often as his schedule permitted. Time spent together opened wide the door to a lasting friendship and led to a trip for Lang and Baarda to Grand Cayman Island. While they paid their own way there, Tell insisted that they stay in his Rum Point home.

After their flight landed, they drove straight to the Grand Old House to say hello and to get the house keys. Tell tossed in a couple of coolers he had filled with abundant food and drinks, including lobsters, wine, and champagne. Within a day or two, he showed up at the house and cooked it for them, arriving by Naul Bodden's Boston Whaler speedboat, with Bunny on board decked out in her bikini.

Tell, on their departure, encouraged his friends to come and visit again. He loved their company. For the couple this penchant led to more island visits, one of which they would never forget.

Tony popped the question on Christmas Day 1992, and Victoria accepted his proposal. He and Victoria made plans for their wedding, but struggled with a strategic nightmare problem, since they lived in Manhattan but wanted to marry on a beach.

"Who do we know with a beach?" they asked.

Lang's mother lived on Long Island northeast of Manhattan, but in the dead of winter neither of them warmed to the idea of a wedding there. Then, the fact that Tell and Bunny lived on Grand Cayman popped up.

"Nah, too crazy to ask," they said. But the more they looked at each other, the more the idea wouldn't go away. Hesitant to call, they agreed to sleep on it. Then the phone rang and everything changed. Bunny and Tell were calling long-distance just to talk. Lang and Baarda's engagement and wedding plans came up, and they ended up telling them about their problem.

"We weren't sure about this, but would you two be willing to let us have our wedding on your beach?"

Bunny and Tell offered, "Are you kidding? We'd *love* to have you get married here! In fact, please come and stay at our place, and we'll cater for you."

Victoria and Tony were amazed by their reaction. "They were so touched that we even would ask them. And we were pleasantly surprised by that," recalled Tony.

In fact, when the date neared, Bunny arranged a bachelorette party for Victoria on 7-Mile Beach. She also stood up and acknowledged how taken she and Tell were that their friends had honored them with their request.

Victoria Lang and Tell prep for her 1993 wedding

Victoria and Tony prep with Tell

Victoria and Tony wanted a wedding ceremony and party for a small circle of family and friends. Once they knew their location, they planned for fifty or so guests to attend on July 4, 1993, on Grand Cayman Island at Rum Point.

They set the plan in motion and mailed out invitations, never thinking that Tell's house, determined to be the wedding location, would become a problem. In the interim between Tell's offer and the Fourth of July, Tell sold his house. He called them as soon as he closed the deal.

"Hello. Tell here. I've got some good news and some bad news. The bad news is that I've sold my house. The good news is that I put into the contract that your wedding must take place there before the new owners can move in."

Dejection became elation. Three days before the event, the excited couple and their wedding party flew down to Grand Cayman, prepared to do a lot of work to fix up the place for the ceremony and the reception.

Like a scene torn from *The Big Chill,* neither stifling heat, humidity, or swarms of mosquito's deterred friends, family, or the wedding coordinators from decorating the Rum Point house with furniture and flowers. Lang's wedding coordinators—like she, producers with television companies—followed her lead and approached the event like a TV production from beginning to end. They stayed overtime and overnight right at the house to accomplish every detail of the project. Even Victoria's mother chipped in her advice.

"If you had to get married on an island, why couldn't it have been f***ing Long Island?" she asked as she swatted mosquitoes and mopped her brow.

But overnight a miracle of sorts happened. "It was surreal," explained Victoria, "because it only lasted for the one day, our wedding day." A shift of the onshore breeze took away the insects. The cumulous clouds disappeared, and the sun shone in an azure sky. The temperature and humidity index relaxed. The wedding day was a picture-perfect day to remember.

Victoria's father, Jack Lang, a future Baseball Hall of Fame sports writer, attended. He gave his daughter away after he walked her out of Tell and Bunny's house, down the beach, and under a grove of coconut trees where the ceremony was held.

Tell staged the fifty-person party and cooked outrageous amounts of food and drink, lobsters included, for the reception dinner. More champagne flowed than most attendees ever saw at one place. Tell's famous Grand Old House bartender served up his infamous "Cayman Mama" drinks, and his one-man-band steel drummer rocked the beach.

Tell and Tony on wedding day

"What an impression Tell made on us. The weather cooperated for our wedding. There were no bugs, no flying insects—a great unexplainable day," recalled the wedding couple. "We had the most amazing wedding, but the party after—WOW!"

"Conga line dancing took us out into the water and along the beach," Tony began, and Victoria finished (giggling). "People were just s***-faced, dancing all over the gorgeous white-sand beach—some of them half-naked doing unimaginable things on the beach—really having a good time!"

Tell, meanwhile, looking like a benevolent general, or a pirate captain, stood beside the newly married couple on a dune and surveyed the crowd with a Cuban in one hand and a Cayman Mama in the other. Pensive, he looked upward at the pastel shades of mauve, orange, and gray reflected off the cumulus humilis whose mirror images sparkled like diamonds off the water's surface as the sun set.

Victoria asked, "What are you thinking, Tell?"

He turned to her, laughed aloud, and pointed to the revelers on the beach, "Those f***ing Rum Punches, they do it every time!" And then he clinked his Cayman Mama against hers, drank deeply, and added, "Reminds me of a f***ing Gauguin."

The whole day, as noted, was "magical." Later in the evening, when the newlyweds stopped by to settle up with Tell, he refused their money.

"Please, it's my gift. You are my produsah. I'm a chef. What am I gonna get for my produsah? A toaster?" In afterthought he added, "Just take good care of my servers."

Wedding Day party!

Tell and Bunny Erhardt at Lang-Baarda Wedding Day party

66

DANCING WITH REGIS

"Ich habe mit Regis mehr als verkehrte mit Nazis."
("I have consorted with Regis more than with Nazis.")

—Chef Tell

Tell could, at times, like or hate the rigors of being a celebrity, but he loved and looked forward to each of his *LIVE! with Regis & Kathie Lee* guest appearances. In the early days, production sets were not sophisticated. Cardboard props worked as well as anything, and Tell, unfazed by the conditions, pitched in and played his part to perfection. He treated his on-camera hosts and behind-the-scene workers with equanimity.

To watch Chef Tell perform on TV was to see a competent, confident professional who lived right in the moment. While others expressed that he was "ahead of his time," in truth he was more "right on time." True, no one had walked the pathway he was on, but he was in his element on TV. His power and personality fit the medium. In this regard, to sample one show appearance allows insight into them all.

Tell, entering the kitchen set with Regis from stage right, is introduced as they walk, "We're cooking today with Chef Tell, who has a wonderful restaurant where my wife and I have gone many times—the Grand Old House in the Cayman Islands."

(Live audience applause.)

"Grand Cayman Island, Regis," Tell corrects.

Suddenly, Tell turns around and as the introductory music plays, he dances with the startled show host, who nevertheless plays along for a few seconds. Short as it was, the dance delights the studio audience and proves Tell's complete ease on national television and with the medium.

Regis, master TV personality that he is, retorts, "Cayman Islands . . . Grand Cayman Island—whatever, Tell. What have you got for us today?" He never realizes that Tell is quite right in renaming the island, because, in fact, Islanders took offense whenever people called their home "the Cayman Islands."

The camera catches everything—this is live TV. Tell plays with Regis, the food, and the live audience for the fun of it, yet he stays in character. Respectfully, he gets to the business of cooking but, in doing so, he also makes reference back to the dancing.

"Regis, you were hot back there with the dancing." As he prepares a lamb stew, he waits for Regis to react. The warm camaraderie communicates right through the camera. People at home see two guys who look and act like friends, which off-camera they are.

Regis plugs Tell's Cayman restaurant several times and relates to his audience that he and Joy, his wife, enjoyed the food there.

Tell rolls with Regis's lead-ins, ever mindful that it is his host's show. Regis says, "Wow, that stew looks terrific, Tell. That should be on the menu down in the Grand Old House."

"The next time you come down there, it will be," quips Tell.

The studio audience and people watching at home laugh.

However, live TV could also be unforgiving when a mistake was made.

Regis drops a blender, which might have thrown off the rhythm of the show, except Tell never skips a beat.

"So, Regis, you just dropped my blender. (Pause.) Go ahead, it's your show."

Regis's momentary embarrassment disappears in the humor. The live audience loves it. The show rolls right along—"No problem," as Tell would say.

* * *

With Regis and Tell playing their selves—decades of experience, skill, and TV personality thrown into the batter—the "cake" baked to perfection.

Tell's cooking segments delivered banter and useful information at a fast pace. Yet it seemed easy-going, never frenetic, never more than the TV viewers could handle, never too fast to learn how to cook the ingredients at home. He controlled the pace, because he intended to teach as he worked. He dove right into food preparation and got Regis to participate with the food by directing him from time to time.

"C'mon, Regis, keep stirring. It's not going to get cooked by itself."

Tell described in clear terms how to use each recipe ingredient, the quantities to use and, more often than not, why. The TV audience grasped what he was doing and what they would need to know and to do to cook the dish at home—a far cry from some of today's food and entertainment chefs—the difference being Tell's intention to actually *teach* cooking.

There was his accent, which, at times, was difficult to grasp, but that made the public pay close attention. Tell's demonstrated level of competence compelled viewers to watch closely. He made very few wasted moves, no errors, and in a few short minutes his food was in the pot or oven—prepped, explained, understood, and full of flavor.

Of course, the completed dishes were pre-prepared, so the audience could see the final product. Here the difference between Tell and other

Strudel ingredients set up for TV shows

chefs, which appeared on the show, was that Tell himself prepared his food, while others brought assistants who prepared the food for the chefs.

In the short span of sixteen minutes or less, Tell could demonstrate, prep, cook, and plate at least five excellent courses of food. His speed and ability could place him well ahead of present-day chefs on TV contest shows like *Chopped*, albeit Iron Chef America's Chef Morimoto against Chef Tell would have been an exciting challenge to watch.

"Tell was right there, showing how the meat was broken down, teaching the details. He was one of the early guys and more thorough than most. If he saw the TV shows today, he would flip," said four-time Emmy winner Chef Staib.

Tell even diced a half-onion with a different technique than current chefs. He explained, "The stem should be under your hand. Score vertical slices toward the stem (which is what other chefs do) but not all the way. Almost to the stem, make a horizontal slice through the middle of the onion before dicing (a step missed by other chefs). You will dice the onion more evenly and yield more cubes in less time. Time ticking is the chef's enemy. It takes money out of your pocket if you don't use it right."

No big deal, you say? When dicing 150–200 or more onions daily in a commercial kitchen, timesaving methods save money for the restaurant operation.

Tell's style led the way and set the standard for other TV chefs to follow. Unrehearsed for the most part, unscripted, and with jokes thrown in, Chef Tell revolutionized home cooking. His measured pace and continuous encouragement as he engaged Regis in two-way conversation outlined the path for success as a chef on TV.

Back in the mailroom, tens of thousands of fan letters and requests for his recipes poured in weekly—not only TV's surest barometer of popularity and ratings, but also a true measure of Tell's intimate connection with viewers.

"Tell was predictable: he knew how to cook, inform, and make it work in whatever time we had for him. He could be called at the last minute, and we knew what we would get. And he was gracious; we liked him coming to our set," Art Moore said.

* * *

"Man, you're pretty fast with those knives, Tell," Regis remarked on-air.

"Well, Regis, I am actually the fastest knife in the west and east," Tell answered. He meant it and could probably prove it.

Not one to miss a quip, Regis later called Tell on what he had said earlier. He challenged Tell to try to beat the show record for speed in preparing and delivering a *three-course* meal, which was established at five minutes.

In the words of Tell's Grand Cayman friend, Boxie, Tell described his record-breaking feat this way: "He spoke with great relish about how he had broken the record on the Regis show. He managed to do it with time to spare, or as he put it (live on the show) 'Man, Regis, if I'd known I had that much time left, I could have done a Bar Mitzvah as well.'"

* * *

Continuing with the sample show:

Without missing a millisecond, Tell then picks up a leek and dices it, saying, "I have to take a leek here, Regis."

Regis retorts, "You have to take a leek right here?"

"That's right, I have to take a leek—there's no other way to say it—and I have to dice it and put it into the pot, just like this."

The live audience can't stop laughing, and the ratings meter shoots up.

* * *

Not even Don Rickles joked as fast as Tell's kitchen one-liners. Regis and Tell loved Rickles's shtick, but Tell could do what Rickles couldn't—he could joke and cook and supervise, prepare, oversee, and plate a full course while holding a conversation with Regis at the same time. Rickles, one of the quickest minds in comedy and a fan of Tell's, never minded.

On the next show appearance, Regis introduced Tell as "one of our favorite guys in the kitchen." On another show, he exclaimed, "That's a good-looking dish there, Chef Tell."

Tell rapid-fire replied, "I'm married now, Regis. Have you seen my wife? There's a good-looking dish!"

The live audience in the studio laughed as fast as Tell dished out the lines, and at home America laughed, cooked, and bought thousands of Chef Tell cookbooks, knives, and endorsed products.

Still, the final test for Tell's cooking—it bears repeating—was the test all chefs must pass: "When the customer picks up his/her knife and fork, does he or she like your food?"

When Joy Philbin or Kathie Lee Gifford stepped up to the counter and sampled Tell's food, their reaction was instant. They *loved* what they tasted more than they had expected. Anyone could see it in their eyes.

Regis often concluded their show segments by reminding viewers of Chef Tell's Grand Old House on Grand Cayman Island. Sometimes he and Tell voiced together Tell's signature sign-off, "I see you!"

Sometimes, when Tell was not even present, Regis talked about the master chef. He described a time his family had spent the weekend on Grand Cayman with Tell, who took them to lunch at a friend's home. On the way home, Tell over-choked the boat's engines and his friend rescued all of them. The back story tells the tale in deep relief.

One morning in the winter of 1990, Tell called Boxall to say that Regis and his family were coming to spend the weekend at the Hyatt.

"I'm going to pick them up in Naul's (Naul Bodden) boat. Could I bring them 'round for a drink on Saturday?" asked Tell.

"In our usual way of teasing each other, I told Tell he couldn't," recalled Boxall.

Tell paused, and then said, "Aw, Boxie . . ."

Boxall let him stew in another pause before he told Tell to bring his guests to lunch.

"Ay, Boxie, that's great. I'll bring dessert," said Tell.

"Tell docked Bodden's boat, looking every inch the gallant captain. Regis, his charming wife, Joy, and their lovely daughters, Joanna and Jennifer, stepped ashore and walked up the beach to the house," Boxie said.

Boxie and Mary had really only heard of Regis from Tell's anecdotes. The few channels available on island television omitted *Who Wants to be a Millionaire*, which wasn't yet household fare on Wednesday evenings on the island. His first thought on meeting Regis was "how remarkable that not a single curl had been dislodged by the fast eight-mile crossing of the North Sound."

Regis realized that Mary and Boxie, an attorney, were not awe-struck fans who would fawn around him, and he and his family relaxed and settled in. After lunch, Tell was to take the family back across to the Hyatt in time for the girls to go scuba diving, but he was the least relaxed of the party and he made the fatal mistake of casting off the mooring lines before starting the boat's engines. The boat drifted away from the dock as Tell frantically attempted to start its engines, which he promptly flooded. Not long after, the starter motors grinded to a halt. The Boxalls watched the entire incident unfold.

"I took off in my boat and caught up with the party. Tell anchored Naul's boat and then the entire party transferred to mine, and we returned to the Hyatt," remembered Boxall.

Boxall returned Tell to Bodden's boat, which started on the first attempt. He thought that was the end of the incident. However, on Monday morning, a friend called to say that her mother had called her from Florida after watching the Regis's show, on which Regis had described his weekend right down to the details of the boat incident and his wonderful lunch with Boxie and Mary.

The final postscript for the Boxalls arrived in the form of a gift from Tell some years later: a copy of Regis's book *Who Wants to Be Me?* inscribed to "Mary & Boxie, 'Good lunch! Regis.'"

67

TELL'S LEGACY: CHEFS ON PARADE

"Ich garantiere Ihnen, der Fisch ist nicht gonna beschweren."
("I guarantee you the fish isn't gonna complain.")
—Chef Tell

Throughout the years after its release in 1982, Chef Tell's best-selling book *Chef Tell's Quick Cuisine* continued to sell well, with sales surges coming after each TV appearance. Among his readership were up-and-coming chefs, who labored long hours in the heat of obscure kitchens, yearning, as Tell did years earlier, to break out. They watched Tell's TV segments, cooked and experimented with his recipes, and absorbed the emerging etiquette of the television medium. As a result of Chef Tell's pioneer work as their forerunner, a few of these chefs earned new levels of public awareness and audiences they had not enjoyed before.

"I think the most wonderful thing in the world is another chef. I'm always excited about learning new things about food," said Paul Prudhomme, the "Father of Blackened Fish." Prudhomme started on TV with his *Fork in the Road* PBS series.

In 1991, Emeril Lagasse stepped away from his executive chef position at Paul Prudhomme's Commander's Palace restaurant in New Orleans and opened Emeril's. Assisted by John Shoup, CEO of *Great Chefs* and his Louisiana *New Garde* TV series, Lagasse auditioned for a Nashville production group, which would later own the TV Food Network that began its run with a self-taught cook, David Rosengarten, and his show called *Taste*. In 1995, *Emeril Live!* hit the airwaves and TV screens and brought New Orleans-style spices to an audience already prepped by Chef Tell's messages about experimenting with spices since 1974.

In 1996, Chef Mario Batali's Italian *Molto Mario*, and Chef Bobby Flay's *The Main Ingredient,* would be added to the roster of the Food Network, borrowing on notions of brand marketing and value-entertainment performances from Chef Tell.

The television landscape experienced a sea change in the 1990s. The time was right for Chef Tell to import his brand and inimitable personality back into the mainland to join the fun. Truth be told, the Food Network offered Chef Tell one of its earliest cooking segments, but he took the ill-fated advice of an associate and spurned the offered contractual terms. In a rare, regretful moment of forgetfulness, he had disregarded Henry Fonda's best advice, "Never be afraid to try something new," as well as his own words, "Say yes; you can always change your mind later."

* * *

In late 1994, Tell and Bunny walked barefoot along the Cayman North Shore beach, letting the soft sand tickle their toes as they discussed their options for the future. Bunny suggested they live back in the United States. She had earned a good income working for two companies down in the islands and sent most of it to her reserve bank account stateside. With her sizable nest egg, she wanted to buy a nice place for them. Her plan made sense to Tell, and they agreed that she should travel up to the States on weekends to start looking at properties.

Like Tell's "obscene white chocolate mousse" made with only four ingredients (egg yolks, whipped heavy cream, chopped white chocolate, and a sugar syrup made from a reduction of boiled water and sugar), a simple life lived well, they both believed, would bring a better life with a good ending. Tell's expression of a more simple life included having his own cooking kitchen TV set and a running show with his name on the marquee.

Grand Cayman, for the time Tell and Bunny lived there, amounted to a world that adhered to a myriad British and Caymanian rules of etiquette.

"Tell kicked me under the table if he thought I was speaking out against Caymanian cultural rules. You could lose your license and business ownership if you didn't mind your peas and queues," remarked Bunny.

Although there were rules that had to be followed, and ethnic mores to align with, life on an island in a warm climate made for a kindness that extended to the way people treated each other.

"There wasn't an elitist feeling among the people there. Since 1987, when I bought my house, it was easy to see wealthy and non-wealthy individuals from all backgrounds, Caymanian and not, mixing socially. People were more likely to invite a passer-by they recognized to join an outdoor party in progress than to ignore him or her," Lenny Mattioli recalled.

You just had to play along with their rules.

Cayman Island ambience included for the most part a safe environment in which people could live and work together. Like any society, there were criminal elements, but these were confined mostly to outsiders from other countries, who struggled economically. At any rate, the percentage was minimal.

British rule, schooling, and behavioral influence, inculcated into the Caymanian culture for such a long time, explained the genteel manner of social relationships on the islands. Tell's restaurant operation was respected among Caymanians. In fact, he employed island residents in various capacities, which went a long way to establishing that trust.

Still, no matter how much money, camaraderie, or gentility he shared, or earned, Tell wanted a TV show of his own back in the States. The next generation of TV chefs had emerged on the mainland, and Tell needed to head back. He kept his name in front of the public with more *LIVE!* appearances by saying yes to last-minute requests in order to keep his brand at the national level. But he also needed to develop new venues back on the mainland so that he could maintain public visibility beyond Regis's show.

68

BACK TO BASIC AGAIN

"Man kann nie genug tun . . ."
("You can never do this enough . . .")

—Chef Tell

Tell underwent surgery in Ft. Lauderdale, Florida in the early 1990s after he felt a sharp pain in his right arm at his Cayman restaurant kitchen while preparing food early in the morning. Chopping vegetables had turned on extreme pain, and he could not even pick up a small pan. Years of chopping, cutting , and slicing foods took their toll, but the advanced tennis-elbow surgery on his right arm delivered not only recovery, but a chance to explore the Tampa Bay lifestyle and business potentials during his one-month recovery.

From 1991 to 1995, Bunny and Tell spent time in Tampa, Florida. Considering retirement there, they set up a company, Chef Tell's Bayside Catering. However, Tell was about ten years ahead of the area's dramatic expansion. Tampa Bay area would become a year-round Mecca for tourists and new residents, but in the Erhardt's time, a real drop-off in food industry sales occurred annually during the torrid summer months, when even top restaurants shuttered until the humidity broke in the fall. In the long run, their plans failed to materialize into the high-speed pace to which they were accustomed; for now, though, they made the best of the non-ideal situation they faced.

Tell had known David Knight more than eighteen years—as far back as the early road-trip days. Knight operated Health Craft, a company with a line of waterless, stainless steel cookware, which operated out of Tampa, Florida.

"Chef Tell helped start this company. We've been friends for years," Knight told a live studio audience during the taping of one of their video co-productions.

In return for licensing his image, good name, and talents, Tell participated with Knight's Health Craft product sales in front of live audiences. He cooked, and Knight demonstrated the cookware. Chef Tell brand knives were also featured and promoted. The setup was an ongoing TV show sponsored by the Health Craft Company—another step closer to Tell's dream of having his own show. Since the production studio was located right in the Tampa Bay area of Florida, the productions were an easy enough reach for Tell and Bunny, who commuted directly between Tampa and Grand Cayman, a jaunt of only 608 air miles.

Tell's pending relocation to Tampa in 1994 garnered press and created media opportunities for both Tell and Health Craft. Tell had already appeared on Channel 13's "Eye on Tampa Bay" on *The Kathy Fountain Show* for Christmas season segments as early as 1991, which featured Tell's Cayman Island recipes. He also appeared in local productions

Tell works a Tampa Bay TV audience

294

with Busch Gardens in Tampa on the *Jack Harris & Company* show in front of live audiences, taking call-in questions on-air.

At this time, Tell arranged a spokesman contract with a European company, Llorenté Bakeware, with a keen view into the future. He promoted their original, Purflex™ silicone flexible bakeware line on TV. Flexible cookware would become a "given" in kitchens and on TV cooking-contest productions in the twenty-first century. Tell was again the leading figure of a new innovation in the culinary arts; this time on the Home Shopping Network, which originated from the area in 1982.

"Tell was working hard all the time," remembered Chef Staib, echoed by a host of other contemporary chefs, relatives, and friends. "He was definitely a workaholic."

Having more free time with Bunny and working with an old friend seemed to mellow Tell. On-air and in the videos, he looked a little bit more relaxed and he worked, if long hours, at least at a catering pace for the time being. His humor remained in good form, and he even took casual potshots, in jest, at his French-cooking friends up in Philadelphia.

"Germans salt their dishes like this." (He picked up a small pinch of salt and let it fall from his fingertips onto the food). He then picked up a larger pinch of salt, stepped back from the dish, and *threw* bits of salt at the dish three separate times, saying with a flourish, "The French do it like this—'*Savon. Savon. Savon.* Two dollars, four dollars, six dollars.' That's how the French chefs do it." (Audience laughter.)

But the laugh, from Perrier's point of view, was that, though Tell had intended to say "salt" three times, he actually said, "Soap. Soap. Soap."—*savon*, in French.

"People, you can put whatever you want on your fish. The fish is already dead. It doesn't care how you cook it. Just play with your food the way you like it. I guarantee you, the fish isn't gonna complain," Tell said to his audiences, and then he proceeded to prepare the same dish differently to show what he meant.

Tell repeated the line during a live Health Craft cooking demonstration at a home show—this time with a twist. Using a grouper fillet, he demonstrated several methods of coating the fish, explaining how each method altered the taste. Tell's teaching point revealed that his madcap joking around was rooted in cooking basics. There was a method to his "madness."

Meanwhile, Bunny scouted locations in Tampa Bay and elsewhere for where the Erhardt's might live. When in the area, Bunny and Tell attended the annual Strawberry Festival in nearby Plant City.

A piece of Americana dating back to 1930, the Strawberry Festival celebrated the more than eight thousand acres of Florida strawberries with an annual harvest of $360 million. Visitors from all over the globe strolled through the fairgrounds and participated in the festivities. Country music superstars performed concerts at the open-air arena on the midway, hosted by famous people from a variety of professions.

Former U.S. President George H.W. Bush was a guest host for the opening concert on the day Bunny and Tell visited. A technical snafu left the president on stage with no one to introduce him. Tell stepped up to handle the scene. He leaped onto the stage and, without benefit of a microphone, introduced the former president, noting Bush and his family dined at the Grand Old House. Bush shook Tell's hand, thanked him for the help, and opened the show. Just for fun, Bunny and Tell wondered if what had just happened was an omen that they should live in the area.

Tell's 1984 demo set at the Strawberry Festival.

While Tell catered and performed cooking demonstrations in Tampa, between work days back on Grand Cayman, Bunny widened her search for places to live to Atlanta, Georgia. Cayman Air offered direct service and Atlanta's suburbs at first seemed like a good place to move. In Marietta, Bunny had considered the hundred acres that she could pick up for only $300,000 almost a dealmaker.

The Erhardts had vacationed in the area before and had met and befriended chef and restaurateur Pano Karatassos. For years, he had displayed Tell's photo on one of his restaurant walls. He was considered an Atlanta mover and shaker, since he now owned three of the most popular restaurants in the area. He agreed to aid their search for a good place to live and work.

Their luncheon with Karatassos was cordial. After, he invited the Erhardts up to his penthouse condo that overlooked the Buckhead commercial district. While the view was spectacular, Karatassos's slant on life was a stretch for them. "What is magical about this view is that from here I can see and watch the parking lots of my three restaurants anytime I wish. I can see who is coming and going day and night," said Karatassos.

Bunny and Tell looked at each other and shook their heads. The way they saw it, they wanted more out of living than twenty-four-seven parking lot vigilance. Not long after their visit with Karatassos, they flew up to Philadelphia for another *Chaine* picnic. The camaraderie and familiar ambience of Philadelphia's *Chaine* ran blood-deep and changed their minds about living in the south. They decided to return to the Philadelphia area where they had already purchased an estate. However, Tell would split his time between the catering business in Tampa Bay and Grand Cayman for the time being.

Practice makes the professional.

69

THE A-TEAM CONCEPT

"Entschuldigen Sie mich, ich weiß du?"
("Excuse me, do I know you?")

—Chef Tell

Waxing nostalgic in 1992, Bunny and Tell took up an offer from new owners and leased the tavern building where they first met, the pre-Revolutionary Harrow Inne in Ottsville. Loose ends were yet to be wrapped up on Grand Cayman, so Tell traveled back and forth every few days to the island until the Harrow was up and running. Bunny oversaw renovations and recruitment at the Harrow.

Using some of their reserves, the Erhardts gutted and retrofitted the downstairs into a kitchen and restaurant suitable for the kind of operation they wanted. Sanders buzzed, carpenters hammered and pounded, and sawdust flew everywhere when Theresa Badmann, Barbie Murphy's look-alike sister, walked in for her first job interview with Bunny. Bunny checked her résumé for experience and hired her on the spot to be a part of a team concept that she and Tell were building to run the Harrow. When Tell returned and saw Theresa, her somewhat-familiar face disoriented him.

"Excuse me, do I know you?" he asked.

"You should. You promised you would," Theresa told him. She then explained about the day at his house on Rum Point. Tell did remember her.

Each team member in the new place would be a 100 percent, experienced professional capable of taking charge of any front-room restaurant function. The team would evolve and be named "The A-team." (Shades of B. A. Baracus, John "Hannibal" Smith, "Howling Mad" Murdock, and Templeton "Faceman" Peck—characters from the contemporary hit TV show, *A-Team*—performed by Mr. T, George Peppard, Dwight Schultz, and Dirk Benedict, which ran from January 1983 until March 1987.)

While Bunny's A-team members liked the simplicity of their uniforms—polo shirts and jeans—and the training directions they received, they were more amazed by how much alike each of them happened to be in personality, skill, and experience. They meshed and synchronized their motions like a fine German timepiece. They practiced their routines in high spirits for the grand opening, which was anticipated as much by the whole crew as by Bunny and Tell.

Opening night was a huge success. The restaurant ran in high gear from Day One. The innovative A-team service matched the quality of the food coming out of the kitchen from Chef Tell's menu and kitchen team. For at least a year or more, the Harrow filled with satisfied customers every open night.

An affordable opportunity to take over a second location, the landmark Upper Black Eddy Inn, opened late in 1994. The Erhardts took it, since it was closer to the celebrated tourist town of New Hope, Pennsylvania, which attracted an affluent, educated crowd—likely gourmands—from as far away as Philadelphia, Manhattan, and Washington, DC. This building was situated right on the Delaware River road only a few miles up river from the town.

"I looked at it seven years ago, when they wanted $700,000. Then it dropped to $285,000. So I say, Okay, I'll put in a bid that's ridiculously low.'"

Tell's bid won.

"'Oh my God,' I say, 'now I gotta do something with it,'" said Tell. Minutes after he settled the property deal, he booked his first wedding there.

The property sat on a river section known as Candy Bend on 3.5 acres adjacent to the Delaware Canal, which ran out back. The

Tell celebrates the Manor House acquisition

building came with an interesting history and a fishing dock across the road on the river. Tell and Bunny renamed it Chef Tell's Manor House. They decided to limit initial operations to half-weeks, weekend brunches, and special events. In fact, the initial plans for the Greek Revival-period building included mini-suites upstairs, a pastry shop, and a casual, coffee-shop atmosphere. The A-team would be its exclusive staff, because Bunny knew she could count on them to offer excellent service right from the start. She and Tell also wanted to reward the team with another income stream.

Team members welcomed the extra work at the Manor House, which was nearby and only operated at different hours than the Harrow. Management staffs were paid extra for running both locations. The arrangement satisfied them, or so it seemed.

The operations manager of the Harrow welcomed the extra responsibilities of running both locations because his paycheck got a handsome boost. He found out, however, that running catered brunches and special events was nothing like operating a sit-down dinner house. The intimate rapport and pacing of serving dinner patrons at the Harrow was far removed from the fast-paced, timed wait-service required by weddings and large-group brunches.

The young manager found that trying to manage the two different styles overwhelmed him. To make matters worse, he developed a testy attitude problem, which boiled over too many times. If he wasn't watched to temper his heat, he spilled over and scalded others around him. However, he did have connections in New Hope, which could bring referred customers to Tell's place.

70

ReNEWed HOPE

"One of the deep secrets of life is that
all that is really worth the
doing is what we do for others."
                                    —Lewis Carroll

Coryell's Ferry (now New Hope)—a collection of art galleries, hotels, and taverns developed on the Delaware River where Highway 202 crosses from New Jersey—was situated about ten miles upriver from where General George Washington with volunteer troops crossed the ice-laden waters on Christmas Day and ambushed the British and Hessian forces camped near Trenton. The place where Chef Tell wished to rekindle the next phase of his personal dream was also the place where Washington turned the war for the revolutionary forces.

The Bucks County Playhouse in New Hope was once the town gristmill. From 1939, the musical theater featured live dramas, comedies, and musical productions. Broadway shows tuned up at the playhouse before heading up to Manhattan's Great White Way. In its heyday, the playhouse was considered "one of America's finest summer theaters," drawing affluent, educated people from a wide geographic area and putting the small town on a much larger map.

The venerable Bucks County Playhouse, New Hope, PA

American Impressionists, *en plein air* landscape painters, Edward Willis Redfield and William Langson Laythrop, started the art colony in 1899. Eventually, artists and performers working in all media were drawn here. In the 1950s, a sizable gay community blossomed and influenced the area's art through restaurants, antique shops, and art galleries. By the latter half of the twentieth century, New Hope's art retailers and restaurateurs thrived at night and on weekends and drew crowds from places farther away as newer highways made the town more accessible.

New Hope was in large part the context from which Tell and Bunny derived the notion that knowledgeable gourmands would come to their two restaurants—because of its proximity to the Harrow and the Manor House. The Manor House was situated right on the road that connected both New Hope and the Washington's Crossing museum and, at that, was located right where River Road traffic had to slow considerably to traverse a bridge over the canal. For that reason, as much as the man's résumé, they hired a manager from New Hope.

When he selected this new area for his restaurants, Tell had counted on finding a class of people that would satisfy the demands of an haute cuisine restaurant, as well as satisfy his personal need for intellectual stimulation. Tell was precocious and paid attention to intelligent conversations about abstract art and current events. He gravitated toward like-minded people.

Not finding those qualities that he sought in the local area, except for only a fraction of the people, Tell would endure more frustration. He was about to enter the most difficult period of his lifetime as he gradually wrapped up his business connections on Grand Cayman.

When the time for his final departure from the Grand Old House arrived in 1994, Tell turned his keys over to his Caymanian partner Bodden, who purchased Alliger's portion of the business after he repatriated to Philadelphia.

Bunny returned to the island for the final farewells among friends, and then she and Tell boarded a Cayman Air flight bound for Tampa where they would pick up Jade, their Presa Canario, and then board another flight to Philadelphia, excited to see what their future would bring. Whatever it was, they vowed they would spend more quality time together and make time for more vacations. That is, once they were settled into the Upper Black Eddy estate they had purchased—a fine place for Jade to play.

71

GOIN' TO THE DOGS

"Es gibt nichts wie die Liebe eines Hundes."
("There's nothing like the love of a dog.")

—Chef Tell

"Jade, our 120-pound 'child,' was with us in Tampa where he was a crazy, young dog running around the neighborhood until he was properly trained," recalled Bunny. As far back as Bunny knew Tell, there were dogs in his life.

Jade loved the open space of the estate in Pennsylvania. He could chase birds, ground animals, and play in the woods out back as much as he wanted. But it seemed to Tell and Bunny that there was too much space for just one dog. They both spent a lot of hours away from home, working, so after only a few weeks, they looked for a companion for Jade and found another Presa Canario.

Jewels was at first jealous of the attention given to Jade, but since Tell and Bunny liked both dogs, the problem fell away. Although he considered Jade his dog, and Jewels Bunny's, Tell sent regular buckets of leftover turkey meat up to the house for both of his "kids."

One July 4th, Jade was found dead on the estate. Tell was devastated. He couldn't easily shake his thoughts of all the past dogs he'd owned. In the heat and humidity of that July, he and Bunny buried Jade in the backyard of their estate. "It was sad, very sad. He loved that dog," Bunny said as her tears flowed.

Tell made up for his loss by finding another dog. On a tip from a friend, he picked up Sydney, a North Carolina Dingo, from the A.S.P.C.A. in nearby Hunterdon, New Jersey.

Sydney with Tell in 1999

Sydney turned out to be a great companion for Jewels. Together they worked "frog duty" in the backyard. Sydney grabbed frogs in his mouth, threw them on the grass, and then rolled over on them for play, before Jewels, who was much harder on the amphibians, got to them—good fun for Sydney and Jewels, a bad turn for the frogs.

Whenever Bunny had to leave without him, Jewels held her hostage at the end of the estate pathway to the main road. She stood in front of the car and barked as long as possible. When Bunny inched her Porsche onto the roadway, Jewels ran after her for many yards. Usually this was safe to do, since there was little traffic on the country road. However, there were blind curves. Jewels was hit and injured slightly on one occasion, from which she fully recovered. Another day, though, Jewels ran alongside of Bunny's vehicle longer than usual and she was hit by an oncoming car that had appeared suddenly from around one of those curves. This time the dog's injuries were too severe to save her. Bunny phoned Tell, who rushed to the scene. They hugged Jewels, lifted her onto his truck, and drove to the vet's office. With tears streaming down his face, Tell carried her inside while Bunny waited.

Dogs that Tell owned seemed to carry forward the habits of the one who came before him. The Presas looked up in the sky and chased birds, and Sydney, after a while, did the same thing along with Jewels. But he stayed away from the main road and ended up living longer.

Tell's final dog, a Rottweiler he named Fifi, was rescued two months later. Merrill, Tell's secretary at the time, told Tell about the dog's plight, which touched Tell immediately. The dog had been rescued from a tree and had a long recovery ahead of it.

When Tell saw Fifi for the first time, she was a mess—very thin and completely untrained. But Tell loved her from their first meeting and a few months later, when she was more stable, he brought her home. There never was any doubt that Fifi was Tell's dog. They were inseparable once they met—inseparable to their last day together. Fifi would outlast Tell by four years, almost exactly to the day.

Bunny's and Tell's dogs were more than pets or welcome diversions from the rigors of their demanding lives. They were a part of their family. In the years that followed the start of their relationship, the dogs offered safety and friendly companionship for Bunny when Tell traveled. When they went out together to a park or just stayed at home on the multi-acre estate, they were "the children" they played with.

Bunny and Tell were in love with each other and with each of their dogs. They were excited about their future now that they could look back and see how much they had come through together. The pieces of their life-puzzle seemed to be coming together, but the crystal ball of hindsight could not prevent the trouble that brewed ahead.

As Jade and Jewels had contributed to the close-knit couple's happiness, Fifi would help them find their way back to each other in the face of the difficulties that were about to befall Bunny and Tell.

Jade

72

DITCHING CONFUSIONS

"Es braucht eine sichere Mann, der diese
Hosen so nah an New Hope tragen."
("It takes a secure man to wear these
pants so close to New Hope.")

—Chef Tell

Less than a year past the Harrow Inne opening, Tell could no longer tolerate his operations director, a small-minded, effete man, who operated in a style that simply did not conform to Tell's manner or policies. In truth, the man had a habit of making mistakes and was unable to take the hard yelling aimed at him. The man just wasn't cut out for the rigors of the job and Tell's, at times, aggressive, managerial style. Tell possessed few options beyond an outright firing when the situation came to a boil over one ridiculous incident.

Tell at this point in his life preferred to wear loose-fitting, colorful chili pepper pants, rather than traditional hound's tooth gear, or jeans. One day the obsequious manager fawned over Tell's pant color choice and how they fit him, and Tell would not have it. Having had enough of the man's games, he retorted within earshot of customers, tongue planted firmly in his cheek, "It takes a secure man to wear these pants so close to New Hope."

That did it. Whatever had been festering inside the manager and between him and Tell blew up in the restaurant. The manager stormed off in a huff toward the kitchen and was never seen again. In his wake, he left behind an empty managerial position at a time when the crew really needed a strong director.

For his part, Tell never acceded to the guy's comments, but he did acknowledge that he may have asked for too much attention that day. Apparently, he wore a new pair of *pink and black* pepper pants with red-hot chili peppers patterned all over the material.

A mutiny at the Harrow took center stage only weeks after Tell closed shop for good on Grand Cayman. Once he began working full-time at the Harrow, Tell wanted to cook high cuisine. In short order, he was fed up with the low-class palates of the local clientele.

However, Bunny, the sous chef, and the back-room crew were satisfied to cater to the tastes of the local people, who were showing up nightly in good numbers. The operation was running smoothly. Regulars were returning, and the wait staff was happy to have a full restaurant to serve each night. For Tell, though, it just wasn't what he wanted to create. He wasn't at the Grand Old House anymore, and the Harrow wasn't Center City Philadelphia either. Tell's frustration eventually forced even Bunny to leave.

She went to work in nearby Peddlar's Village in Lahaska. She had sided with the other chefs, believing that it was the only way to keep the Harrow viable. When Tell was still working at the Grand Old House, she "owned" the Harrow as her "baby." With the help of the A-team, she had managed it into a viable operation, and wholesale changes could bring disaster.

More than that, Bunny was looking out for the health and wellness of her husband when she left. She saw that Tell was upset by the situation and that his health had declined—a diabetic condition was not yet diagnosed. Leaving the Harrow was her way of showing Tell how strongly she felt about the pressing issue as much as to protect him. She hoped to keep the direction of the restaurant moving forward and to let it continue winning.

Once Bunny left, Tell revamped the operation, which, at first, was a mistake. He lost some of his chefs and a few non-critical, front-room crew. He brought in new personnel, some of whom Bunny had warned against hiring. If these new staff did not work out, it would be on him.

If nicknames count for description, the new operations manager was soon nicknamed "Bubblehead" by the front-room servers. However, Tell was less concerned about the front room. In his mind, finding another chef to run his kitchen was paramount. A faxed résumé delivered him.

Chef John Barrett, a thirty-three-year old resident of New Hope, interviewed with Tell at the Harrow, and Tell hired him on the spot.

"Tell is a chef's chef, someone I wanted to work with," Barrett said in an interview at the time.

Although Barrett had to give two-month notice where he was working, Tell liked his Bellevue Stratford experience and his Creole/Cajun-cuisine innovations that were highlights on his résumé and would be fine additions to Tell's menu.

Barrett fell into his career by way of an after-hours job in a hospital kitchen. At the time, he was still a high school student. He worked as a vegetable runner, pot scrubber, and dishwasher, giving him a chance to observe a working kitchen, much like Tell's beginning. He gleaned enough knowledge about the work that he applied for whatever position he could get at the Fairmont Hotel in Center City Philly—the same building that experienced the ill-fated Legionnaire's Disease outbreak in 1976, then known as the Bellevue-Stratford Hotel. In 1979, hired by Austrian Chef Leo Kessler, Barrett worked side-by-side with certified master pastry chef Gunther Heiland. He set his sights on a personal goal of attending the Culinary Institute of America and saved enough to pay for the school's rigorous program. After graduation as an associate chef, Barett, hired again by Kessler, worked at the Playboy Hotel in Atlantic City. Through a Book and a Cook promotional program run by the hotel, he met other renowned chefs Emeril Lagasse, Kevin Grahame, and Rene Dupuis. The experience furthered his ambitions. He moved on to Café Nola on South Street in Philly.

"The café was an independent owned by Judy De Vicarus, an interior designer, and Bill Curry, a columnist with the *Philadelphia Inquirer*. They featured New Orleans Cajun and Creole cuisine specialties," said Barrett, who had worked closely with master chef Terry Chompson in New Orleans where he completed extensive Cajun cuisine training.

At the Harrow Inne, Barrett was hired as Tell's chef de cuisine. The Harrow menu of typical German fare—Weiner Schnitzel, sauerkraut, Stuttgarter toufe, slow-roasted duck, spaetzle, and the like—was something Tell wanted to change. Barrett's Cajun creations based on crawfish interested him and were added to the menu.

"John's strong point is seafood and he is very, very creative," Tell noted.

The relationship became collaborative. Tell taught Barrett several new skills and groomed him to take over daily operations behind the line. In turn, Barrett brought in more menu innovations.

Tell's commitments to appear on TV with Regis in Manhattan, at times, were unscheduled. On those days he did appear, Barrett and the crew prepped Tell's food and loaded it into the large cooler that he would use at the TV studio.

Tell ordered whole legs of veal because he knew how to dress them out, cutting the meat to the best effect. The process was new and a little intimidating to Barrett, who had never seen how to do such work despite his training at the CIA. "Tell would have been considered 'old-world,' since the CIA program was geared more to specialization rather than holistic kitchen skills. Even purveyors were packaging meats into smaller pieces to compensate for this lost art," said Barrett.

Barrett asked Tell to show him how to dress out the leg. Noting the young man's eagerness to learn, Tell was more than happy to teach him.

Barrett's attitude led to Tell's invitation to him to attend the Grand Cayman Island wedding of Tell's partner Naul Bodden. Not having been to the islands, Barrett was stoked to go. Even their flight to the island impressed Barrett—Tell traveled first-class all the way. Barrett accompanied Tell right into Cayman Airway's Admiral Club for VIPs and found a world, that he had never experienced.

"I saw how everyone seemed to know Tell and how they treated him respectfully. I got my first taste of the celebrity lifestyle up close and personal and I was impressed," said Barrett.

The bachelor party on Grand Cayman the night before the wedding was a highlight event. Several blasts of rum and coke left both Tell and Barrett hung over.

"You wouldn't know that by looking at Tell and watching him work the next morning. He was the consummate professional," added Barrett, recalling the arduousness of the work they'd done side-by-side that morning. With 450 island dignitaries coming to the event, cases and cases of chicken, side items, and desserts had to be prepped, starting at daybreak.

Barrett—a thirty-something at the time—would never forget what he observed and experienced on the Cayman Island trip with Tell. Back at the Harrow, working in the same kitchen with Tell, camaraderie and friendship became another learning ground for Barrett, some of which was downright humorous.

"The duck we prepared at the Harrow was salted overnight, which drew out the extra skin moisture. We then poached it in honey water on high heat; this produced a golden brown caramel color. As the dried skin became thin and crispy the duck meat remained moist. The duck was next placed on cooling racks to rest, which helped retain the juices. Tell would come along and tear off the parts that went over the fence last and eat them. Tell, one could say, liked to eat the duck's ass," Barrett laughed.

The people Barrett met in his time within Chef Tell's celebrity world inspired him to continue with Tell as long as possible as chef de cuisine at the Harrow. His duties included oversight of all back-room operations, such as ordering supplies, menu, cooking, and the creation of innovative dishes. Despite Barrett's skills and enthusiasm, the Harrow's financial situation waned. Lack of abundant financial resources painted a bull's-eye on the restaurant's back.

On top of his money and mutiny problems, a private dissatisfaction gnawed at Tell. He felt he was not getting the intellectual stimulation he required outside the restaurant. He was in the beginnings of a mid-life crisis and felt he needed something more to satisfy an itch that he couldn't define. His confidantes offered only empathy and opinion, exhorting Tell to "work on solutions, not problems," which did nothing for his dissatisfaction.

A more explosive situation underlay the apparent one. Tell had worked up an increasing interest in another woman. This woman tried more than once to get hired at the Harrow when Bunny was in charge. Now she ate there regularly. When Tell's distraction surfaced, it caused a minor rift between Tell and Bunny.

Unfortunately, with Bunny working at Peddlar's Village, the woman in question, Catherine, talked Tell into hiring her. Sadly, Tell was headed toward an ugly incident.

On her way home from work at the other restaurant late at night, Bunny saw Tell's car parked outside of the Harrow. She pulled into the lot and parked. Expecting some free time alone with Tell, she approached the building. Near the entrance, a flurry of activity inside the closed restaurant caught her eye through the large front window. She discovered Tell *in flagrante delicto* with Catherine on the restaurant bar

Bunny was devastated.

Tell had once again tossed away his moral compass. With such a public act, he risked his restaurant, his liquor license, his marriage, and any television future. What if someone else—a journalist, say—had discovered them?

Once again Tell had forsaken his wedding vows. This time there would be no denying of the evidence, which was right in front of Bunny, who went inside and confronted him.

When temptation wins, one comes face-to-face with one's weaknesses. Tell had again given Bunny reason to not trust him and he pushed her away with his act of infidelity. He could only hope that she would forgive him in time so he could return to the comfort of her arms. This time he would have to come to grips with the greatest mystery a man struggles against in the war of the sexes: what is the true price of love?

As he lay downstairs on the couch—alone, eyes closed—Tell stared at mental images of his dead mother hanging over his body and he felt the recoil of his treasonous behavior.

Consumed by the darkness of the dark place he was in, after a while he began to feel that this was where he needed to be. For the first time in his life, in an inexplicable way, Tell came to feel that he was precisely where he needed to be. It seemed to him that he had, at last, located himself—knew *where* he was and *that* he was somebody's husband.

The intensity of his personal revelation broke his body out in a cold sweat. For the first time in what felt like eons, he felt a relief from things that haunted him. He was not sure why, but he was sure he had somehow changed. Tell Erhardt had hit rock bottom with nowhere to go but up.

Up from here was to figure out *who* he really was in the scheme of his life and Bunny's. The road "home" was going to be rocky and imperfect, but he felt certain that he was *willing to take the first step in the morning*—the last thought on his mind as he closed his eyes. He slept a long time that night.

For her part, Bunny had suffered the price again and wondered how much more it would cost her to love her man. She did not forsake her husband, despite having every reason and moral ground to do so. She shouldered his burden as if it were her own, stood by his side, and extracted only one condition: Bunny would take over the Harrow again.

* * *

Bubblehead departed when Bunny stepped back inside of the Harrow. Wanting to bring in a local manager with catering experience, Bunny contacted Christine Hess, whom she had befriended during her hiatus from the Harrow. She had observed that Hess possessed a strong work ethic and seemed to have a keen mind for marketing.

Hess agreed to meet Tell only so long as Bunny would act as chaperone. She had done some due diligence on Tell prior and heard that he was awful to work for—that he was a "tyrant," "terrible," and "overbearing." She preferred, however, to find out for herself. What she did know was that she worked seventy hours a week with another caterer, and pretty much anything had to be better than that, since her current position kept her away from her children—she was a single mom.

It happened to be Oktoberfest the day Hess stood at the bottom of the narrow stairwell inside the Harrow Inne kitchen and waited for Tell to come down to meet her. Tell hollered that he was coming and when he clogged down the wooden stairs, his tall barrel-chested body was clad in brown leather lederhosen, a colorful embroidered blouse and knee-length stockings.

Hess's first thought, *Holy sh**! He's so big and intimidating,* almost forced her to walk away. The sight was too incongruous for her to believe. "Here was this NFL-sized, middle-aged man with salt and pepper curly hair and a Fu Manchu-style moustache, in short-shorts, way taller than me, with two barking dogs in tow," she recalled.

Tell looked right through her, flashed his famous smile, and said, "Welcome to the Harrow."

Hess was at least intrigued after the introduction. She let Tell guide her on a tour of the restaurant. He told her about his other restaurant located a few miles away and suggested they go there for the meeting. Not willing to get in a strange man's car—even if he was married to Bunny—Hess told him she would follow in her car. Bunny called down from upstairs and said she would join them there.

Tell and Hess sat in the middle of the spacious blue, gold, and white dining room with large horizontal glass panes overlooking the fall foliage across the Delaware. The main building of the Manor House was built as a 1830s Federal-style inn, though this room had been added in recent years.

The interview went much like a boxing match at first—a little sparring and a few jabs here and there—before any serious discussion of opportunity or details.

Tell opened, "Can you train people?"

"Yes, I can. I've managed catering crews."

"Can you work full time?"

"Yes, but something less strenuous than what I have going now. You see, I'm working about 60–70 hours a week and I have two children. Is that going to be a problem?"

"No, this is no problem. Your résumé looks good."

"I've heard you're hard to work for."

Hess watched his body language.

"Who says these things?"

"This is a small community, and rumors fly. I was doing my homework on you." Hess came back, "Are they true?"

"You don't know anything about me, do you? I guess you never watch television."

"All I know is what I've heard, and I need a better job than what I have. I'm pretty good at working hard, as you can see," she countered, pointing to her résumé.

"Well, I've been on television a few times, have had other restaurants in this area, and Bunny and I have just come back from a few years with our restaurant on Grand Cayman Island." He paused and then added, "Do you know Regis Philbin?"

"No. Who's he?"

"That's okay. A lot of people don't know Regis like I do," smiled Tell.

Tell showed Hess some clippings and explained some of the things he'd done in the Philadelphia area. Now that she understood his reputation, she relaxed.

"Can you handle swearing?"

"Excuse me?"

"Can you handle swearing?"

"Yes, anything but the 'C' word. I will leave you if you use the C word. I'll quit on the spot."

Tell acknowledged her and threw a #10 envelope in her direction, banged the table, and complained loudly about the "a**hole manager I f**king had to fire. What a "f***ing c***!"

Hess got up without hesitation and headed straight for the door.

Tell shouted after her from the table, "You're staying! You're hired! I was testing you."

Hess stopped and turned.

Tell explained what happened with the previous manager and pastry chef and that he didn't like confrontations. He told her that he wanted to know if he was hiring a replacement with integrity—someone whose word he could count on. He also told her that he wanted to find someone to help make the restaurant operation a lot easier for him and for Bunny.

Hess returned to the table but stayed on her feet. Still a little ruffled after Tell's sudden outburst, she asked point blank, "Are you for real? Because if that ever happens again, I'm gone."

Bunny, who had slipped into the room unnoticed, walked over to the table and reassured Hess that Tell had only tested her.

Tell found Hess refreshing. He repeated that he liked what he heard and saw. He told her that she was hired, if she wanted the job. He offered two consecutive days off weekly and $100 more than she was getting with her current employer.

Before she could respond, he also offered her his first piece of advice, "Always say yes. You can always back out later, if you need to."

Hess started the next day and stayed for several years. At first she felt intimidated to come in as the "newbie" floor manager of the A-team. Knowing the details of the team's concept, she understood that the rest of the team had operated together for at least a year before her arrival. But she also knew she was as professional as they, and that once she and the team met, they would probably get along.

Under Hess's direction the team veterans—Karin, Theresa, Faye, Mary, and sisters Melissa and Sharon—continued to flourish. Loyal, trustworthy, caring, and hardworking, Hess considered them a dream to manage—one could rely on them no matter what. After all, Bunny had hired each one of them.

A-team members Debbie, Karin, Fay, Kim, and Theresa (2011); missing are Mary, Melissa, and Sharon

A-team members offered to do extra errands for Bunny and Tell even on their days off. In turn, if any of them had a personal problem, they were assured that Tell had their backs. As long as they produced, they knew Tell would care for them better than another restaurateur might. With the A-team, Tell and Bunny had created a living machine to which he could add his heart and passion and receive in return a precision crew willing to help.

Hess was delighted that the rumors she'd encountered before she was hired were unfounded. "Chef Tell turned out to be one of the nicest men I ever met."

Bunny, like Tell, was meticulous about details. She checked and rechecked dozens of items as if there was a quality control list in her head. She loved to ensure that nothing was overlooked for their guests, which, at times, made personnel feel they were micro-managed.

The fact was they *were* being micro-managed. There were hundreds of ways that a large restaurant operation could lose profitability, either through improper and unsupervised handling of customers, materials and supplies, or food purchasing, over-stocking the pantry and cooler, or outright thievery. And that didn't include variable cost factors like local, county, state, and federal taxes; insurance and license fees; and donations to charity. A restaurateur who didn't micro-manage didn't survive long.

After her break-in period on the job, Hess wanted to bring a different management system to the Manor House. Because of her catering background, she knew a different system would suit catered table service better than the Harrow's dinner system.

Banquet servers were for the most part to be seen but not heard. Table servers, however, like in the Harrow, were expected to work with each party and encourage their diners to make desirable food and drink selections that were profitable for the house.

Hess's systematic approach allowed for less hands-on oversight by Bunny, since the delegation of authority was laid out clearly among the staff. Personnel knew who wore what "hat" and could, therefore, rely upon each other more. They could be certain that detail work in another's area was covered. Hess's new method oiled the machine and increased morale as a result of greater production. The system allowed staff to cover the duty stations of another when emergencies popped up.

Hess's method allowed Bunny to breathe. By defining zones of responsibility and placing personnel over those zones, Bunny could see at a glance that the details were, in fact, getting proper attention. As a result, she returned to her primary hat as Tell's wife, which in turn, gave him some relief.

The method Hess brought in also made "bad apples" stick out like sore thumbs, especially at the Harrow. Catherine, who was caught fooling around with Tell, was found to be helping herself to extra tip amounts on credit card purchases by changing the totals. Upon further investigation, Hess discovered the woman had a cocaine habit, was still coming on to Tell, and stole money from the register. Later, the gossip grapevine relayed the tale that she had moved on to work at another restaurant and got caught doing the same thing, for which she was fired. A local Porsche dealership was handed bad checks for her car repairs. When confronted by the dealer, she reportedly replied, "So sue me!"

In Christine Hess, Bunny and Tell found a front-room manager who cared about their well-being as much as they cared about their crew. For Tell, a lifetime search for reliable friends culminated with the sense of a "family" that he could take into the twenty-first century. The A-team was smoking hot, in his estimation, and worth every penny of the extra income stream he set up for them in the Manor House operation.

73

MANOR HOUSE ON THE DELAWARE

"Ganz einfach. Sehr einfach. Sehr gut."
("Very simple. Very easy. Very good.")

—Chef Tell

Chef Tell's Manor House soon became the premier special-events location in Bucks County and a noted stop for politicians on the Pennsylvania campaign trail. However, years earlier, its reputation was known far and wide for other reasons.

The Delaware Canal's wide berms were used in the late nineteenth and early twentieth centuries to haul coal down to the port of Philadelphia. The Manor House served as one of several structures built along the almost fifty-mile canal to provide overnight rest stops for the families who worked the mule-drawn boats.

The building's design accommodated the diverse needs of its clientele. First floor taverns served up ale, basic foods, and bar fights. Second floor bedrooms sheltered sleepy families. Third and fourth floor rooms hosted "ladies" who "entertained" men for pay.

The Manor House at 1800 River Road, situated near the halfway mark of the waterway, maintained a fast pace during the canal's busiest years of 1890 through 1913. Not all rumors of the establishment were substantiated, but the death of a madam, who ran her girls from the third floor, survived the test of time.

Although never formally validated until Tell's proprietorship, instances of sightings accompanied by creepy feelings were fodder for speculation among the construction workers who labored to renovate the building. The madam apparently inhabited the building—she was very much alive if only in spirit—and, later, food servers and chefs, particularly pastry chefs, had to deal with her presence.

Pastry chefs revolved in and out at the Manor House. The madam delighted in creeping them out by appearing whenever they visited the men's room. Perhaps a former pastry chef she loved had jilted her or skipped out without paying for his time with one of her ladies. Hard to figure out why, the sightings were real enough, and the turnover rate of pastry chefs gave Tell and his managers fits.

Bunny sensed the madam's presence right from the start. Oddly, she was able to get the madam to agree to turn the lights of the place on or off for her as needed. On occasion, Bunny had to open the building very early in the morning before sunrise or close it very late at night. Compliance from the madam could, therefore, easily be monitored.

In the dark one morning before sunrise, Bunny drove to the restaurant with her sister, Ali, along the way telling her about the madam. She turned toward the dark building and said aloud, "I'm coming in." The lights went on inside the restaurant.

"C'mon, you just have an automatic lighting system installed," Ali remarked.

"Ali, we don't have any system. Those lights went on because the madam put them on. We have a deal."

Ali couldn't believe she just witnessed the lights go on because of a ghost. Once inside, however, Bunny let Ali inspect the electrical wiring throughout the entire building, including the other floors and the basement, to prove that she hadn't lied. A paralegal with an eye for reality, Ali couldn't find evidence of an automatic on/off light switch. Having run out of options, she got creeped out. She sat down, the hairs on her arms raised, and she shuddered. Bunny had not been kidding. Ali was impressed.

Still, nobody figured out what it was about the pastry chefs who continued to come and go as long as the Manor House was in business. The last one was "pushed" into a large vat of batter. No kidding.

The Manor House pulled visitors from a multi-state area. The license plates of cars and buses that filled its ample parking lot proved the point. In fact, opening day saw more than 120 guests arrive for brunch alone. The Cajun, German, and French cuisine that Chef Tell's team put forth generated a viral stream of compliments on the Internet.

Fundraisers for politicians were naturals for afternoons and weekends, either indoors during inclement weather or outside in the Beer Garden. *Forbes* magazine editor-in-chief Steve Forbes attended a capacity-bursting luncheon of 175 held during the Republican presidential primary in 1996. Tell orchestrated Hess's introduction to Forbes, who instructed her, "The one who is the most important and powerful at the table, any table, is the one sitting furthest from the table's edge. He's the most important and can afford to sit relaxed and comfortable that way."

Forbes then asked Hess which man was the most important at the table where he sat. Hess looked around and pointed out an older gentleman dressed in a natty suit. Forbes smiled and nodded. Hess had pointed out long-time, Pennsylvania Republican Senator Arlen Specter. From his position within the legislature since 1965, Specter had swung a lot of votes to favored campaigns, and Forbes hoped to carry a Republican primary voting nomination with his help.

Tell took no prisoners and he didn't take sides in politics. As a restaurateur, he fed political hopefuls from either side of the aisle.

* * *

The A-team split its schedule across the two restaurants and worked a variety of situations as a result. The arrangement afforded opportunities for more work for those who earned it. Of course, everyone had to get trained on the service differences. Between special events at the Manor and day-to-day dining service at the Harrow, Hess shared her knowledge gleaned from her banquet days, which came in handy at one particular wedding scheduled for a sunrise ceremony.

Yawns and early morning coffee were on tap as the morning shift left the WaWa store on Highway 412 and headed to the Manor

House in the pitch black before dawn. Save for an overhead lamppost light, which stayed on all night at the restaurant site, illumination was minimal. Stretching sleepy muscles, crew members threw open the basement doors, descended into the low-ceilinged basement—too low in which to stand erect—and took charge of the folded and stored event tables. Those strong enough carted the tables to the outdoor gazebo garden. The other servers set up linens, dishes, glasses, and silverware on the tables.

Since the wedding ceremony took place before the restaurant would open that morning, staff stood at the fringes of the guest crowd and watched. When the post-ceremony breakfast reception completed, the well-rehearsed setup and breakdown process continued and was finished in time for brunch service inside the restaurant. The same staff members doubled for the day service.

The sleep-deprived staff worked its way through a twelve-hour shift that day, but there was an upside. Tell's policy for events was that open champagne bottles not emptied could be enjoyed by the staff after all work was finished for the day. A few extra bottles were opened in the last few service minutes, which ensured a generous supply of champagne for the exhausted staff. Bunny and Tell, aware of what was going on, this one time let the crew slide.

Quid pro quo.

74

NO LONGER *CHEF DU JOUR*

"Dies ist nicht ein deutsches Restaurant, obwohl ich ein
("This is not a German restaurant, although I am a German.")
—Chef Tell

Tell understood that marketing his public image was part and parcel of any successes he'd had in the past. At this point in his life, he was used to it, but his restaurants faced a problem as time marched on—his public's taste buds changed. As the 1990s slipped away, they wanted less and less sophisticated dining. They wanted what they *thought* was "real German" food and not much else. They wanted Wiener schnitzel, which is actually from Austria.

Like a hot dog from Coney Island, Weiner schnitzel was the commoner's choice of good food. Its preparation was a no-brainer for Tell. But he didn't want to pound and bread veal cutlets—they were not haute cuisine—for a living. He wanted to plate creative ingredients for appreciative audiences.

As much as fine thoroughbreds wish to run among the best of fields, or Olympic athletes desire to compete against the best of competitors, Tell expected the affluent cognoscenti of New Hope and surrounding towns to patronize his restaurants. Unfortunately, their lifestyle landscape also had changed. The area wealthy had purchased the latest digital amenities, which meant they could entertain at home.

Large screen television monitors, Bose surround-sound speaker systems, DVR recorders, DVDs, improved satellite broadcasting and home theaters, coupled with a dumbing-down of the American palate, made dinner dates inside restaurants scarce. Other than special occasions, dining out was just too much of a hassle to do often.

The hand that fed Chef Tell's early career was now choking it. Television offered too many choices, and people stayed at home—not to mention, as they became more and more popular, home computers, the Internet, digital games, and movies-on-demand.

Running two suburban restaurants became a more difficult feat. That's why Tell ran a catering service out of the Manor House location.

Celebrity chefs catered to a new generation of TV viewers. For them, Chef Tell's footsteps were the only pathway to follow. Television's next generation had taken its cue from lessons that Chef Tell had pioneered. Even names like his contemporaries Wolfgang Puck and Paul Prudhomme were more prominent now, but a new wave lead by Emeril Lagasse, Mario Batali, and others fashioned TV appearances out of the Chef Tell blueprint.

At the moment, Chef Tell was no longer *chef du jour*. He felt underutilized. He didn't have his own TV show on-air to pick up the slack of his rural location in Upper Black Eddy. The area Tell and Bunny settled into was too remote from the city of Philadelphia to attract city gourmands. There were too many other restaurant choices along the main arteries leading out from the city to make a trip worthwhile all the way out to Ottsville and Upper Black Eddy.

Locals who did brunch in Tell's Manor House—denizens of the Homestead General Store frequented by Tell for personal sundry purchases and a place to keep his ear close to the ground—expressed point blank the caliber of the local palate in the words of one of them, "Food is food. That Chef Tell? I tasted his food. It was good, but in the end, food is just food."

The problem was more than a local lack of taste-bud sophistication and expectations, as high-caliber chefs discovered across the nation. Fewer people engaged in discourse for hours over a dinner table. The cultural importance of the leisure-dining experience had declined. Weiner schnitzel and beer had become, for an ever-widening circle of influence, good enough.

The better chefs' culinary sophistication—at least, in pocket areas of the country—was marginalized by the proliferation of corporate-owned chains of themed restaurants, like Olive Garden, Red Lobster, Steak & Ale, et al, which offered Howard Johnson–like menus: brand-recognizable food at affordable prices, which was good but not great. The result was a dumbing down of the American palate into categories of lesser expectation. If all you knew was Olive Garden, for example, you thought Italian was limited to what was on their menu and missed the wider panoply of the rest of the cuisine.

"This is not a German restaurant, although I am a German," Tell explained over and over to tour bus groups at the Manor House. Still, the problem of what patrons expected and what the chef wanted to cook persisted.

The way Hess saw it as manager, what they had was a marketing problem, not a problem of economics or taste. Although Tell wished to attract a customer base that preferred the cuisine he liked to cook, and the customers they were seeing wanted convenience food, Hess saw a third avenue that might cut through the fog. She suggested a marketing campaign of emails and a newsletter, which would offer cooking tips and cooking classes at Wiener schnitzel luncheons, marketed with the *promise* of a Chef Tell appearance. The concept was to get as many people as possible to at least arrive for lunch and then, while they were eating Wiener schnitzel, educate them into something better that might upgrade their palates for another visit or dinner at the Harrow Inne.

Putting Tell's image and personality up as a cooking class "carrot" was a unique use of his celebrity. Tell went along with the idea. It worked well for the daytime crowd and chartered bus tour groups soon booked the cooking class lunches. Additional special events targeted at women's groups were another prong of the marketing campaign that worked. The content of a typical promotional piece delivered the message clearly:

"International television and culinary arts celebrity Chef Tell Erhardt will conduct a celebrity cooking class and prepare gourmet dishes to benefit Animals in Distress on Saturday at his Manor House, formerly the Upper Black Eddy Inn, along River Road (Route 32) in Upper Black Eddy. Guests are invited to arrive by 3:30 p.m.

Chef Tell will entertain and educate with cooking demonstrations of various courses from the dinner menu. Guests will receive a personally auto-graphed copy of Chef Tell's cookbook and recipes from the day's menu. Lunch will include salad, assorted pasta dishes with a variety of sauces, Weiner schnitzel or a fish entrée, a side dish, garnish, and dessert. The menu will please both vegetarians and non-vegetarians."

Women responded. Women's groups from all over the area booked classes and luncheons at the Manor House. Bus tours visited from as far away as New York City—a two-hour journey—when the marketing campaign tapped into Tell's residual celebrity status from his appearances on *LIVE! with Regis & Kathie Lee.*

The compromise was simple: Tell's crew served only the entrées the public wanted, and Tell prepared and cooked high-end cuisine in front of live audiences while they ate. In other words, he would do live with his own customers what he did on TV. If people wanted him as much as they wanted the Wiener schnitzel, he was willing to give them what they wanted.

Still, the main draw for most fans was the chance to have one's photo taken next to Chef Tell. Hess often ribbed Tell for doing the photo sessions.

"Oh, please take a photo with me, Chef Tell," she repeated in the kitchen until he laughed.

Tell could take the joke as long as the bills got paid and as long as Hess compiled the scrapbooks and press releases that captured these marketed publics—a publicity gambit to sell his own show to network affiliates in the future.

Feeling closer than ever to his goal of his own TV show, Tell looked at these luncheon demonstrations as practice for that day.

75

FRIENDS IN NEED DO WHAT FRIENDS DO.

"Light it up!"

—Chef Tell

Susan and Richard Winston—yes, *that* Winston of *the* Winston Jewels family—lived in New York City and kept a car there for weekend drives to the countryside. In 1996, on a Saturday filled with bright blue skies and warm sunshine, they drove to New Hope. An article in *The New York Times* that Susan read only that morning gave a good review on the restaurant at the Black Bass Hotel, naming it the "Jewel of the Delaware." They hoped to try out its cuisine.

After hours of walking the narrow lanes of New Hope, popping in and out of art galleries and antique stores, and a late lunch at the Black Bass, they were prepared to return home. Wanting to take a different route, they headed up-river along River Road and reminisced about the past. "Sunny," the 1960s hit by Bobby Hebb, played on the radio.

As Nature would have it, a flood had rerouted the road and made the drive longer than expected. Richard wanted a break and Susan welcomed the idea since she felt parched. Something liquid would quench her thirst. Just ahead the sign for Chef Tell's Manor House caught Susan's eye.

"Honey, pull in here. I know that name!"

Richard turned into the spacious parking lot. Inside, he headed for the men's room, and Susan walked to the bar and sat down.

"I'll meet you right here at the bar," she said.

Years earlier, Susan had been a fan of Chef Tell on TV. She recognized him when he turned and faced her for the first time.

"What would you prefer to drink, madam?" Tell asked her from behind the bar.

"A martini—in fact, two—one is for my husband," Susan replied.

"Coming right up," he told her. While preparing the drinks, he conversed with her. "Where are you from? What brings you here today?"

Susan related the events of their day and, in the midst of her story, Richard joined them and was introduced by his full name.

"That so? Well, Mr. Richard Winston, are the jewels as valuable as they say they are?" quipped Tell, thinking that Richard wasn't really a part of the famous diamond necklace family.

"Well, actually . . . they really are, sir." Richard sipped his martini, reacting positively to its taste, " . . . Man, you make a good martini!"

"Thank you. I like them dry myself," Tell answered.

With time, Tell was convinced that he was, indeed, talking to a bona fide Winston. A half hour rest stop for the couple became an hour when common interests—fishing, politics, cognacs, history, general biographies, and books about World War II—were discovered and shared. The hour became dinner and then a late-night, after-hours repartee, which extended into the early hours of the next morning.

Tell suggested they stay over and return for brunch Sunday morning. He recommended the nearby colonial Bridgeton House on the Delaware. The Winstons found the place suitable for a night, with its comfortable rooms and a manicured garden overlooking the river.

The Winstons returned for Sunday brunch and were greeted by Bunny, who was the hostess. Only after their food was served did they realize that Bunny was Tell's wife. Though their conversation with Bunny was broken up as she handled incoming customers, the subject was food. Susan exclaimed about Tell's German dishes that she "loved the subtleties of the spices and sauces. Besides, the baked goods were fabulous."

Upon hearing of her keen interest in the nuances of herbs and spices, Tell took her outside on a small tour of his backyard next to the restaurant. He shared with Susan his little-known hobby—his own herb garden behind the Manor House. He confided later that it reminded him of gardening he'd done with his mother after the war and later other gardens he'd tended as an apprentice.

Brunch service was complete by mid-afternoon, and the foursome spent more time together. When the Winstons bid *adieu*, they knew it would only be a short time before they met again. Plans were in place to

Tell and the Winstons shared this pontoon boat.

Tell with Richard and Susan Winston at the Manor House 1997

go fishing with the Erhardts, as work permitted, as well as continue their discussions, which had already spanned a broad range of historical and contemporary subjects. It seemed Tell and Bunny had found a reliable couple, which would at least satisfy some of his intellectual yearnings, while shad fishing on the Delaware from a pontoon boat they would share as owners.

* * *

A well-to-do couple, which frequented the Manor House, wanted to celebrate Valentine's Day in 1997 at home with a catered party for six guests. They commissioned Tell's catering service, which rounded up a small crew, picked up a harpist for ambience, planned the setup, worked out the menu, and prepped, cooked, and prepared the delivery of the food for the evening soiree.

On Valentine's, Tell and crew arrived in his favorite company vehicle, ready to set up and serve with precision at the couple's home. The used ambulance was painted pure white with a large blue Chef Tell logo emblazoned on both sides.

You laugh? The ambulance was a masterful stroke of logistical brilliance. Built-in compartments fit the dishes, silverware, food, and glasses and held them intact when on the move. Whoever rode in back could drink and party all the way home to the restaurant on the way back from catered events—like from the Valentine's Day affair.

The party lit up the night. The couple and their guests loved the food and appeared happy with the crew. The team had done their job well. While they were cleaning up, the couple paid Tell and retired upstairs to bed. They told him to lock the door on their way out and not to forget the gift they had left in the dining room on a side table.

On the final inspection sweep, the crew spotted the gift—a doobie on a silver ashtray. Only one problem remained—what to do with the doobie? Tell said, "Light it up!"

76

THE GOOD, THE FUNNY, THE BAD, AND ROYALTY

"Kein Problem. wie Wasser eine Ente hinter sich."
("No problem. Water off a duck's behind.")
—Chef Tell

THE GOOD:

Tell's restaurant and catering crews understood team dynamics. They knew a lot of sub-products went into the making of an end product and that applied knowledge was needed to pull it all off. They had learned much of what they knew from Tell. If there was wine to be bought, he took A-team members with him and taught them how to purchase wine. He shared lessons about different port wines, how to go about getting permits, and how to obtain liquor licensing—who to talk to and why. Tell put all he knew on the table for his team members and the responsibilities that went with the knowledge.

"It was like getting a free education that I've used for the rest of my life," recalled Hess.

Free meals, too. Often, when the restaurants were dark on a Monday, Bunny and Tell invited Hess to join them for lunch at Siam Cuisine in

Doylestown. The early course Tell selected on one occasion was chicken satay with peanut sauce. Next, the flour dumplings were light and the Tom Yum (lemon grass soup) refreshing. Tell ordered a lot of food in his usual fashion. His favorite dish was duck, and the place had at least five different duck dishes, so Tell ordered them all. Hess was amazed when so much food arrived, but she was about to learn how to eat a meal chef-style, the same way Victoria Lang learned.

Tell took a small amount of one offering into his mouth, tasted it, and passed each new plate of food to the left so the process could be repeated by all three of them with every dish on the table. Christine was astonished that she ended up feeling full even though not one complete round was consumed. She couldn't eat it all, but she was able to try several dishes at once and thereby discovered what Thai foods she liked, or didn't like, in one sitting, as Tell narrated the meal.

Tell spread his knowledge around liberally for different reasons; in Hess's case, to help her raise her children.

Tell remained accessible to his employees at any time. One night in the middle of winter this promise was put to the test. After a long and grueling day and night of work Tell had just tucked himself under the covers when the phone rang. An employee's car was stuck in a snow bank at midnight during a blizzard, and he asked for help. No questions asked, Tell bundled up and drove out to get him. In turn, when the employee was asked one morning to pick up bread from the bakery on the way to work, the bread arrived in no time.

Hess spent hours listening to Tell share anecdotes, from which she gleaned useful information. She looked forward to her one-on-one time with him. Little by little, she observed the kind of person he was by his interactions with others. There was the time, for instance, that some of her friends arrived as a group and ordered the Chef's Table Special—what the chef wanted to cook. Tell over-delivered and undercharged them as a favor to Hess. "Chef Tell, if he liked you, in many ways would offer his help without explanation or demand," she said.

"He would just be there for you," said Hess, "and the A-Team made sure we were, in turn, there for him and Bunny."

Tell was selfless about assisting his personnel through tough times. He paid a higher-than-average electric bill for a single-parent server, who in the dead of winter faced her heat being shut off. When asked about payback, Tell said, "When I'm gone, you pass it on."

One long-time employee found herself in the middle of a nasty divorce and needed a place for her and her children to live. Tell offered the down payment for a home that was available down the street from the restaurant. Although this offer was not taken up, the employee was forever grateful.

Going to appearances on *LIVE! with Regis & Kathie Lee*, Tell took different employees with him as assistants. Hess was offered the chance. In a way, her decision was based upon Tell's earlier advice in her first meeting with him, "Say yes first . . ." Given the opportunity, she took it. Others looked upon off-camera assistant duties as extra work, but she considered it more of an honor and a privilege. In the process, she learned about a whole new world she had never seen before, and a lot more about Tell as a person.

"It was amazing to watch how he was treated off-camera. The show staff took turns and clamored for their opportunity to assist Tell with the show's preparations. I think it was because of the way he treated them, spending extra time with them off-camera when he didn't have to," said Hess.

Another whole book could be filled with stories and anecdotes about the favors Chef Tell bestowed on people without any request for favors in return. All of its content would stem from his simple desire to help people, because that was his way—a far cry from some other celebrities of his day.

The good times included trips back to Germany where Tell stayed with his son and his wife and their son, Tell's grandson. Tell visited them for the last time in June 1997, and the visit was a highlight for Torsten, who took off from work for the week to spend as much time with his father as possible.

"We went to the Mercedes museum in Stuttgart and a Middle Age festival. We took walks together, as he could," he said.

Tell's health was compromised at the time, which shortened the walks, but the rare family time was a welcome retreat from a lifetime of workaholic hours endured under the pressures of almost daily performance.

"My son, Max, wasn't in school yet, so he was with us all the time, and Angelika and I cooked for Tell almost every day—a thing Tell hardly ever got to experience."

Lucky for Tell, Angelika and Torsten absorbed some of the cooking genes that Tell possessed, for they turned out some fine dishes for him, which he enjoyed not having to cook.

"Angelika comes from the Frankfurt area. In spring a very typical dish known as Frankfurter Green Sauce combines sour cream, a little salt, fine-chopped boiled eggs, and seven fresh minced herbs mixed into a sauce. At that time, white asparagus, which only appears four weeks annually, were available. Knowing that Tell loved white asparagus, we prepared them especially for him. Our plate was beautiful: Frankfurter Green Sauce poured over grilled chicken breast accompanied by freshly cooked white asparagus and new potatoes, skins on," recalled Torsten.

Tell loved the sauce. He never knew about it and never had tasted it all his life.

"He also loved when we made real Italian Tiramisu for him. And *Cantucci al mandorli* (biscotti with almonds). He loved my *risotto mare monti* (with shrimps and mushrooms) served with a corn salad under a warm shallot raspberry vinaigrette."

Home cooking. Nothing better.

THE FUNNY:

In the Manor House one evening, Theresa Badmann was handling a champagne bottle that Tell found deep in the wine cellar to impress her VIP party. Although she was trained on the handling of wines and table etiquette, this particular bottle of Dom Perignon packed a kick. No sooner had she loosened the wire on the cork, it recoiled.

The cork sailed across the entire thirty-foot dining room with a loud *pop!* It landed in another lady's salad, kicking up dressing onto the hapless woman's attire. Of course, pricey champagne foamed out of the bottle, surprising everyone, including one very shocked Badmann, who, unthinking, reacted by capping the bottle with her mouth.

"Oh no!" screamed the wife of the man for whom the bottle was intended. All conversations in the restaurant ceased as heads turned in her direction.

In a still-life frame, Badmann, dressed in her official tuxedo shirt, colorful tie, and black pants uniform gear, stood at the table in front of the VIPs, with their oversized bottle of Dom Perignon stuffed in her mouth. Her puffed-out cheeks turned red with embarrassment. She then swallowed and tried to apologize, but the celebrated man of honor would have none of it. With a wave of his arm, he forgave her and said, "Please pour."

The event was the talk of the night among the patrons. The talk at the VIP table, between sips of Dom, centered on comparisons of movie scenes as hilarious as the scene they had just witnessed.

In the end, Badmann smacked her lips and smiled when she saw the huge tip the party had left her. They even thanked her for the memory as they departed.

Badmann never found out what Bunny and Tell had to say about the incident but that she kept her job for a good while longer probably said it all.

THE BAD:

In August 1997, *Philadelphia* magazine printed an article titled "Reinventing the Veal" by William Bunch, a politico who sharpened his nib freelancing. Across well-researched pages, the scribe painted Tell as an "affably roguish Bad Boy of the Philadelphia restaurant world." He wrote that Tell was "fiscally challenged" in his attempt to make a Philadelphia comeback to a level of prominence he had enjoyed almost all of his professional life. Not one mention testified to the fact that Tell had *created* that pioneering prominence from scratch.

Nothing had been handed to Tell on a platter. He earned his way to celebrity status with hard work, unique skills, and his outgoing personality.

Not one real-life, humanitarian, Chef Tell anecdote emerged within the crafted prose. Reading the article, one had to wonder—was it designed to spin the reader's head like tossed salad greens, or grind away at Tell's comeback chances like old sausage?

The return of one of America's most-admired TV chefs, whose indefatigable schedule of touring for years had brought home the bacon in so many ways for the City of Philadelphia and its restaurateurs, should have been heralded, not punted. The keys to the city would have been more appropriate, for Tell, who with Baum, Perrier, Arnoldi, Foo, Patruno, Poses, and Gruben had advanced a culinary legacy for legions of Philly chefs to come and walk in their giant footsteps.

The revival that circle of professionals created from their kitchens, Chef Tell expanded nationwide into America's living rooms. In doing so, he created the *foundation* for a budding national interest in food, dining, and cooking that has never faltered. His influence expanded television's interest in food and chefs. In turn, television exploded beyond the old technology of towered broadcast signals, got into cable and satellite transmissions, and, beginning with Chef Tell, reached an ever-widening and awakened audience that clamored for more culinary artists. Black-and-white to color, analog to digital, from vacuum-tubed screens to high-definition monitors to mobile handheld devices—the world of television cast aside its early cardboard-propped sets for a multitude of hi-tech stations and channels that broadcast twenty-four hours a day at light speed into the twenty-first century and kept going.

The irksome words of the writer, about the chef who stood in front of the camera when the notion of a TV showman chef was brand new and untarnished, failed to perceive and acknowledge Chef Tell's iconic place in America's history.

Tell dismissed the scathing article, "No problem—water off a duck's behind." His take was that it was just black ink on white paper—colorless and tasteless—and, by the way, thanks for the free publicity.

But was it an underhanded "hail to the king," a chip on a writer's shoulder? To be fair, the story might have suggested merely Philadelphia toughness in print—a reflection of that love/hate syndrome unique to the City of Brotherly Love. Whatever the writer's real intent, the message's effect begged the reader—or just Chef Tell—to change lanes, slow down, and stop, none of which Tell ever considered.

Tell's attention never drifted from serving his fans. He knew they were smart and never cooked down to them. They knew what to expect when they picked up their forks and knives and dug in at one of Tell's five restaurants: the chef was going to, if they were lucky, spend some time at their table, say something irreverent, and make them laugh. Tell's followers wanted entertainment, great food, and a good time. Chef Tell, they knew, would show them the way.

At the turn of the twenty-first century, less than three years after the scathing "exposé," Chef Tell was chosen one of the Top 10 Chefs in the World for A&E's *A&E Top 10: Celebrity Chefs* by Arts & Entertainment Network in conjunction with Weller/Grossman Productions.

Tell's latest line of sauces won numerous Scovie Awards—"judged on design, creativity/visual impact, originality, quality, content, navigation, and use of technology"—in the following year, 2001, the *first year he entered* into the competition. His Caribbean Ketch-Me took first place in the Hot Sauce classification; Chef Tell's Spanish Ketch-Me won second place in the World Beat classification; Chef Tell's Italian Ketch-Me placed second in the Pasta Red Sauce classification, and Chef Tell's German Ketch-Me won third place in the World Beat classification.

ROYALTY:

Chef Tell would have thought the following words of one of his long-time A-team staffers a much better representation of him than the pundit who interviewed him in 1997:

"Tell held paid-for Christmas parties for the staffs and their families. He cooked for us. He conducted summer parties for us. He took us on canoe trips on the Delaware, with drinks.

"The only thing we could complain about was his wearing that darn Speedo swimsuit! We begged him to put more on (laughter), but he took it well as we manned the oars, and *he* sat under the parasol, cognac in one hand and a large Cuban in the other.

"Did we treat him like royalty? You bet.

"We would have done anything for him, to keep him alive among us. There was that much love."

Manor House Christmas Staff Party

With the advantage of hindsight, a few of his accomplishments, though hindered and marred by negative events, set the stage for the climax of the chess game that was Tell's life.

77

THE ROAD BACK RAN
THROUGH BETHLEHEM

"Sie müssen so stolz auf dich."
("You must be so proud of yourself.")
—Chef Tell

Back in 1998, the good news was the Manor House rocked. The bad news was Tell, unable to move forward uncompromised over what he wanted on the menu, considered closing the Harrow. He felt that he was much closer to getting his intended TV show, which was to be named *In the Kitchen with Chef Tell*. Indeed, his next big break did happen.

Bob Croesus grew up thinking that he had a knack for television and that he liked to follow celebrity's lives—Chef Tell's was one of them. Like most Philadelphians, he had watched Tell's cooking shows on Philadelphia TV and became a fan. Tell's career seemed to him, as he grew up, the perfect mix of technology and personal preference, and he hoped to meet him one day. However, by the time Croesus completed his college education, Tell had disappeared off the media radar and left the country.

Croesus didn't know what happened. He only knew that what had seemed promising in his training days, that one day he could play a part in Chef Tell's career, had somehow vanished.

Where did Tell go? Croesus wondered for almost ten years. And then his dream returned, because Tell moved back to Bucks County in 1993, and made his presence known through Harrow Inne advertising and publicity in 1994.

Now I have my chance to work with him, he thought as he prepared for the first show they would film together in March of 1998, thanks to local business investors. By now an executive producer at MBC Teleproductions in Allentown, Pennsylvania, Croesus had planned and sold the idea of a series of TV shows with Chef Tell, which they would shoot inside a kitchen they built together in the Manor House.

He took a step back and admired how Tell spoke with tones of quiet

Chef Tell and lobsters

respect to the rest of his crew. The addictive combination of celebrity, food, and potential fortune was, for Croesus, "weirdly exciting, and even more exciting to see Tell back in action. After all, this was like working with a childhood idol."

Croesus continued, "Off-screen, Tell had become a normal guy again—someone trying to make a comeback after years of being away. On-screen, he was like a horseman grown up in the saddle and ready to ride at whatever speed the horse wanted to go. We all got caught up in being a part of an epic comeback."

Tell turned to Croesus, "Listen, 'Greek' (Tell's affectionate nickname for Croesus), have you noticed they're not making real cooking shows anymore?"

"What do you mean?"

Tell answered his own question with another question, "What if we did a cooking show that was fun and easy and showcased recipes that everyone could do?"

Croesus laughed. "You mean something straight-ahead; something lighthearted with recipes that even I could do?"

"Exactly, even you, Greek!" Tell was aware that his producer was incapable of boiling water.

One young crew editor named Kelly, who was aware of Tell's celebrity résumé, was eager to meet him and introduced herself before shooting began.

"Hello, Chef. I'm Kelly. I edit your show."

"Z'at must be a privilege," Tell responded in a heavier German-dialect accent than normal.

Kelly looked troubled and didn't understand. "I mean I'll be editing your film, Chef," she added.

"Den you mus' be zo proud of yourself."

Tell watched for a reaction. Getting a nervous grin out of Kelly, he smiled and put his arm around her shoulder.

"We're gonna have a good time with you editing my show, Kelly. You're my 'editor!'" She began to understand him.

"Kelly, bring some friends with you for dinner at the Harrow some time."

A few nights later she did. A male friend, who was like a brother, accompanied her for dinner at the Harrow. Tell picked up their check. Her friend was impressed, Kelly ecstatic.

The next day on the set—never one to miss a punch line—Tell asked, using his most gruff German accent, "Zo, about ze gentleman you vere vith last night, vas he a 'prozpect' or jus' a quickie?"

Kelly laughed and said, "None of your beeswax, German." Tell laughed back.

No matter how far they were going to go with their syndication plans, the crew knew it would be fun getting there with Chef Tell—a far cry from other productions Croesus had experienced.

Chef Tell was as rare as a gemstone in an acre of dirt, and that was the reason Croesus was able to convince his production company to invest in the new show, despite the fact that Tell had not been seen on syndicated television for a number of years. He had a charisma that carried.

"We'd like to shoot an audience test to see if we have sustained interest," said the suits with the purse strings. "This would be a kind of comeback teaser, to give us an idea of how well Chef Tell plays out with today's audience." They were being cautious but they weren't saying no.

Because the station's budget allocated to Croesus in March allowed for only six half-hour shows to showcase Chef Tell's test run, Croesus held down costs by filming, for the most part, with a small crew of two cameras. Three months later, the results came in. Response was very good. The public, it was apparent, remembered Tell and wanted to see more of him.

The station then backed Croesus with a larger budget for thirteen additional shows. An eighteen-wheel TV production truck loaded with millions of dollars of equipment took over the parking lot and a full camera and grips crew set up inside of the restaurant kitchen. In a couple of days in July, Tell and Croesus put in the can a week's worth of shows. Morale was high, and Croesus was ecstatic. The show's progress reminded him of his feelings when he first conceived the idea. "I didn't really know how it was going to go, but I felt a tug from my childhood that told me I had to do it, and let the chips fall where they may," said Croesus.

78

ONE-TAKE TELL STRUTS HIS STUFF

"Du machst dir zu viel, Griechisch. Dies wird gut."
("You worry too much, Greek. This will be fine.")
—Chef Tell

In between filming, Croesus arranged phone meetings with independent syndicators who could sell the show for airing on their affiliated stations. He found one based in Houston, Texas, who shared his vision for a series of cooking shows tied in with another Chef Tell cookbook.

The day the "big shoot" for the Houston prospect arrived, the crew set up early in the morning. Croesus sat next to Tell in make-up and noticed that his star appeared nervous.

"Are you alright, Tell? Are you ready for this?"

"Sure I am, Greek. I'm a world-class chef, you know. I'm gonna do magic cutting and dicing." Tell bear-hugged Croesus. "Don't worry, Greek, you'll pick up the cooking jargon soon."

With that, Tell stepped onto his set and into his on-air persona of Chef Tell. In front of his crew, which he put at ease right away, he complimented Croesus on his kitchen set in a manner that suggested he loved every aspect of the television experience. Having done the "drill" thousands of time before, he stood at ease and smiled to the camera.

Tell started the cooking demo on cue. Halfway through the first show, the director and Croesus saw that some of the food was starting to burn.

Should we stop the production or keep going? ran through Croesus's head, but the director kept filming.

Tell wasn't at all concerned that part of his meal or sauce was charred. He never skipped a beat in his monologue, "That looks nice and crunchy—just the way I like it—and we're gonna put a nice sauce on it." "Very nice, very easy—you can do this," he told the camera. "I tell you, we need 'smellivision' here, this smells that good."

After the director yelled "cut," Tell yelled across the set, "You worry too much, Greek. This will be fine. Just remember, Greek, here I am the cook, and you are the produsah. Jus' make me look good."

At the end of a long day of shooting several segments, Tell asked Croesus, "How do I look on camera?" (Croesus didn't know it at the time, but Tell had let his guard down for a second. He had belied his calm exterior with another question inferred between the lines, "Do I still have what it takes?")

Croesus told him he looked fine and was doing a great job. Tell reminded him then that people always called him, "One-take Tell."

As Croesus walked to his car after the day's work was completed, he realized that Tell was right. He had shot several long sequences, cooked different dishes, and talked non-stop all day long, using only one take every time.

Croesus felt triumphant. He had worked with his hero and gotten to know the charm of Tell's personality up close. He had watched Tell create what he never before experienced on a set—*professional fun.* He realized there was real substance to his childhood hero, after all.

Back at his office, Croesus took a phone call from the Texas syndicator. There had been a major buy-in from a large PBS station. Croesus smiled and pounded his fist down on his desk, because Chef Tell, his man, was coming back stronger than before and was about to go nationwide. The world was about to witness the comeback of Chef Tell—this time on his own terms and with his name on the marquee.

In the Kitchen with Chef Tell aired on forty PBS stations across America in a very short time and continued on-air for years. Even though

Tell had disappeared to the Cayman Islands and was off-camera for eight years prior, former viewers had not forgotten him; they only missed him.

In the Kitchen with Chef Tell

Tell was the show. His was the "x-factor" to which audiences responded. The featured recipes, the pots, the pans, the set, and the food were props. Tell Erhardt—the one and only Chef Tell—was the one the viewers wanted, because he was the one who empowered them.

Now that his name was featured in the show title, the persona of Chef Tell merged with the man—what viewers saw, at last, was Tell Erhardt being himself. However, the wheel of fortune is always spinning, and Tell's life was about to change forever.

79

THE DELAWARE RIVERBANK INCIDENT

"Get me eine verdammte Flasche meiner besten Cognac!"
("Get me a f***ing bottle of my best cognac!")
—Chef Tell

The 58.89-mile Delaware Canal is duly registered for its place in history and its role in the development of Pennsylvania's important anthracite coal industry. The man-made waterway ran parallel to the Delaware River from Easton, where it connected with the Lehigh Canal at Bristol. Before steam engine "iron horses" superseded them in the early 1800s, three thousand mule-drawn boats, each hauling eighty to ninety tons of anthracite coal, made the trip up and down the canal through a series of tended locks. These mule-drawn boats had hauled one million tons of coal annually during the Civil War years.

On October 17, 1931, the last of the commercial boats was pulled down the canal through the twenty-five locks. Since then, tourist boats guided by period-costumed volunteers plied the waters less and less frequently, until operations stopped altogether after 2006.

One early Oktoberfest Sunday morning in 1999, at the Manor House location, Tell walked across River Road, intent on disposing waste in the (illegal) burn barrel located at the bottom of a ten-foot slope on the bank of the Delaware River. On level ground covered with soft, conker shells, not noticing a small hole ahead of him, Tell stepped on one of the slippery shells and fell off-balance into the hole, "snapping his leg like a twig" at the ankle.

Delaware River site of Tell's nasty fall

Lying on the wet ground, he knew that it was too early for any of his crew to arrive and that the only other person around was the janitor working inside the restaurant. He lay in severe pain for over an hour without help, just out of reach of the still-smoldering cigar he'd dropped when he went down.

The morning brunch scheduled for 10 a.m. brought the crew in around nine. Hearing their voices, Tell waved at them, and they waved back. He waved more, and they waved more, not realizing he needed their help. Finally he hollered loud enough that they heard his plea, "Help me! And get me a f***ing bottle of my best cognac!"

Once they understood there was trouble, the A-team sprang into action. One called for an ambulance; another ran inside, found the cognac, and handed it down to another who ran outside, across the road, and down the hill with the bottle. Still others gathered around their fallen chef.

Tell chugged down the cognac—about a half-bottle of the stuff. He lay back and barked out orders.

"Where's Christine?"

"Here I am," Hess replied.

"Get these people organized and back up in the restaurant. The brunch is scheduled for 10 a.m., and you've less than an hour to be ready."

"Will do, chef." Turning to the staff, "Well, let's get going then. You all know what to do up there."

Servers, chefs, and bartenders took one last look at Tell on the ground and then helped each other climb back up the dewy slope. Hess stayed behind as Tell lay on his back on the wet, grassy ground and stared at the blue sky and sycamore and oak trees as he listened to the leaves rustle.

"We called Bunny and the EMT. An ambulance should be on the way."

"My f***ing leg hurts, but not so much now with the cognac. When Bunny gets here keep her up there and tell her to run the restaurant. Tell her I'm alright."

"I can do that," Hess replied.

The EMT squad arrived and attended to Tell. Once Hess saw him into the ambulance, Bunny arrived.

"And make sure the brunch goes well, okay?" were the last words Hess heard as the ambulance departed and she took Bunny into the restaurant where she updated her on Tell's condition.

The hospital where the ambulance transported Tell did not have a full-time orthopedic surgeon on staff. Most small medical centers do not, so one was called. As a result, Tell lay in his bed in pain until 5 p.m. When he was less under the influence of the cognac, a nurse introduced the acetaminophen, Percoset—a narcotic painkiller with a slightly lower addiction rate than morphine—into Tell's body. Around 6 p.m. the surgeon performed major surgery on Tell's broken leg.

During subsequent visits, the same surgeon explained to Tell that he was "progressing fine" after he heard Tell's complaints of unusual pains in his leg. He scribbled out more prescriptions for Percoset and handed the sheets to Tell, who was not offered any other option.

Wracked with pain, in the weeks that followed Tell added another "medicinal" remedy—frequent daily doses of Bombay Sapphire gin. The volatile combination of the narcotic and alcohol-induced hallucinations prevented Tell from working in the kitchen. His right leg was considerably shorter than the other now and constantly hurting. Tell was forced to walk with a permanent limp and the assistance of a cane.

Bunny worked double shifts to keep both restaurants afloat. Weekends, she managed the Manor House; evenings, she worked at the Harrow Inne. She let the A-team help her as much as possible while Tell brooded and talked with his lawyers, who pushed along the pace of his lawsuit against the surgeon whom he thought had botched up his leg. However, justice moves slow and the case would not be settled for years.

80

HITTING BOTTOM

"'Warten Sie ein paar Tage' erzählt er mir. Inzwischen
bin ich in der Hölle leben."
("'Wait a few days,' he tells me. Meanwhile, I'm living in hell.")
—Chef Tell

The turn of the century brought more changes. Despite his physical condition, Tell continued to produce TV show segments from the Manor House kitchen set. He also made appearances on other TV venues, notably Regis Philbin's show and *The Donny & Marie Show*, among others.

As the rumor went for one of his appearances, Tell is announced to his live audience and viewers with an ersatz introduction that makes light of Allentown, Pennsylvania—where Tell's TV show aired. His host deflects the sting, asking Tell about a recent high-profile assignment he completed.

Tell says, "Well, I recently catered the bar mitzvah of Regis Philbin's godson. It was a very loud and boisterous crowd, not unlike Regis himself."

Tell explains how he prepared, "I have been experimenting with fusion cuisine, taking some staples from my native Germany and mixing them with other things."

One host, looking for a laugh, then makes an offhand reference about Tell's Germanic heritage and his catering of a Jewish bar mitzvah.

Tell, who always took such things in stride, says, "Well, as you know, I have lived in this country for many years and I have consorted with Regis on his show more than with Nazis. But it was a challenge, I can tell you! I started off with a béarnaise of mushrooms seasoned with pepper and cinnamon and topped with mango."

One host grimaces and chides the other for it, but Tell continues unfazed, "The important thing is to play with the food. Always be fun and free and see where your taste buds take you. That is how I ended up with a Spicy Jerk Duck served with bratwurst and apricot chutney—the unexpected combination of flavors, which surprised many of the mitzvah guests."

While talking, Tell prepares a hors d'oeuvre of sauerkraut and raisin rolls with a side of ketchup—the same dish that he had made for the reception. The host expresses concern about the calories.

"Yes, but everyone needs to indulge now and then," said Tell, who demonstrated that one only needs to buy or prepare a crepe, "in the French tradition, as we like to say. With this dish I tried to capture the animation—the hoopla—of French cooking, and then grounded it with a populist, home-style, American ingredient—ketchup."

Having some fun with his hosts, Tell then plants his tongue firmly in his cheek and says, "I recommend Hunt's. It's cheaper. Or for the very best American ketchup, you need to get McDonald's Fancy Ketchup packets—but this is a lot of handiwork . . . the squeezing."

Incredulously, one of the hosts professes McDonald's is a favorite! Tell simply goes on, "Now, you take the sauerkraut, which you can also buy in the store—though it would not be as good as if Chef Tell made it, of course—and you fill the bread with it. You can also use hot dog buns for this, or pita bread. And if you want to be extra adventurous, you can spread some applesauce on there. But we are keeping things simple."

The same host remarks about having a large family, while the other is silent, watching Tell continue his work, "Then you get some raisins. I prefer the dark kind, but you can also use golden, if you must, and sprinkle them on top."

One host asks if it might be better to mix them in, which Tell mostly ignores, preferring to finish his description. "Finally, you slice the roll and serve with ketchup on the side. And you can follow it up with a nice tawny port"—at that, Tell presents the dish to the camera.

The same host can no longer hold back and blurts out, "Are you sure this was a bar mitzvah? None of this sounds very Jewish to me."

Tell would not let that remark pass: "You, who know nothing of Jewish cuisine, you say you are a 'Soldier of Love,' but I am finding otherwise."

The other host quickly plays up to Tell. "Just ignore that; that's the reason why we have trouble getting decent guests! Emeril Lagasse has blacklisted us," not realizing the current guest, Tell, has just been dissed on national television.

To make matters worse, the other host then digs a deeper hole, "Well, even though your guests have not been saved, they at least deserve decent cooking."

Tell whips a dinger right back at him, "Herr Host, if there is any saving to be done, it is this sorry-ass show and your ridiculous singing," which he caps off by flinging sauerkraut at the host's eyes.

The alleged rumors of the incident ring true: TV hosts could not prepare for television Chef Tell–style, he never worked from a prepared script.

* * *

Tell appeared on QVC more than once, which came about as a result of Home Shopping Network appearances he had done earlier in the Tampa Bay area, and the fact that the QVC studio was located within driving distance of his home. Thursday, September 14, 2000, Tell prepared to do two episodes at QVC. He gathered his fresh food and utensils that he would need for the demonstration and loaded them onto a rolling cart.

The floors between the set-up area and Studio K2 were not on the same plane. A ramp built to accommodate carts getting to and from the two areas—twelve feet long but only eighteen inches wide—had to be traversed to arrive at the show's set.

The gray-painted surface was not level, and hidden indentations made it difficult to maneuver a loaded cart of the size and weight Tell pushed. Also, prior to his segment, water or grease had fallen unnoticed onto the ramp and had not been cleaned up.

As Tell pushed his heavy cart up the ramp, he slipped on the wet, uneven surface. Unable to grab any handhold on the way down, he landed hard on his back and his previously injured leg. He was unable to move for several minutes. Eventually, a few QVC employees managed, with help from Tell's personal assistant, to have Tell sit up. Though he tried, he could not stand on his own. Medical personnel arrived on the scene and further assisted Tell. At Tell's demand, they allowed him to get to the set, so he could do his TV show segments.

Tell completed his televised morning segment barely able to stand. He was experiencing a lot of discomfort, and by the afternoon the dull pain in his lower back hadn't gone away. Because of his previous leg injury, he carried a supply of strong painkillers. He gulped a couple down to ease his back pain, enough to get him through the next segment of the day. As his pain increased throughout the day, he took more painkillers. Somehow he drove home and then hit the bed around 9 p.m.

At 5:30 a.m., Tell awoke and realized his muscles were stiff and that he still felt the dull pain in his back. He was unable to move around very well. His ankle was bruised, swollen, and tender to the touch. Looking at his back in the mirror, he found it similarly discolored, swollen, and bruised.

A subsequent examination at the doctor's office revealed the cause of the persistent pain in his back. Two nerves in his lower vertebrae were pinched and one disc had moved out of alignment. Unbelievably, the doctor prescribed yet another pain killer and said, "Wait a few days. If it doesn't improve, we'll do an MRI in ten days."

Meanwhile, Tell lived in hell. The combination of pain, Percoset, and gin, coupled with the frustration of having to stay at home, stimulated the darker recesses of his mind. Every day for weeks, the drinking and prescription drug combination ruled his days and, by night, darkened his attitude and outlook on living.

Bunny, meanwhile, was burning her candle at both ends, trying to keep up with two restaurant operations and the added traffic on her plate. In the middle of the turmoil, the Harrow Inne folded. Medical bills and overhead could not be met, and the bank foreclosed.

Chef Barrett came off a July weekend mini-vacation and was informed by Tell's secretary that the restaurant was closed. The Manor House continued, however, and Tell paid Barrett whatever he had coming to him and then some.

"John, you were the best chef I ever had," Tell said. Those words summed up the close relationship that he and Tell enjoyed. Together they had spent time inside the kitchen, had traveled first-class, met scores of celebrities, and also enjoyed the camaraderie of talk and time away from the demanding strictures of the business. Indelible memories of knowing such a personality as Tell left many lifelong impressions and a professional admiration in the mind and heart of the younger Barrett.

"I met a good guy who was ahead of the curve, ahead of his time, who taught me a lot. Chef Tell? I will never forget him," said Chef Barrett from the kitchen of the Black Bass Hotel near New Hope, where he landed as the executive chef.

Bunny's flame for her marriage almost snuffed out from the over-whelming odds against her. Trying to make ends meet beyond the one remaining restaurant, she spent more time with real estate sales—she had gotten her license when separated from Tell. Caring for the estate, the dogs, the bills, her husband, and her own survival—there was very little emotional fuel left in her tank. Yet, she had not witnessed the worst.

Into her overwhelmed condition, a charging wounded bull—Tell on a deadly cocktail of Percocet and booze—entered her house. He accused her of infidelity. All of the time away from the restaurant, all the time alone dwelling inside of his pain amid mental and emotional re-stimulations, had pushed Tell to accuse Bunny of the ultimate marital betrayal. Never in a million years would she ever have entertained even the thought.

Tell's words almost broke Bunny's heart. She had fought and fought and struggled to keep them afloat but now, with this accusation, she was ready to throw in the towel.

"Where do you expect me to go then, Bunny?"

"I don't care where the hell you go. Go live in the Manor House. You've got an apartment up there. Just leave."

For Bunny, life would go from bad to worse in the immediate future before she could right the ship again and keep it afloat.

"I was doing everything to stay sane and make money. I was fired, rather dismissed, from working at the restaurant while we separated. It was not fun," she said.

"I worked two, sometimes three jobs to make money and pay the mortgage. When Tell left, I found out that he had not paid the mort-gage for the house in two months. The payment for the third month was due in two days. Not paying the third month would have put us into foreclosure."

She didn't find any sympathy at the bank when she called.

"I told them I would pay the full amount, and they said they would not take my payment; it was too late. It was Friday, and Sunday was the last day."

She did what she had to do: "I went to the bank on Saturday. Because there were no managers there, the clerks registered the payments." The house was saved in the nick of time. Bunny's resourcefulness and quick thinking—skills learned from hours spent inside of Tell's restaurants—had saved the house and the acres of the estate they had worked so hard to earn and keep.

As this occurred, Tell gathered his belongings and moved out of the main house. He went down to the river site and moved in alongside the specter of the madam—fitting, because he had become a ghost of his usual self.

* * *

Believe it or not, beneath the trauma, the lawsuits, the accusations, and their outcomes, Bunny and Tell remained in love with each other. They just didn't know day-to-day what to do about their lives. The underlying love and the common welfare of their beloved dogs kept them in touch. While the dogs stayed with Bunny on the estate, Tell made sure that both dogs and Bunny were cared for by seeing that food was delivered daily from the restaurant to the house.

Still under the influence of his pain and painkillers, Tell took in a girlfriend, who lived with him on the third floor of the Manor House. An attractive, educated nurse who had been a regular patron of the restaurant, she was someone with whom Tell found a companionship of sorts. Unfortunately, she wasn't his wife and she wasn't the one whom he truly loved.

Tell was at a crossroad in his life's path. If he was to come up to even having a chance of getting Bunny back, he was going to have to find out who he really was.

Actually, this was, for both of them, their defining moment. But coming to grips with it right away would not be possible.

81

THE MADAM WREAKS HAVOC

"Ich hatte eine ganze Flasche Jägermeister am geworfen
'Dame.' Was für eine Verschwendung."
("I'd thrown a full bottle of Jägermeister at the 'lady.'
What a waste.")

—Torsten Erhardt

As soon as he could, after hearing the succession of bad-news stories, Torsten and his wife, Angelika, visited Tell. Hearing that they were coming from Germany, Bunny invited the couple to stay with her in the large house on the estate. However, Tell insisted they stay upstairs at the Manor House with him.

After an exhausting twenty-hour trip, the couple discovered their accommodations to be woefully underwhelming. Their room, if you could call it one, occupied barely enough space for a bed and a dresser and was located right above the kitchen next to the cramped business office. Tired and defeated, they bedded down for the night and slept as best as they could.

After another two nights in the makeshift *boudoir*, they opted to take a trip south to Williamsburg and to see Virginia's other historical sites. Later, driving north along the coastline, they stayed overnight at Cape May, New Jersey. The next day they enjoyed the beach and sand dunes at Surf City, drove further north to visit a close friend on Long Island in New York, and then returned to the Manor House.

After the crowd thinned on that humid night, Torsten and Angelika reconnected with Tell. Dinner was cordial over flowing red wine. Tell's new lady-friend—"Nurse Germany" to Freddie Duerr, who had been hired to fill the void left by Barrett's departure, Bunny, and the staff, because she was a dialysis nurse—added spice and intellect to the table talk. Laughter punctuated the conversation, and the tale of the resident madam-ghost came up.

Torsten, who heard about the restaurant being haunted ever since Tell took over the place in 1993, was inclined to believe what he wanted to believe. Since he had not seen the purported ghost himself, he was a non-believer.

Early the next morning, Torsten tossed in bed fitfully and couldn't sleep. He stood up quietly, not wanting to awaken Angelika or his father sleeping above him on the third floor. The way to the bathroom crossed a large storage room filled with boxes of liquor, extra chairs, and furniture. Ahead of him a foot away from the restroom door, he saw a glowing light. Suddenly this "light"—five feet tall and ambient—flew straight at him and right through him. Startled, he screamed. He grabbed a bottle from one of the boxes and threw it in the direction of the apparition. The bottle smashed against the wall with a loud crash.

Angelika ran in from their bedroom and wrapped her arms around Torsten, who said he was freezing cold. He had goose bumps all over his body.

Tell found both of them shivering and wondering what to do. He yawned and, heading back upstairs to bed, said, "Aaahhhh! That was the lady. That happened before." He yawned again, "I cook breakfast for you later—*Schlaf gut* (Sleep well)."

Looking back on the night, Torsten said he was impressed. "She ran into a six-foot-nine German guy, who almost peed his pants, but afterward I found out that I'd thrown a completely full bottle of Jägermeister at the 'lady.' What a waste—Germans are afraid of God and nothing else in this world."

Like father, like son, except that Angelika and Torsten moved out of the Manor House that morning and checked into a B&B on the other side of the river, where they stayed for the last two nights of their trip.

In the days that followed, Tell brooded. Though he hadn't shown much interest that night, the incident of the madam's intimate appearance had shifted his outlook. His behavior toward others changed: he no longer took his relationships as much for granted as he had in the past. Self-inspection of what he really wanted most in his life—*who* he really wanted—lead to Nurse Germany's departure, and his decision to seek another doctor and work on improving his health. On a personal note, he wanted to feel better physically; on another note, he wished to look better for Bunny and to be able to do more with her.

82

RESURRECTION

"Es wird wahrscheinlich nie einen anderenwie ihn."
("There will likely never be another quite like him.")
—Anonymous

His familiar guardian angel, Serendipity, revisited Tell. The cascade of troubles that began with the broken ankle accident proved to be temporary setbacks after he changed his habits and decided to shape up.

In the medical office where he received a complete physical checkup, he acted like his old self, the good self, drawing out smiles from others with his one-liners.

"Do you know why the Swiss invented Rösti (pan-fried potatoes and hash browns)? So they have an excuse to eat half a pound of butter for lunch!" he told the doctor.

At least the nurse laughed.

The joke backfired when the medico told him that his cholesterol was 635 and his triglyceride level was a whopping 723. To make matters worse, the doctor informed him that he had a diabetic condition.

"If I tell you all the things you shouldn't do, you would probably die of withdrawal symptoms," admonished the doctor, who handed him a guide list he wished Tell would follow. "Cut back on drinking alcohol—scotch, martinis, gin, for starters, have to be gone. You have to exercise. Take walks with your dogs along the canal behind your restaurant. Cut down daily caloric intake and drink more clean water."

"Yeah, I know, Bunny tells me to do that every day," Tell sighed. But this time he knew he was a walking time bomb of high blood pressure, diabetes, and heart disease and he vowed to make the changes.

"My doctor, due to excessive weight, cholesterol, and triglycerides, has me off nuts, chocolate, whole milk, cream, beef, pork, and caviar. No alcohol too. But I always have a glass of wine with meals. It's incredible. You can't eat anything this way."

Tell complained but he followed the regimen.

A year later, Tell's weight had dropped from 300 pounds to 240, a healthier weight for a man who was 6'3." More importantly, he had spent free time exercising, reading how to eat healthier, and eating a better diet. He added garlic to his cooking every other night. He sliced ginger root, let it soak overnight in water, and drank it every morning.

"The Germans say, '*Alles heilt*,' which means, 'It heals everything,'" he told friends.

Six days a month, he drank ginseng extract twice daily, and his cholesterol dropped to 218 with triglycerides at 264. He weaned off the Glucophage medication for his diabetes by breaking away from salt and butter. He replaced these with olive oil, fresh herbs, peppers, and other spices. He added another round of exercise as a daily discipline.

"I will not promise it will work for everyone," Tell wrote, "but it sure worked for me."

The visible difference in his shape and his mentality was unmistakable. The leg pain persisted, but he had learned to manage living with the constant, severe pain he felt every day. He was not out of the woods, but he intended to keep the diet and exercise changes to enable him to so impress Bunny that she would reunite with him. His good work not only changed his emotional outlook and prospects, but also brought him good news from an unexpected source. He remembered reading somewhere, "Good things happen when you take care of yourself."

* * *

A dinner patron at the Manor House turned out to be a surgeon connected with one of Greater Philadelphia's best hospitals at the University of Pennsylvania. He recommended a second opinion and X-rays on Tell's injured leg and offered a free consultation.

Tell took the surgeon up on the offer and visited the hospital. Complete X-rays found that the eighteen-inch metal pin, which had been placed in the right leg during the surgery after his fall, was installed incorrectly—perhaps even grounds for another lawsuit (besides QVC). The pin was spiraling up toward his knee and was about to break through his skin.

No wonder Tell was in pain.

A beloved and talented chef known all over the globe had been unable to work, barely able to walk, and under the influence of a powerful drug/alcohol combo to ease pain because a surgeon's malpractice left him with a shortened leg due to missing bone length. The subsequent side effects of the doctor's mayhem, and Tell's malaise, contributed to regretful activities and marital unhappiness that almost crashed the most important relationship Tell lived for in his personal life.

Faced with horrible 50/50 odds that he would lose his leg—odds explained to him by the new surgeon—Tell opted to endure the risk and resetting of the broken ankle and another surgery to install a new pin. In the end, his leg was spared amputation, but that wasn't the last surprise. The best miracle came after the surgery when serendipity made an unprecedented fourth appearance in Tell's life.

One of the nurses at the local hospital where the botched surgery had taken place stepped forward and volunteered information, which settled the investigation. The nurse told the attorney that she was present during the first surgery and that the surgeon had arrived drunk from a party. In other words, he performed major surgery on Tell's leg while under the influence of alcohol. Unbelievable.

Tell retaliated. He had been disgruntled and in pain since October 1999. He filed suit against the surgeon who botched his leg surgery and the hospital where it took place. Another suit in excess of 1.5 million dollars, which referred to the low back pain as a result of the fall at QVC, was filed with the Court of Common Pleas of Bucks County. Although backed by the report of Dr. Steven J. Valentino, who performed the corrective surgery, the two cases remained open and pending as late as mid-June of 2001. Three more years would go by—and Tell's hair would turn white—before the suits settled.

The suit against the hospital settled for what was, in Bunny's estimation, "not enough money, but [it had] become more important to devote our attentions to getting our marriage back together."

That reconciliation was not easy, but Bunny and Tell did work their way back and even felt they came out of it stronger than before. Together again, they visited family in southeast Florida and considered a permanent move south.

Tell interviewed at the famous Culinary Institute in Palm Beach, Florida, where he suggested he could conduct cooking classes. While he was offered work there, a long-term position was not in the offing.

The Restaurant School at Walnut Hill College in Philadelphia, however, did accept Tell's résumé and credentials. In fact, the school's administrative staff looked forward to his teaching of their cooking interns. They were only too happy to have "one of their own"—a local restaurant/kitchen legend—on board.

Pennsylvania's four seasons—not palm trees, humidity, and warm surf—were in the cards for Bunny and Tell, but, at least, here serendipity showed up often.

Bunny and Tell opted to weather whatever might come their way in Pennsylvania and to keep breathing.

But, serendipity had already visited four times. Had their luck run out?

83

A *"JE NE SAIS QUOI"*

"Wenn das Glas voll von Limetten ist stop me."
("When the glass is full of limes stop me.")

—Chef Tell

A year later in 2004, a Delaware River flood of historic proportions destroyed the Manor House operation, followed by another ruinous flood a year later.

Christine Hess was out of work and she still had two daughters to house, clothe, feed, and educate. She approached management at The Buck Hotel for a job.

During the course of her interview, Brian Ruhling Sr. the owner, asked, "Does this mean that Chef Tell is available?"

"As a matter of fact he is," she said.

Without missing a beat, Ruhling made a deal with Tell, who was able to bring in Hess. The name of the upper dining room changed to Chef Tell's

The Buck Hotel, Feasterville, PA

Top of the Buck and cooking classes were added. They were back in business again.

Serendipity had appeared an unprecedented *fifth time*! Even Tell had a hard time explaining it, and no one could deny that Chef Tell led a charmed life by any standard.

Tell wowed them here at The Buck

Tell's first cooking demonstration at The Buck was a success because of, as he put it, "f***ing CNN." (Although ironic with his pronouncements, he loved that people showed up. He just didn't want to make a big deal of it.)

Tell with Regis's producer Gelman on an outdoor *LIVE!* set

A crowd of women with their Chef Tell recipe books in hand filled the lobby and overflowed out the doors on day one. Small ads, which announced the grand opening with Chef Tell, and of course, f***ing CNN, had brought the ladies out. Held back by a velvet cordon across the bottom of the grand lobby stairway, the frenzied bunch buzzed with excitement. Seating upstairs was first-come-first-serve, and early arrivals hoped to be seated close to Chef Tell. After all, a "rock star" chef was a rare commodity in the sleepy Philly suburb of Feasterville.

Once the cordon was removed, the mad rush up the stairs filled more than one hundred chairs in less than a minute.

The chant of, "Chef Tell, Chef Tell, Chef Tell!" didn't let up until the man himself walked out onto his "set" to thunderous applause and screams.

Chef Tell put on a great show. From beginning to end, he delivered non-stop cooking tips and fast action. His usual barrage of irreverent remarks and throwaway one-liners delighted the ladies, who had come to see their idol in action. No one went home disappointed.

Tell at least appreciated the adulation. He would most times go out on the floor, turn on the charm, pose with fans, and answer questions. This time, though, after the cooking demo was complete, he said to Hess in the kitchen, "Time to do the f***ing, 'dancing bear' routine."

Tell walked out to the front room, smiled for the cameras, and gave his fans what they wanted. He was working harder physically than they would ever know.

About an hour later, with a cramped signing hand and his fill of autograph requests, Tell stormed back into the kitchen. He handed Hess an autographed photo of himself and said, "Here's *your* f***ing autograph!"—because they both knew she had never asked for one and never would.

Tell flashed his million-dollar smile when she looked up. They laughed so hard they cried. After she wiped her cheeks, Hess remarked, "Well, at least we know the marketing campaign works."

Tell had faced hardships that might have turned another person sour on the game of living, but now that he was winning—and for Tell winning meant confronting, moving forward, and keeping your mind on the ultimate prize until you win it—more than ever he wanted to taste the sweetness of victory: to have his own show. With Croesus he was doing it. He also had wanted to win Bunny back and he had done that.

Still, more than anything, he wanted what eluded him for all of his life: inner peace and understanding.

Later that opening night, after work was done at The Buck, Tell sat with employees at the bar and waited for the final sales figures. He nursed a plate full of lime slices and a glass of gin and tonic. With each new pour, he added another lime to the glass, telling the bartender, "When the glass is full of limes, stop me."

The take that day was very good. Tell broke out a cigar and lit it. He knew Hess, who was seated next to him, hated the smell and smoke, but tonight neither of them cared.

"Well, we fooled them one more day," he announced to no one as he stood up and hobbled out. He was tired, ready to go to bed and, inside, unrequited.

For nearly a quarter of a century, Tell had cooked and served German, Caribbean, French, Austrian, and continental courses of incomparable quality to hundreds of thousands of customers. He had seized opportunities and demonstrated his competence, live and on TV. He had shown the world a rare combination of training and personality, coupled with a flair for living large. He had *panache* and charisma. Tell's *"Je ne sais quoi"* was worthy, flaws and all. Yet he needed most of all to find a lasting measure of personal peace.

Advantage Home Care promo

Mercy Catholic: When Tell was
helped, he returned the favor.

84

IMPERFECT . . . STILL WORTH IT

"Ii placea sa faca alimentare și oameni fericiți."
("He loved to make food and people happy.")
—Chef Vasile Bageag

Monday is a "dark" (closed) day for most restaurants. Monday's anticipated fishing trip, planned for several weeks by a group of chefs, who worked together in downtown Philly, brought thoughts of hours of pleasure on the Delaware River. Without deadlines or fire-breathing executive chefs looking over their shoulders, leisure time and tight lines would be the only thing on their minds for at least twenty-four hours.

Unfortunately, Romanian chef Vasile Bageag and his buddies learned that Mother Nature would not cooperate with their plans. Daybreak brought a surprise mix of drizzle, wind, and dark clouds guaranteed to obscure any warm rays from the sun. The thought of standing waist-deep in the cold river waters drenched their dream day like a mixed salad under a deluge of balsamic, and turned off the group members' hopes.

A straw poll scratched the fishing plans. Instead, the circle of friends retreated to a nearby tavern.

Maybe the weather will change after a drink or two, Bageag thought as he lifted his first pint of beer to his lips. Midway through the second pint, he heard the TV weatherman predict rain for the rest of the day.

Glances outside at the darker-than-ever skies convinced the rest to stay put in the tavern. By lunchtime they were flying, powered by cognac and whiskey chased with strong beers. Fishing had not crossed their minds since mid-morning. Nonstop anecdotes and outlandish stories held forth late into the night.

Rather than sleep off the last twenty hours in his car, Bageag took the wheel and ventured up the ramp onto I-95. Not too far down the highway, he totaled his car. With few bruises to show for it, and no injuries to others, Bageag walked out of jail later that morning with a DUI on his record, a suspended license, and no means of private transportation.

Bageag was a wartime survivor with a carefree demeanor much like Tell's. Lean, five-foot-eight, a former Romanian Navy veteran, he took up cooking after he escaped death from Communist religious persecution in 1981. He worked in the downtown Philadelphia eatery where he found living a much safer proposition among his friends, at least up until his recent accident.

At the eatery, because of his formidable skill with knives and an uncanny ability to combine different foods into tasteful dishes, he'd been noticed. He had a bright future there—until the news of his DUI got him fired. Further camaraderie with his coworkers was thereafter put on hold. Without a car, it was going to be difficult for him to get another job in a kitchen, but he was not worried. He had been in worse situations. He started faxing his résumé all over town.

The résumé that Tell received on his fax machine was an answer to one of his prayers. He needed a sous chef at The Buck—someone reliable enough to cook and to oversee the operation behind the line, since Tell wanted to hobnob with the women out front. He also needed to sit down with customers rather than stand up in the kitchen, since his right leg had developed phlebitis.

Tell phoned Bageag and asked how soon he could come over to The Buck. Bageag explained his predicament, being without a car. Tell suggested the proper bus line to take and told Bageag he would wait for him.

Bageag "auditioned" with tarragon chicken, lamb pilaf, mixed green beans, and tomatoes that he cooked for Tell. Once Tell tasted the food, he leaned toward hiring him on the spot. Although The Buck pushed an American cuisine weighted more toward steaks and side dishes than European delicacies, Tell's palate told him all he needed to know about the younger Bageag's skills. But he needed proof that Bageag could manage kitchen personnel, so he inquired about his background and his journey to America.

From Bageag's answer, Tell learned that his mother had survived Communist turmoil and atrocities for more than half her life. She had helped her son escape the tyranny and come to America. She operated a vineyard and produced wine in the old country, at times in lots of two thousand liters. He told Tell, however, that he was not much of a wine-drinker—he preferred beer. He was, on the other hand, a connoisseur of cognac, which, of course, suited Tell.

Tell enjoyed Bageag's company the more they talked. Introducing different chefs to Bageag in the course of their meeting, he also observed how this new prospect interacted with them and was satisfied that he would be able to manage them. Further, Bageag had not held back when asked about how he got into his current situation. Bageag's honesty got him the job.

Tell hired Begeag and told him to stay and work the night. When the work went smoothly, it sparked the kindling of a good and long relationship.

* * *

While Upper Black Eddy will never be found in the Guinness Book of World Records as a party-magnet town, Buck employees and their friends thought it was a good enough place to wind down. Blowing off tensions and stresses built up from serving ever-growing numbers of hungry women at The Buck was reason enough to party, but a better one was to honor the memory of Chef Tell's Manor House.

When the Delaware River floods of 2004 and 2005 rose past Tell's place nestled under white oak, red maple, and river birch trees, the hard work and sweat-soaked hours of labor that had gone into making the place work were washed away. The building was now condemned and later would be torn down, but a farewell party could still be held.

The obvious place to have the get-together was on Tell's thirty-six-acre property up the hill. Bageag, Tell, and Bunny greeted the rest of the crew on Sunday as their hard-work shifts completed. Food, wine, and German beers on tap flowed into the wee hours of Monday.

Most revelers enjoyed a great time and then simply passed out in their cars parked on the grounds. For the trio of close friends, the perfect time for an early morning cook-in had arrived. A good meal would remedy their feelings of loss for the restaurant and replace the emptiness in their stomachs.

Either chef would have cooked for the other, but Bageag took charge. He placed a pan over a hot burner, poured in some fresh virgin oil, mixed in chopped sweet and hot peppers—the way he knew Tell liked them—and finished off his Sicilian-style calamari appetizer with a splash of white wine and flame. For Bunny, he made her favorite of his signature creations—a "mad roasted" eggplant salad.

Next, Bageag mixed finely ground beef with lamb and spices, formed the meat into small sausages, and sautéed them. The aromas alone could satisfy, but Tell and Bunny ate as Bageag watched with a smile, taking a little for himself.

Warmed apple strudel with a dollop of rice pudding on top capped the nosh.

Bageag cleaned up all of the party remnants in the kitchen and departed. After the guests were gone, and Tell and Bunny were alone, Tell walked outside and played with Sydney, throwing sticks that she retrieved again and again. Bunny watched through the dining room window.

Out of habit, and because they were not ready to sleep, Bunny pulled out two shovels and a couple of other gardening tools and handed some to Tell. In silence, they worked the rose garden not far from the bonfire site where Tell and Bunny often sat and talked as they sipped wine and watched the fire's flames reduce to glowing embers. On those nights, silent fireflies lit the evening air. When the sky was pitch black, Tell and Bunny gazed up to the Milky Way and watched shooting stars that appeared close enough to touch speed across the sky.

Bunny and Tell were the stars that touched each other. As she worked the garden beside Tell, Bunny asked herself *why do I stay with Tell?*

85

TOUGH LOVE & PURSUIT

"Love is an act of endless forgiveness, a tender
look which becomes a habit."
—Peter Ustinov

Tell trusted people, but some used him. By the same token, he did not easily trust those most trustworthy—his family.

"Tell had a fear that I would leave him if he failed at anything. That is what I felt was happening when—because he did 'it' the three times that I know of," Bunny recalled wistfully, not able to bring herself to say the word—infidelity.

I've stayed with Tell because I see through his weaknesses, she told herself. She thought that he seemed to collapse when hit with a financial brick wall, discovered a theft or a friend's betrayal. In other words, he caved when he was demoralized. These things do happen, but when temptations conquer willpower, one only comes face-to-face with more of one's weaknesses, not strengths.

Bunny kept thinking about Tell's strengths, about the good times that they shared. As their years together added up, those moments, remembered, became comforts—reasons to overlook shortcomings in the heat of day-to-day living together. She looked over at Tell and watched him—tilling the soil, pruning the roses, deep in his own thoughts—before she let her thoughts flow across her mind like a river.

We went to Mangia Bene, a restaurant in Flemington, New Jersey at least three times a month. We've gone to Italian, Thai, Chinese, Indian, and French restaurants—any cuisine that Tell would not cook. We drove on our days off, talked about history, international events, wine, the books we were reading—anything. We listened to music on our way to lunch or an early dinner.

Her thoughts shifted.

He loves Haitian art and modern art by Michèle Vaserely, which I can appreciate. We've got lots of mutual friends. We can talk—that's more than I can say for a lot of others we know. He still turns me on.

Then she remembered more about his larger value to the world around him, *Chefs play a kinder role in society. He gives to charity with his time and food. He sees what people need on a daily basis . . . hears the stories of what is happening around him and always wants to help.*

The scope of her thinking expanded: *In his profession you can never please everyone, all the time. Food is such a personal preference . . . how can anyone strive for perfection in such a field . . . but he does.* She was beginning to understand him now; understand why he had put them both through such ups and downs.

And then his real value finally sunk in: *Few rise to the top, which is a fleeting moment at best, but the one with the God-given gift—because that is what it is, and he is one of them—truly plays with fire!*

Tell wondered why Bunny sat back right then and looked as if a lightbulb had gone off in her head, but he said nothing. Instead, he delved into his thoughts about her, about love, about right and wrong, about his son, his grandson, and where he was right now. He considered that he enjoyed, more than anything else, Torsten and Angelika cooking for him while he played with little Max. They loved to cook *for him.* Tell even dubbed Torsten's risotto "100 out of 100 points."

The others left me, or I left them, but Bunny threw me out and still stayed—she didn't leave me. Nurse Germany left me cold, gone. Nicoletti—what a shame. Catherine—she stole me blind.

His thoughts were all over the place. From time to time, he looked over to Bunny, realizing—imperceptibly at first—that he had erected his own obstacles. *After all,* he thought, *the one constant in my messes was me. The other characters in my life's play have changed, but standing at center-stage . . . was just me.*

A wave of affinity that he loved Bunny in a way that he had not loved other women washed over him. He had said as much to trusted confidantes, but never realized the meanings of his words until this moment. Alone yet near her, he caught on to the depth of his love for this woman next to him.

Georges Perrier had told him another day, "This is the nature of our business, and what's in our blood. Forlorn days? Yes. Infidelities? Oh sure. But underneath, we [chefs] are all good men."

Tell found comfort in those prophetic words, because they returned a measure of self-respect to him. Another time, Perrier had spoken aloud what he thought, "My friend, Tell, you are married to a saint." And he agreed to himself that *Perrier is, in fact, right about that.*

Susanna Foo also had commented, "Tell had other trials with women, but he always kept coming back to Bunny, because his love for her was the real thing."

Bunny saw the good in Tell, "He had a giving side. He gave of his time to charities even when he had no time. He was generous with his friends to a fault. He gave of his time and money to animal shelters, shelters for women, the Lutheran and Catholic churches, community clean-up projects, Save the Swordfish, and Philabundance."

She continued, remembering a time that they had just arrived in Vermont, where they liked to go for winter activities, "A phone call from Regis's assistant said they were in a bind—they had no guest for a show. She asked Tell if he would appear on short notice. Tell agreed to go, no questions asked. We left for the studio in Manhattan immediately. That wasn't the first time he helped his friend. He did it simply because Regis was a friend who asked. Tell would do that any time, from anywhere, to help a friend."

Through their highs and lows together since 1982, Bunny watched Tell work hard like the workaholic he was. Now she could see that he still loved to jump in and try new things.

"I came to realize that looking at life through Tell's eyes was a child's view of the world—so full of fascination and wonderful imagination. His whole world was something to be curious about and it rubbed off on me."

However, remnants of his early life lingered in his mind and could be restimulated at any time. When they activated, life became unpredictable and simulated a roller coaster.

Bunny continued, "He had this bad side of him that would self-destruct, or make him give up, when things went badly."

Although decisive in the kitchen, beyond it Tell enacted unresolved "maybes" left over in his mind, like the major upheaval that left his brother and him on non-speaking terms. His inability to help Nicoletti before she died, and his inability to prevent people stealing from his business despite his having helped them, made it difficult for him to get close to others, especially family.

To his mind's way of thinking, family was not trustworthy. He just could not cross the broken chasms of his memories. Instead, Tell purchased his "license to survive" the only way he knew how—he offered food and laughter to anyone he liked. Yet, he did it all on his own terms, always. Aside from Bunny, Tell seldom allowed others to see the vulnerability that he felt. There was the public persona Chef Tell, and, for Bunny, there was the man she loved, who loved her in return.

Like most chefs, running the finances of his restaurant business was not Tell's forté. The only economics taught in cooking apprenticeships in his day was the economical use of whatever was in the cooler or freezer. Consequently, he handled foods very efficiently. No waste in the kitchen was one of his trademarks, but he didn't do as well with money beyond that.

"I almost think he was just too busy—too happy, really—inside the kitchen to have time to care enough anywhere else," Bunny surmised, echoing a common opinion about chefs, especially the really good ones.

"Handling the business side of our work is not what we do best," offered Chef Foo.

Chef Perrier concurred, "I prefer to put my hands on the pots more. Administration just makes me very tired."

Then again, one wouldn't expect Willie Shoemaker to fill out the Morning Line or Mickey Mantle to make out the game roster for the New York Yankees.

Ask the really good ones: they will tell you the greatest chefs are artists. Artists are trusting, vulnerable, sensitive beings with unique insight. They create in time zones far into the future, dreaming the dreams for society. Yet in present time, artists are vulnerable.

What would we do with Michelangelo and Van Gogh or Escoffier, Beard, Point, Child, or Chef Tell if they returned? How would we treat them? Knowing who they are, would we protect them and let them do what they do best? Or would we try to change and mold them—*again*—like square pegs into round holes?

Asked about Tell's importance in her life today, Susan Winston offered a significant reply: "How valuable was Chef Tell, then and now? Here it is almost five years past his death, and I still want his cooking, still miss his food," she lamented, ". . . and I've tasted some of the best of the other contemporary chefs."

Tell's long-time Grand Cayman friend, Lenny Mattioli, noted: "Tell was a truly unique professional in the kitchen. If a customer's complaint with his food was knowledgeable and informed, he could take criticism. But if the customer, for instance, said, 'There's too much parsley'—and there wasn't any in the dish—Tell engaged."

In the words of another important friend (who wishes anonymity), "Tell's legacy should not get smaller; it should grow. Why? Because he was a decent human being, born into the roughest of worlds; because he fought his way to a better place and then shared his spoils; because he grew up surrounded by unhappy people, yet tried his best in his way to bring happiness to others—and in the largest part, he succeeded at that.

"Even in the middle of situations that he created, he ensured things would come out better than they were before—that people survived better or easier in the end. With Tell, things might have gotten awfully messy at times, sure, but most of his outcomes went right. Chef Tell made things go right. I miss him now and I will always miss him."

86

COMMUNION

"Never bereue, was Sie tun, es ist es nicht wert."
("Never regret a thing you do. It's not worth it.")

—Chef Tell

After another appearance on *LIVE! with Regis & Kathie Lee*, Tell drove to the Kule family's summer house on Long Beach Island in Ship Bottom, New Jersey. Once there, he met up with Bunny and other family members. Dan, his brother in law, had returned from a half-day fishing trip with his nephew, Bobby Pfeil, with a mess of twenty-five bluefish. Tell volunteered to prep and cook the fish.

Climbing the outdoor stairway to get a stored sauté pan, Tell felt dizzy and out of breath, his skin flushed. Red-faced and perspiring, he sat down, inhaled a few slow, deep breaths, and looked past the sand dunes at the blue waters of the Atlantic.

Dan witnessed Tell's trouble and walked over to him.

"Tell, are you okay?"

"Yeah, yeah sure; I'm alright," he lied.

He told Dan that he just got winded and needed to sit down for a minute, but he was afraid. Dan joined him on the stairs but he didn't press Tell.

Tell spoke, "You know, Dan, I am at peace with myself and my love with Bunny." He paused and breathed deeply again. "I tell you another thing, Dan, never regret a thing you do. It's not worth it."

Before Dan had a chance to ask Tell what he meant, Bunny came outside and asked for Dan's help inside the house. Dan stood up to go, and he hugged Tell.

Feeling sturdier, Tell finished his climb upstairs and down. He was soon in the kitchen, cooking bluefish. The incident and the conversation were left forgotten.

Had he experienced similar warnings before, when he was alone?

* * *

On October 20, 2007, Tell's protégé, Chef Freddie Duerr, opened his first restaurant, the Rising Sun Inn in Franconia, Pennsylvania. The renovated dining room and large stone fireplace retained the character and charm of the 1739 structure's colonial days. It had been a former stagecoach stop known as Gerhart's Tavern and it housed the Liberty Bell overnight during the siege of Philadelphia in the fall of 1777, when American troops moved the iconic symbol from Philadelphia to Allentown to prevent its capture by British and Hessian troops.

Duerr's detailed attention to the grand opening was admirable. In particular, he reserved the table nearest the fireplace with a name plate inscribed, RESERVED FOR CHEF TELL.

When they arrived, Chef Duerr greeted Bunny and Tell, who handed him a bottle of Rhinelander White, as they stepped into his unique, bison-themed establishment. He guided them through the building, including upstairs. From the window of the Liberty Bell room on the second floor, he showed them the adjacent eighteenth-century barn that he had refurbished into a room suitable for up to one hundred guests for special occasions like Oktoberfest and weddings.

In the main dining room, Duerr showed the reserved table to Tell. The surprised look on Tell's face summarized their twenty-four years together. Duerr's gesture moved Tell almost to tears. If tears did well up in his eyes as he and Freddie hugged that would be forgiven but certainly never forgotten. At the time, Tell was not able to express into words what the gesture meant to him, but he felt the satisfaction of knowing that he had paid forward to his chosen apprentice, now good friend, all of the knowledge that he had received from others in his lifetime of kitchen work—*especially from his dear mother.*

Duerr lingered at the table and reviewed the night's menu with his VIP guests. In Tell's honor, he offered not only Tell's signature Schweinepfeffer, but also Lobster Chef Freddie's Way—Chef Tell's Way, which was, *really*, Chef Herold's Way—and New York Sirloin of Bison *au poivre* (peppercorn crusted with brandied demi-glace), which was, for real, Freddie's Way. Also, Carrots Timbale—puréed carrots in heavy cream with nutmeg. His own rendition of a recipe handed down from Tell's grandmother, Freddie's German Apple Cake, complemented the dessert list.

The Saturday-night gala was standing room only. The Erhardts enjoyed Chef Freddie's beautiful restaurant and his well-prepared foods. In the kitchen after dinner, they expressed compliments to the smiling chef and his crew for a "job well done."

Tell and Bunny agreed to return a week later to dine with Duerr on October 27. In the days of the week that followed neither Freddie or Tell called each other.

* * *

On Friday, the 26th day of October, Tell awakened at twilight—5:47 a.m. In the dim light of the predawn, he saw from his upstairs bedroom window that the fall leaves on the ground were damp from the coolness of the night. He showered and dressed alone.

Bunny had stayed overnight in her rental property on Long Beach Island. She had a small following as an agent with a local broker on the island, and one of her connections led to the purchase of the island property.

By 6:30 a.m., Tell had cooked himself a breakfast and cleaned up the kitchen. He left the house twenty minutes later. He walked across the dewy lawn to the old barn building which, in part, served as a carport for three vehicles. He selected the silver BMW X5. He pulled backward from the barn and then drove slowly forward on the gravel pathway to the edge of his property where the main road ran past his land.

Because there was limited visibility at the main road, he looked both ways before proceeding west toward Highway 611. At the light, he turned south and headed toward Sam's Club in Willow Grove, where he intended to pick up supplies for the catering business with his Commercial Vendor Card. On the way there, he punched on Sirius Radio for music and then phoned Bunny.

When her cell phone rang on the nightstand, Bunny answered half-asleep, "Good morning, man." Tell smiled. He recognized the familiar salutation that Bunny always said to him. He made small talk about Fifi, who had climbed onto the bed and lay next to Bunny, until she woke up enough to roll over, sit up, and ask about his plans for the day.

Bunny rubbed her eyes, yawned, and stretched as Tell told her about his shopping plans at Sam's and about the cooking class he would teach at the Walnut Hill College later that morning at 11:00 a.m.

They agreed to talk after his class and again later in the evening.

"He told me he was almost at Sam's Club, so I knew where he was. And then I told him, 'I love you. Go be a star'—something I told him before every television appearance."

Those were the last words Bunny would ever speak to Tell.

Once the supplies were loaded into the SUV, Tell left the Sam's Club parking lot. He would have headed south toward Walnut Hill on Highway 611.

With his favorite 1961, Willie Nelson–penned song, "Crazy," sung by Loretta Lynn on the radio—"I'm crazy/crazy for feeling so lonely . . . crazy/ crazy for feeling so blue"—this day he headed north, instead, toward his home.

Tell never made it to his cooking class at The Walnut Hill College Restaurant School in Philadelphia. By noon, Bunny had not heard from him. Traveling from Warminster along Route 611, a short shot to home, something undetermined and unusual happened to Tell—the only evidences were a long scrape and a cracked window and mirror along the passenger side of his BMW and the items he purchased that morning at Sam's Club, which were still in the car.

The local hospital on the highway where he drove was the same one where Tell received the botched surgery on his leg. If he was experiencing chest pains or having trouble breathing, he did not stop there to get checked out, although that might have saved his life.

After he parked the loaded SUV in the barn carport at his estate, Tell did not stop and talk with the tenant living in the barn's converted apartment as he had done frequently in the past. He was, therefore, alone when he crossed the grassy yard from the barn to the stone and mortar main house.

He was not well. Something so troubling was occurring that he didn't have the presence of mind to call Bunny or 911.

* * *

Bright daylight burned through the tall windows of Tell's wood-beamed home as he entered and stumbled past the empty dining table and then the cool stove's silent gas burners where the kitchenware was washed, dried, and stowed away.

Tell stepped up one small stair into the pre-Revolutionary living room, staggered across the small room, and leaned heavily on the wood desk where he studied and wrote his recipe books. He looked westward at the early-American wood fence that bordered his property and blinked several times as he tried unsuccessfully to draw deep breaths. He turned to his right and looked at the dusty memorabilia—his life as a chef, TV celebrity, father, husband, and family man, which spanned more than half a century, was set up on the built-in shelves.

Not well at all, short of breath and gasping for air, Tell clutched his right hand to his chest and left arm and scanned the walls of the room. Off-balance and turning to his left, so disoriented that he did not reach out for his nitro just a few steps away, he collapsed onto the leather couch, Fifi's bed, and closed his eyes forever.

Silence overcame the room. Dust motes drifted across the sunbeams streaming into the room. Somewhere a bell tolled.

* * *

Tell Erhardt's lifetime was a steeplechase, and the gun went off the night he was born. But not for a million reasons would Tell ever want to cut short his daring run because he loved every minute of his incredible life; he loved the journey.

His shooting star simply burned out sooner than expected.

In a 2004 interview for *The Intelligencer*, reported by food writer Betty Cichy, Tell assessed his accomplishments: "I am content with my quieter life and my satisfaction in knowing I played a leading role in a culinary revolution that turned chefs into TV stars. All these chefs today—Flay, Puck, Lagasse, Batali, and the others—I wish them success. I had my run. It was a good life. As I got older, I got better."

Ruhe in Frieden. (Rest in Peace.)

EPILOGUE - PART ONE

PALPABLE GRIEF

"He was the first of the great showman chefs.
Up until his era, chefs stayed in the kitchen."
—former *Philadelphia Inquirer* restaurant
critic Elaine Tait

The weather on Friday, October 26, 2007, was clear, still sunny from the day before. Bunny was working out on Long Beach Island, New Jersey, in the shoreline community of Barnegat Light. She had traveled there a few days earlier to oversee renovations on her beach rental property, which she dovetailed with work at the Prudential real estate office in the same town. Working full time in Philadelphia, Tell had little time for his dog Fifi, so Bunny took Fifi, whom she liked to have with her on the trip to the shore.

On this day the temperature hovered in the 40s to low 50s. The late-night weather report had promised rain sometime on Friday afternoon, so Bunny's plan was to check with the renovation crew early, work her shift at the real estate office, and then leave Saturday morning for home. She had only been at the beach for two nights.

The bottom of the beach house was getting gutted when Bunny arrived on-site from her overnight stay in a house she had listed in Surf City—a place that the owner let her stay in during her renovation project. The same familiar workers had already renovated the top floor and they were ripping out the first-floor kitchen and bathroom now.

Bunny had scheduled morning floor time at the Prudential Zack Barnegat Light office on Twenty-Ninth Street and had to be there from 9:00 a. m. until 1:00 p. m. Traffic to the office had been slow and Bunny was feeling antsy. She was relieved when her associate, Rick, arrived early for his floor shift and did not mind her leaving early when she asked.

Since the crew at the beach house would need her input on how to proceed later after work, Bunny called and spoke with them briefly again on her way to pick up Fifi to take her to the beach. A usual walk for both of them included the beach access on Twenty-Ninth Street, and Fifi was excited and ran ahead of Bunny once she sensed their destination.

Knowing that she could still reach Tell before he would be at work, Bunny tried to reach him by phone several times as she drove between Tenth Street and Twenty-Ninth.

Fifi ran wildly and playfully on the beach. She circled around and around and ran down to the ocean shoreline water and back up to her . . . teasing Bunny to hurry up and play with her.

The sky, the temperature, the breeze in the air, and the beach invited— the proverbial calm of warmth and bright sunlight before the storm.

Suddenly, walking down the dunes entrance to the beach, a very bad feeling slammed into Bunny. She felt in the worst way that Tell should be there with her. Frustrated that he was not, she yelled out to him, "Tell, where are you? You should be with us!"

Though the feeling gnawed at her, she played with Fifi at the beach for about half an hour before leaving.

Returning to the Tenth Street house, she met again with her handy man, Ed, and his crew and went over what needed to be done or purchased to complete the work. She then drove with FiFi to the Home Depot off the island to pick up items for the house. Along the way, she continued to try and reach Tell.

Heading off the island and crossing the causeway, Bunny concluded something was amiss. She had the carriage house tenant's phone number and she knew he would be home. Not knowing what was up, she decided that even if Tell thought she was crazy, she would have the tenant, Tom, go over to the main house and knock on the door to advise Tell that Bunny was trying to reach him.

Bunny asked that Tom call her back when he got over to the house.

Tom called when he reached the house and knocked on the door. He said that he was knocking, and no one was answering.

Bunny then asked Tom to walk inside and yell in to Tell, which he did. No answer.

Bunny then asked Tom if the BMW X5 was in the driveway, hoping that it was not. But Tom said yes.

Now Bunny felt a sinking feeling that something definitely was not right.

Tom stayed on the phone with Bunny as he walked back to the house. He was on the phone with her when he walked through the empty kitchen into the living room.

"Tell is on the couch, Bunny, and he is not moving," Tom said.

"What do you mean, 'he's not moving?'" Bunny asked.

"He's not moving."

Bunny asked him what he meant again, and he told her that he was not moving.

Tom had walked over to Tell and determined there was no pulse.

Bunny asked, "Is Tell dead?" and he replied, "Yes."

Bunny screamed, "Are you sure?"

He repeated, "He is gone." And in a panic, he asked, "What should I do?"

Bunny told him that he must call the police. She said she would call George, Tell's close friend, and that she would have him go over to the house immediately to help him.

With that, Bunny hung up the phone. Pouring rain lashed out at the parking lot of the Home Depot and at her windshield. Bunny sat unblinking and sobbing.

With Fifi coiled in fear in the back seat, Bunny called her Dad and spoke with him at length. She then called her eldest sister, Tee, and told her that she would need her help, which she received immediately.

Bunny then placed the call to George and asked, "Please go and make certain that Tell's body is not taken from the house until I make it home."

George, on the other hand, tried to advise Bunny not to drive home in bad weather. He also offered her caring consolation, but Bunny decided that she had to make it home, no matter the weather or her condition.

First, she had to drive back to the beach house and retrieve her belongings, not knowing when she would return. There she informed Ed, who was in shock right away, asking twice what had happened.

On the difficult drive home, Bunny prayed for the strength to complete the drive as she fought back blinding tears. She clutched the wheel and tried the best she could to breathe normally.

"I picked up my things on the island, made sure Fifi was alright for the long trip, and backtracked off the Island. The bad weather stayed with me all the way home. The usual 2.5-hour trip stretched out to more like four that night.

"There was a desolate long stretch that went through the Jersey Pines—a state park/Air Force base—there I called Torsten and told him that his father had died. We spoke for about forty-five minutes, which helped me.

"At the house, when the Medic asked if I wanted an autopsy, I declined."

Tom, earlier, having called the local authorities after hearing again from Bunny, went back into the house to stay with Tell's body and wait for George. The men then waited with the authorities for Bunny, who, when she did arrive about four hours later, was stopped on her property before she made it to the main house.

"I finally made it to the house around 10:00 p.m. The police stopped me at the barn and in the rain asked me questions before they would let me see Tell. They asked me if he had an insurance policy. I asked them if they thought I killed him and laughed, saying deliriously, 'That would be something Tell would laugh about.'

"Finally, they let me go into the house."

Pastor Rex, who had been called by Bunny and arrived in the interim, did not wish for Fifi to be let into the house, but Bunny insisted that she must see him, so she would know what had happened. Fifi came in, smelled him up and down, and lay down next to him at his feet.

"He was found in the house and he looked peaceful," Bunny said to Victoria Lang, one of her closest friends, by phone. Victoria, of course, was stunned but listened and consoled Bunny.

Tell was found on the couch, leaning back like he had found some rest. After Tom and George, the police, and the detectives departed, Bunny was alone with the pastor, Fifi, and Tell. She placed his head on her lap and said her private goodbye. Earlier, she had phoned two friends, J. D. and his girlfriend, Bernadette, to come and stay with her, but they would arrive later.

"I was left with the pastor, Fifi, and Tell. The Pastor said he would call the local funeral director, and they would take Tell. We waited for more than two hours. Finally, they arrived around one a.m.

"The elder, seventy-something funeral director showed up with his son and informed us that we would have to put Tell's body on a gurney, so the body could be taken out. I was told by the son that he needed help moving Tell—he has too heavy."

The Pastor and Bunny took the chef's legs and completed the *uneasy* task of getting the body onto the gurney from the couch, almost dropping him.

"My friends finally showed up, and Pastor Rex left with the funeral people."

Bunny stayed up for a little while and talked things out with her friends and then retired to the upstairs bedroom with Fifi.

* * *

The interns at the restaurant school, who wondered why Tell had not shown up for classes on Friday—until the news hit the media and the Internet—offered to cater the planned reception.

"To me, Tell Erhardt seemed to be a constant success," said Restaurant School president Daniel Liberatoscioli, "... he was a dynamic, outgoing, vivacious character and he grabbed every opportunity with two hands. He was a great role model for our students."

Over the next few days, Christine Hess and the A-team assisted Bunny with the logistics of planning and staging a funeral service and reception, which would be attended by three hundred people. Reverend Rex arranged for Tell's church service to be held on the morning of his birthday at St. Luke's in Ferndale.

Bunny's three sisters flew in from Florida and California to be with her. One of her four brothers and his wife lived close by—they helped as requested. On Bunny's request, another brother wrote the eulogy that he would deliver at the church's memorial ceremony.

* * *

On November 5, 2007, Tell's birthday, the air was cool, but the sun felt warm in a cloudless blue sky. During the church ceremony, bright orange leaves fell from Tell's favorite tree back at the estate.

About noon, three hundred friends, family members, chefs—some from as far back as the earliest Marriott days and the later Cayman Island days, business associates, and cooking interns from all over the globe gathered to bid their friend and mentor farewell and to celebrate his life.

The scalloped edges of white, open-sided canvas tents erected for the event fluttered from breezes that soft-shoed through the leaves of the estate's scattered black oaks. Men, women, and children mingled in honor of the man they knew was a damned good chef. They were certain they would miss his cooking as much as miss him.

Guests reconnected with friends long out of touch. New acquaintances shared small talk and anecdotes. Immediate family and relatives closed quarters. No one talked about tomorrow—only the immediate past held their attention.

Tell's interns prepared and cooked German sauerbraten, sautéed Wiener schnitzel, and the fallen chef's signature dish, Schweinepfeffer mit Spaetzle, which had been cooked by Chef Bageag from a menu developed by Chef Duerr. They also delivered his large cake, which they had planned to surprise him with on his birthday.

The liquid comforts of Rhineland whites, rosés, and reds, alongside endless barrels of German beers, beckoned. Glasses and steins rose in toast again and again to their departed friend.

Amid the conviviality, palpable grief hung in the air. Jagged holes of loss gaped where the larger-than-life, mustachioed man had carved a place inside of the attendees drawn in by the vacuum of his absence.

The disc jockey spinning vinyl for ambience scratched her turntable to a halt. She picked up a microphone and talked about Tell. At first few listened, but as her quiet words rippled across the party, people leaned forward, eager to hear every syllable.

Interns capping Sterno tins, packing up serving dishes, and breaking down empty coffee urns drifted toward the main tent. Catering personnel washing dishes, drying glasses, and restocking the kitchen shelves in the main house walked outside and stood among them.

Between every spoken sentence the rustling leaves of the tree situated in the center of the crowd punctuated the air above Tell's loyal ninety-pound Rottweiler Fifi, who lay with her head upon her paws and watched.

The disc jockey concluded, and people were laughing. F-bomb recounts of famous Chef Tell quips sprinkled among ribald anecdotes and bombastic incidents left people guffawing and wiping soft tears away from their eyes.

Another guest stepped up and took over, "Well, I have my own Chef Tell story, and here goes . . ." And then another and another stepped up. By the time the sun slipped below the treetops west of the manor's

Mr. and Mrs. Tell Erhardt

Tell and Torsten Erhardt

stone-walled border, twenty or so people had regaled the rest with reminiscences, told through laughter and teary-eyed pauses.

Then there was nothing more to be said or done but raise the final
toast and say with glasses held high, "*AUF WIEDERSEIN, TELL!*"

The essence of Erhardt's persona lingered on lips and minds well into
the late-evening hours. The eldest of guests had bid adieu. Hangers-on—
mostly family and servers close to Bunny—lingered in the master chef's
dining room and kitchen. Unwilling to fall asleep, they watched the large
bonfire's glowing flames through the windows and heard its wood crackle
and shift as sparks headed for the Milky Way. In a way that was personal
to each family member and close friend who lingered, unwilling to let
go and go home, the bonfire represented the arc of Tell's life: tinder burst
into small notes of fire, which then roared into a high-heat display of
marvelous, tall flames stoked by combustible materials and relationships,
literally singeing those who ventured too close—and, in the end, passing
skyward as flickers of fading light.

"To me, it really felt like his spirit was set free as those sparks raced
to the sky," said Tee Pfeil, the eldest of Bunny's sisters.

Inevitably though, November's chill captured what was left of the
evening, and the glowing embers whispered down to lifeless, gray ash.

EPILOGUE - PART TWO

PEACE & UNDERSTANDING

"All of the contrasting poles of his life were sharply etched: the restless departures and the search for stillness at home; the diversity of experience and the harmony of a unifying spirit; the security of religious dogma and the anxiety of freedom."
—*Siddhartha*, by Hermann Hesse

There is more truth inside each of us than we let ourselves know. That which opens our hearts and uplifts us to care for others beyond ourselves is innate. Chef Tell sensed this.

At first, he sought the answer to war—for war surrounded him at birth. When war fell upon his home and later raged inside him, he reached out through worlds of sensation—food, women, celebrity, parties, and drink—but was not satisfied.

Over time, windows opened. True love and friendship broke the ice. Though he nearly drowned before he realized that he must give true love to receive true love, he conquered the mysterious waters of love.

Tell entered and passed through many portals in his lifetime. With each progression, he picked up discarded, broken pieces of a puzzle that he discovered, at last, to be his self. By assuming responsibility for each

Bunny attends a 2008 Farewell Event for Tell on Grand Cayman

piece, his certainty of self as a being continued to rise right up to the day his body gave out.

Chef Tell's personality and experiences crystallize his link to such illustrious chefs and food personalities as da Como, Carême, Escoffier, Point, Beard, and Child. But will the next generation of TV-chef, cooking personalities—Batali, Bourdain, Colicchio, Lagasse, Pépìn, Ray, Ripert, Flay, Morimoto, Stone, Guarnaschelli, Sanchez, Burrell, Zakarian, Freitag, Garcés, and Cora, to name a few—acknowledge his historic feats and crown him "America's *Pioneer* TV Showman Chef"?

Does it matter if they do, or if they don't? He already left more than a legacy of recipes and television segments in his wake. Would it even matter to Friedemann Paul Erhardt? His personal answer would likely be, "If it makes someone happier, of course it does."

We do know this: the small German boy with very large dreams to touch millions of lives, to cook for the world, and to make people laugh . . . made his dreams come true. Ten days shy of his sixty-fourth birthday, he discovered the certainty that he had so long and so hard fought for: the peace and understanding of knowing who he really is.

What more could he have wished for? What more could we wish for him? *What more can we hope for ourselves?*

END

AUTHOR'S NOTE

Not everyone believes that spirits survive body death, but the spirits sure do. For seventeen months, Tell told me so.

Tell's welcome company as I worked brought me laughter, fits, sleepless nights, and tears of joy—at times, almost more than one could bear in small windows of time. I wouldn't trade the experience for the world and I will never be the same because of Tell Erhardt.

This book was a personal journey for me. The research and writing of his life story revealed the generosity of his spirit. Tell will likely remain an indelible part of my life for eons to come.

Maybe you, too, will feel the same way; maybe, having read his story, you do now.

* * *

Lest anyone think that Tell never "gave back," he was a big supporter of Philabundance. The Philabundance mission is "to reduce hunger and food insecurity in the Delaware Valley [Pennsylvania] by providing food access to those in need in partnership with organizations and individuals. Philabundance is the region's largest hunger relief organization. In fiscal 2011, Philabundance acquired 21 million pounds of food, distributed 19 million pounds in its service area and exported 2 million pounds of food to assist other area food banks."

Shira Rosenwald, marketing manager for Philabundance in 2011, wrote, "For a golf event, Chef Tell donated a dinner party cooked by him as one of the prizes. He attended the event and helped get the price of the item up nice and high. After the winner was announced, Tell went back to the runner up and said that if he'd pony up the difference—an additional $100—Chef Tell would cook for him, too! So it was a great event with a big impact."

A line that pretty much sums up Chef Tell's entire lifetime.

To make contributions, contact Philabundance at www.Philabundance.org.

* * *

In 2004, Iron Chef Cat Cora, Food Network's first female Iron Chef, founded *Chefs for Humanity* to bring the culinary community together in an effort to raise awareness and provide resources for educational, emergency, and hunger-related causes. The organization is committed to promoting nutrition education, hunger relief, and emergency and humanitarian aid to reduce hunger worldwide.

The Author donates a contribution to Chefs for Humanity for every book sold, in honor of Chef Tell, who would have helped Iron Chef Cora's organization. To make further donations to Chefs for Humanity, contact:

Chefs for Humanity
c/o Jamie Wolf, Esq.
Pelosi, Wolf, Effron & Spates, LLP
The Woolworth Building
233 Broadway
Suite 2208
New York, NY 10279

LAST WORDS

t Tell's final birthday reception, invited guests publicly shared fond stories about him. At the author's request, several guests graciously agreed to share their reminiscences for the book. Here they are in their own words:

Tell Erhardt was a man of truly excellent passion! Tell used his ability to make people feel at home. He was our number one greeter each week, and the people loved him. Never did he show anything but open kindness to everyone who came through the door.

This was another trademark of this great man. His welcome attitudes made you feel at home in any restaurant he opened and managed. He was dedicated to whatever he did, and it had to be the best, no questions asked. Tell was a perfectionist.

He was elected to the Council of the congregation and became a fearless leader. At times, members would try and negate the progress of the congregation, only to be confronted by this imposing figure of a man, who would just as soon invite you to worship here or lead you to the door inviting you to find another place to worship. Other members of Council found courage to provide strong leadership in tough times, due to his style and faith commitment.

The children loved him! He would address them with a gentleness and kindness that was never lost upon them. Tell was always looking for answers to life's persistent questions. In his way, it seemed he thought that a child might hold the key.

There was more to Tell than just the food and fun. He was looking for something, at times impatient at not finding the answer. During his time with us at St. Luke, I saw a man bigger than life, which could lead people with courage and strength while being a gentle and kind man of faith. I wish we had more time, for I miss our conversations and I miss his leadership. While we could disagree on some things, he would listen and grow, whether learning or leading.

Tell led the Peach Festival Committee, taught baking to the children and gave cooking classes for adults. He volunteered for every activity that involved food and festivities. He helped me entertain the pastors of the Lutheran Conference at a luncheon that is still talked about—the food was beyond measure and his presence made things memorable.

Tell helped prepare the Mother/Daughter Banquet each year and ran the kitchen with skill and patience. His temper could at times flare up but always to the betterment of those to whom it was directed. Tell knew what worked, and what would not—better to listen and work with him toward a successful activity than to disregard his advice and counsel in matters of food.

Somehow life is emptier these days without Fifi greeting me at the door, the aromas of Tell's kitchen, and the invite to a glass of scotch before dinner. I gained much from our relationship in both body mass and wisdom!

—**Pastor William Rex, St. Luke Evangelical
Lutheran, Ferndale, PA.**

* * *

Tell's students sure knew what he wanted—a big, fat party full of food, drink, friends and fun, that was all Tell. It was typical of the kind of generous affair Tell would throw for his friends and a party he would have been the center of. It was clear that he was missing. As much as we all were enjoying the lovely weather, the beautiful setting and the fabulous food, it just wasn't the same without Tell there. His large presence was bigger than life—and that life was gone. My dear friend was gone. The mood lightened a bit as everyone started passing the microphone around and recounting favorite Chef Tell stories. Here was mine:

When my fiancé, Tony, and I decided to get married, we wanted it to be on a beach. The only people we knew with a house on a beach were

Tell and Bunny. When we asked if we could have the wedding at their house in Grand Cayman, we wondered if they would agree, but they were thrilled! Typical Tell and Bunny. And in typical Tell style, he catered the affair grandly. Everyone was having a fabulous time and eventually wound up in the water fully clothed. Tell and I were standing on a small hill on the beach looking at my father and my girl friends frolicking in the water, and Tell said to me: "Those f***ing rum punches, they do it every time!" I cracked up! And, typical of Tell's generous nature, when I asked him for the bill at the end of the night, he waived me off, saying: "I'm a Chef—what am I going to give you for a present, a toaster?" That was Tell. He would give you the shirt off his back.

—**Victoria Lang and Tony Baarda,**
personal friends

* * *

Light peeked through the floorboards of the guest room [upstairs] in Tell and Bunny's historic farmhouse, so did the kitchen vapors. I was awakened at about five in the morning by the enticing smells of stock reducing and the sound of his clogs hitting the wooden floor.

I remember a particular morning with my young son at my side, who also tended to awaken early, tiptoeing down the tight circular stairway—because my sister [Bunny] who was accustomed to these noises was still asleep—to join Tell in the kitchen. We made eggs and he ribbed me, as he always did, with his off-color jokes and teasing. It was his way. If Tell didn't like you, he ignored you. If he liked you, you got teased and chided.

I remember when I first met him. I was in boarding school. His height was the first thing that made an impression on me. God, he was tall. My roommate, who knew of him from Chestnut Hill, where he ran the hotel for many years, said to me, "He's not 'that' famous." What did she know, she was a girl who put butter and cream cheese on a bagel and then covered it with salt. She thought a gourmet delicacy was dipping Fritos into cream cheese. Yes, he was 'that' famous. If he began his career today, he would have a show of his own, like Rachel Ray. Let it be said, that without Chef Tell, Julia Child, the Galloping Gourmet, and Wolfgang, there would not be a Rachel Ray, an Iron Chef, or a Hell's Kitchen.

Tell was above all, generous. He was always out at a church picnic or a fundraiser for someone. He had a caustic streak and he could definitely rub people the wrong way, but his benevolence made up for it. He was a man you could never forget, if you met just once. You would like him or hate him, or both, but you simply could not experience him and not leave with a lasting impression. He was a man who lived his life according to his own dictate. Sometimes this created waves—sometimes tidal, sometimes ripples—often humorous.

Following my mother's funeral, Tell and the rest of the family were relaxing poolside at the Gulfstream Bath and Tennis Club in Delray Beach, Florida. The manager of the club came over and whispered to me to follow him. In a quiet hallway he discussed with me the problem of Tell's wearing his very European Speedo.

"They are not permitted at the club," he said.

I felt like saying to him, "Jesus, buddy, the guy is six-foot-seven [he seemed 'that' tall] and has a bad attitude—YOU tell him he can't wear that!" Instead, I nodded my head and calmly went out to ask Tell to cover up a bit.

Tell's response was, "Tell the manager to go f*** himself. You pay for this club so I will wear what I f***ing please." And, that was that.

Tell swam and sunbathed in that Speedo the rest of the afternoon without a care. To this day he is the only person who has ever gotten away with a Speedo bathing at that club.

—**Francesca Kennedy, sister-in-law**

* * *

Tell was a big bombastic guy who could cook like hell! And I miss him just thinking about him.

—**Lenny Mattioli (a.k.a., "Crazy TV Lenny"),
personal friend**

* * *

Tell and I hadn't met before when I walked by a table where he was sitting with customers in the Harrow Inne—I was there for Bunny's surprise birthday party upstairs. His first words to me were, "Hey, good looking." I knew he must be Tell and I thought *what a flirt!* He saw me upstairs afterwards with her brother, my fiancé—awkward.

I was surprised and happy in 2003, when he attended my wedding, and the following year at a family gathering, when he was very welcoming to me. The day of the final celebration, I fell in love with FiFi and felt for her losing her master. I was drawn to Tell's beautiful and favorite tree and, in the evening, to the huge, symbolic bonfire. It was a memorable day with so many of his friends and their humorous stories.

—Sherry Kule, sister-in-law

* * *

While attendees shared their funny stories about Chef Tell—*boy, he would have loved to sit in on that!*—I sat at the back of the house with the people I worked most closely with; the people who had seen the worst and best of me, and I the worst and best of them: the chefs.

These were the guys that got the details of Tell's vision correctly . . . sitting outside the kitchen's back door, away from the other guests; sharing my depth of sorrow.

We didn't just lose a boss or a man, whom we respected, or an icon, we lost the man who told us like it was. Tell didn't sugarcoat or garnish his criticisms, advice, or his rewards. Instead, he enabled us, sharpened our skills. He helped us envision ourselves in the positions we wanted to rise up to, not just in our careers, but in our relationships, our communities, and our industries.

I could not listen to the others' stories that day; it was too soon for me. I knew the others were in pain and needed to laugh, but my pain was different and, although I needed to laugh, I could do it only with the people who were there for me when the job was hard.

We felt we had lost the man who mentored us, educated us and pushed us. Tell allowed us to experience really running a restaurant. That was not necessary to our

Christine Hess, manager and marketing director of Tell's last two restaurants

positions; yet he showed us tricks beyond what another boss might not take the time to teach.

Oh how we will miss his stories!

Most of all, Chef Tell shared his passions. And isn't that the single-most, magnetic trait among humans? Passion!

—Christine Hess, Tell's restaurant manager and personal friend

CHEF TELL'S
SEVEN-COURSE DINNER*

APPETIZER:

Stuffed Cucumbers

    3 large cucumbers
    1 8-oz. package cream cheese, softened
    3 tbsp minced onions
    ½ tsp paprika powder
    White ground pepper (to taste)
    1 cup finely chopped dill
    Lettuce leaves for garnish

Trim the ends of the cucumber and cut the cucumbers in 1½-inch lengths. Peel the skin off one half of each segment. Remove the seeds from the center of each section about ⅔ of the way down leaving the bottom intact. Turn upside down to drain.

Whip the cream cheese until it is fluffy. Add the onions, paprika, and pepper. Form the mixture into enough balls to fill the cucumber shells. Roll the balls into the chopped dill and place in the cucumber shells.

Line small serving plates with lettuce and distribute the cucumbers. Serve very cold.

SALAD:

Daikon with Citrus

> 4 cups grated daikon radishes
> 2 tbsp grated orange rinds
> 1 cup orange segments
> ¼ cup olive oil
> White ground pepper (to taste)
> Chopped cilantro for garnish

Mix the olive oil with the orange rind and white pepper. Add the shredded daikon and orange segments. Mix it together and let it sit for a few minutes. Serve on lettuce leaves with cilantro for garnish.

SOUP:

Red Lentil Soup with Yogurt

> 2 tbsp olive oil
> 1 chopped onion
> 1 celery stalk, finely diced
> 1 large carrot, peeled and finely diced
> 1 bay leaf
> 1 cup red lentils
> 5 cups chicken stock (fat free)
> 1 tbsp chopped cilantro
> 1 cup plain low-fat yogurt
> Cumin and freshly ground black pepper (to taste)

Heat the onion, celery, and carrots in olive oil; sauté until tender.

Add the bay leaf, lentils, and chicken stock. Cook on low heat until the lentils are done (about ½ hour). Season to taste with the white pepper and cumin. Remove the bay leaf.

Now you can purée the soup in a food processor or serve it as-is. I like the latter.

Pour soup into the bowls and add a generous spoonful of yogurt to the top. Sprinkle with cilantro and serve.

SEAFOOD:

Sautéed Bay Scallops

4 tbsp olive oil
1½ lbs bay scallops
1 cup finely chopped carrots
1 cup finely chopped celery
1 cup sliced mushrooms
½ cup white wine
¼ cup chopped fresh dill
White pepper (to taste)
2–3 drops Tabasco sauce

Heat the sauté pan and add the olive oil. When it's hot, add the scallops and pepper. After sautéing for two minutes add the carrots, celery and mushrooms. Sauté another 3–4 minutes and add the wine and dill. Sauté for a few more minutes until it's done and serve immediately.

If you don't have a large sauté pan, use smaller ones. Or make two batches so the scallops will not overcook.

ENTREE:

Baked Chicken Dijonnaise

1¾-lb butterflied* chicken
A few drops of olive oil
Fresh ground black pepper (to taste)
8–10 cloves garlic, chopped

½ cup French Dijon mustard
Chopped parsley for garnish

Place chicken in an ovenproof baking dish. Sprinkle the chicken with black pepper, chopped garlic, and a few drops of olive oil. Generously brush the top with the Dijon mustard.

Bake at 375 degrees for approximately 1 hour and 20 minutes or until done. Remove from the oven and let sit for a few minutes so the juices settle. Sprinkle with chopped parsley and serve.

If you want—this way it's healthier—you can remove the skin from the chicken before starting.

* Butterflied: the backbone is removed from the bird. Place the chicken on its side. With a large knife, cut on both sides of the backbone the length of the chicken and remove the backbone.

VEGETABLES:

Sautéed Spinach with Red Peppers

1 lb. fresh spinach, cleaned
1 large red pepper, diced
½ onion, sliced
1 tbsp olive oil
Fresh ground black pepper (to taste)
2 cloves garlic, chopped

Heat the olive oil in a sauté pan. When hot, add the garlic and sauté until it is a light brown. Add the onion and the red peppers and sauté a little longer. Add a handful of spinach and sauté until it is wilted. Add the next handful of spinach and sauté until it is also wilted. Continue doing this until all the spinach is wilted. Add pepper, salt, and serve.

STARCH:

Brown Rice Pilaf

1 cup brown rice (Basmati or regular)
¼ cup onion, diced
¼ cup carrots, diced

¼ cup celery, diced
2 cloves garlic, chopped
2 tbsp olive oil
3 cups chicken stock (fat- and sodium-free)
Fresh ground black pepper (to taste)
Chopped cilantro as garnish

Heat the olive oil in a small pot and add the garlic. Sauté until the garlic is light brown in color. Add the onion, celery, and carrots and sauté for 2–3 minutes more. Add the rice, chicken stock, and pepper to taste. Bring to a boil and turn the heat to low. Cook it for approximately 25–30 minutes or until done. Sometimes you may need a little more liquid; just add some water. When it's done, let it sit for a few more minutes and serve with cilantro as garnish.

DESSERT:

Black Forest Apples

8 apples
8 tbsp raisins
8 tbsp sliced almonds
8 tbsp honey
8 tbsp Kirsch (cherry brandy)

Preheat the oven to 350 degrees.

Cut a lid off each of the apples and reserve. Peel each apple ⅓ of the way down. Core the apple with a melon-ball cutter, being careful not to cut through the bottom of the apple.

Fill each apple with one tablespoon of raisins and one tablespoon of almonds. Pour one tablespoon of honey into each apple and sprinkle one tablespoon of Kirsch over each apple. Put the tops back on the apples.

Put the apples into an ovenproof baking dish and pour in about ¼ inch of water. Bake about 25 minutes, or until the apples are tender.

GUTEN APPETIT!

GLOSSARY OF CULINARY TERMS

Ambience -
the atmosphere of a place.

Aperitifs -
small drinks of alcoholic liquor taken before a meal.

Appetizers -
small portions of food taken before a meal.

Apprentice -
a person who works for another to learn a trade.

Back Room -
where food is prepared; the kitchen.

Bake -
to cook by dry heat in an oven.

Behind the line -
where food is cooked; the line is where prepared foods are picked up for serving.

Bitter -
a harsh acrid taste; one of the four basic food tastes.

Blend -
to mix smoothly and inseparably together.

Boil -
to cook something in boiling water.

Boil down -
to reduce the quantity of something by boiling off liquid.

Bouillon -
a clear seasoned or unseasoned broth made by straining meats cooked in hot water.

Braise -
to cook by sautéing in fat and then simmering slowly in very little liquid.

Broil -
to cook by direct heat on a grill or in the oven, heat overhead.

Broths -
thin soups of concentrated meat or fish stock.

Champagne -
a sparkling dry wine.

Chef -
the cook who is responsible for planning menus, ordering food-stuffs, overseeing food preparations, and supervising the kitchen staff.

Chef de cuisine -
head of kitchen.

Chef de partie -
a chef who oversees a particular part of food preparations; a line chef.

Chop -
to cut into pieces with quick heavy blows.

Cognac -
a fine distillation from wine or fermented fruit juices; a fine brandy.

Commis -
an assistant to a chef; a student chef.

Cook (v)-
to prepare by the use of heat; (n) someone who does this.

Cooking Olympics -
international cooking competition.

Cuisine -
a style or quality of cooking.

Culinary -
literally, of the kitchen.

Culinary Arts -
skillful employment of food preparations in the kitchen.

Cut -
to divide or detach with a sharp-edged instrument.

Deglaze -
to add wine or liquids to cooked juices to make a sauce.

Dessert -
the final course of a meal, usually sweet.

Dice -
to cut into small cubes.

Entrée -
a dish served as the main course of a meal.

Fillet -
to cut away a boneless piece of meat or fish.

Foie Gras -
the liver of specially fattened geese or ducks.

Front of the line -
where prepared dishes are picked up off the line for serving.

Front room -
the dining room; where dishes are served.

Fry -
to cook on a grill or pan over direct heat, usually in fat or oil.

Fusion cuisine -
a combining of two or more ethnic cuisines in a dish or method
of cooking.

Garnish (v)-
to provide a food that adds flavor or color to a dish; (n) the food
so used.

Gastronomy -
the art or science of good eating.

Gelee -
a jellied (sugared and boiled down) food substance.

Gourmand -
a person fond of good eating, sometimes excessively.

Gourmet -
high-quality food, or the preparation of such foods.

Granité -
a flavored, icy, mid-course dish offered to cleanse the palate between main courses.

Haute cuisine –
fine, gourmet cooking that is prepared artfully.

Ladle -
a long-handled utensil for dipping into and conveying liquids.

Liqueur -
strong, sweet, and flavored alcoholic liquors; after-dinner drinks.

Marinade -
a seasoned liquid in which meat, fish, or vegetables are steeped before cooking.

Marinate -
to steep in a marinade.

Master Chef -
a uniquely trained, skilled, and qualified chef.

Mince -
to cut or chop into very small pieces.

Mix -
to form or combine ingredients loosely.

Nouvelle cuisine -
modern French cooking employing reduced stocks, herbs, and the finest freshest ingredients.

Palate -
the sense and ability to discriminate food tastes.

Pantry -
a room in which dry foods are stored.

Pare -
to remove the outer layer or coating from a food.

Presentation -
the way a food dish looks or is shown upon delivery.

Recipe -
a set of instructions for preparing something, like food.

Reduce -
to evaporate water from sauces, soups, etc. by boiling.

Repurpose -
to alter the usual usage of a food or ingredients.

Restaurateur -
owner or manager of a restaurant.

Roast -
to bake uncovered by dry heat, causing browning.

Salt -
an element that gives a liveliness or pungency to ingredients; one of the four basic tastes.

Sauce -
any preparation eaten as a gravy or a relish on foods.

Sauté -
To cook or brown in a small amount of oil, butter, or fat.

Simmer -
to cook in a liquid at or just below the boiling point.

Slice -
to make thin, flat pieces of foods.

Sour -
an acid or fermented taste; one of the four basic food tastes.

Sous chef -
the second in command in a kitchen.

Spam -
a canned solid block of pork food; trademarked name.

Spice -
pungent aromatic substances of vegetable origin.

Stock -
broth prepared by boiling meat, fish, or vegetables, used as foundation for soups and sauces.

Samosa -
an Indian fried turnover filled with minced meat, vegetables, and spices.

Sweet -
flavors characteristic of sugar, honey, etc.; one of the four basic food tastes.

INDEX

Rum Point, xvii, 176, 213, 216, 224, 225,
    229, 234, 262, 263, 264, 265, 276,
    278, 299
Rum Punches, 198, 234, 280, 395
"Run for the Roses," 189, 190
Russell Baum, ix, 78, 101, 102, 103, 104,
    122, 123, 125, 143, 150, 163, 166,
    213, 214, 215, 216, 217, 335

S
San Francisco, 190, 221, 222, 223, 224
Saturday Night Live, 127, 170
SchweinePfeffer, 57, 377, 386
Scovie Awards, 336
scrapple, 107
scuba, 10, 175, 176, 186, 196, 197, 198, 199,
    200, 224, 287
Secret Service, 4, 187, 244, 263
Senator Arlen Specter, 127, 185, 321
serendipity, 63, 119, 143, 358, 360, 361, 363
Small Talk, 84, 92
Solingen, 188
Southern Women's Show, 139, 143, 168
Speedo, 199, 217, 232, 337, 396
Steve Forbes, 321
Steven Stills, 243
Strawberry Festival, 295, 296
Stuttgart, xv, ixx, 1, 2, 4, 6, 7, 19, 20, 21, 23,
    25, 30, 33, 37, 58, 63, 187, 268,
    310, 333
Stuttgarter Nachrichten, 4, 26
suicide, xxviii, 6, 27, 28, 41, 55, 126, 129, 219
Suladda May, ix, 174, 175, 214, 241, 419
Samosa, 214, 404
Sun Tzu, 244
surgeon, 55, 347, 348, 359, 360
Susanna Foo, ix, 81, 99, 122, 123, 124, 125,
    161, 372
Swabian, 152, 153, 269
syndicated, xvi, 45, 92, 94, 95, 340

T
Tastykake, 107
Tell Erhardt's International Cuisine, 99, 109
Top of the Buck, 363
Torsten, ix, 53, 54, 62, 197, 198, 199, 200,
    333, 334, 355, 356, 371, 384, 419
Tortuga Rum Cake, 263
TSOP, 89

U
Ulrich, 26, 27, 29, 30
UNICEF, 74, 75
Upper Black Eddy Inn, 299, 325

Ustinov, 71, 75, 76, 370

V
Valentine's Day, 148, 330
Vanessa Williams, 141
Vanity Fair, 236
Vasile Bageag, ix, 366, 367, 368, 369, 386
Victoria Lang, ix, 271, 272, 273, 274, 276,
    277, 278, 279, 332, 384, 395, 419
Viktoria trophy, 22

W
Walt Disney World, 169, 170
Warner publishing, 133
WaWa, 321
Wiener schnitzel, 323, 325, 326, 386
wild boar, xx, 84, 86, 164
William Penn, 105
William Rush, 106
Willie Nelson, 259, 378
Windows of the World restaurant, 169
wine, xxvii, 10, 34, 48, 58, 62, 63, 76, 84, 86,
    99, 100, 101, 102, 103, 118, 119,
    124, 128, 144, 145, 164, 169, 176,
    183, 184, 190, 191, 194, 214, 221,
    222, 223, 237, 239, 255, 262, 263,
    273, 276, 331, 334, 356, 359, 368,
    369, 371, 400, 401, 412
Wine Spectator, 259
Winston, ix, xxiv, 327, 328, 329, 374, 419

Y
Yul Brynner, 71, 76

ABOUT THE AUTHOR

Ronald Joseph Kule was born in Bogota, Colombia, the son of a Polish-American, Navy-veteran father and a blue-blooded, Chilean-Colombian mother. He grew up in Levittown, Pennsylvania, the second eldest of eight.

Kule pitched lefty in Little League, played on school football teams as both linebacker and quarterback, but retained a stronger interest in his father's jazz record collection and the performing arts, having performed lead roles early in grade school musicals.

At Oakland University in Rochester, Michigan—once touted the "Harvard of the Midwest"—he was a founding student member of Charter College. Two years later, he transferred to New York City and pursued applied philosophy studies and employment. In Manhattan, he enjoyed a part-time modeling and acting career, spurning a generous offer (naively) from the William Morris Agency before heading out to the West coast.

Continuing advanced philosophy studies in Los Angeles, he also began what would become a successful, forty-eight-year sales/sales training career, which lead to the first of his published books (a sales-training text) and the development of his acclaimed, sales-training workshops. He sold well enough to travel through thirty-five countries and deliver seminars and speaking engagements in seventeen, including mainland China and Russia in the 1980s.

Aided by his many ventures, Kule wrote and published poetry, short stories, and articles here and there. In between, he trained in acting (L.A. Academy of Dramatic Arts under Fred Cook), drawing and painting (Mission: Renaissance Art Academy under Larry Gluck), and screenwriting (Hollywood Screenwriting Workshops with Ernie Lehman) to enhance his writing skills. Writing for the pure love of words, he aimed not to waste the twelve years of Latin he had received in school!

Finally, in 2009, he turned off the sales career and turned to writing books full time, which, fortunately, he has pursued with some success. (See Other Books by Ronald Joseph Kule.)

The hallmark of Kule's success in both careers is the result of, in his words, "Caring for my prospective customer or reader enough to accomplish mutual understandings that satisfy. My greatest thrill comes from writer's 'psychic pay': when my words uplift and change lives for the better."

OTHER BOOKS BY
RONALD JOSEPH KULE

onald Joseph Kule co-authored *Carolina Baseball: Pressure Makes Diamonds*, with award-winning sports journalist J. David Miller, foreword by three-time NCAA Baseball Coach of the Year, Ray Tanner. The book assists The Ray Tanner Foundation (http://TheRayTannerFoundation.org) to fund and build a Miracle League™ ballpark for physically challenged kids in Columbia, South Carolina. Miller and Kule followed with the eBook *Pressure Makes Diamonds A Timeless Tale of America's Greatest Pastime.* (http://www.amazon.com/Pressure-Diamonds-Timeless-Americas-ebook/dp/B00Λ63ΛWH2) Both books are the meticulous account of the 119-year history of University of South Carolina Gamecocks baseball from inception in 1892 through the Gamecocks' back-to-back NCAA National Championship wins in 2010 and 2011.

Kule wrote and published *Carolina Baseball 2012 Poetic Justice*, an eBook account of the Gamecocks' 2012 season run for an historic three-peat national championship, in which Carolina ended as runners-up at the NCAA Division I College World Series Finals in Omaha. (https://www.smashwords.com/books/view/208586)

His *Sell Better, Sell Easier, Sell Everything Artfully*, sales-training book undercuts other sales-training methods and introduces exclusive selling exercises developed by the author to improve selling skills immediately. English, French and Spanish editions are available online at Smashwords.com.   https://www.smashwords.com/profile/view/ronkule

English hardcopy and eBook editions are also available online on Amazon. com as *Sell Better, Sell Easier, Sell Anything Artfully*. (http://www.amazon. com/Ronald-Joseph-Kule/e/B007OA69AY The hardcopy Italian edition, *Vendere Meglio, piu facilmente e con Maestria*, is available in Italy through www.venalereconmaestria.com.

Kule's short story, "ThunderCloud and the Old Man," was published in *Better World Stories* by Artists for a Better World International. His poetry credits include entries in *Bamboo Souls* (2005) and *Spirit of Humanity* (2008) published by Artists for a Better World International and *The Little Book of Cleveland Street Poetry*, Volume II (2009) by Artists In Action International. His eBooks *Romance & Sensuality: Volume One of a Series of Poetry Collections known as Haikulisms™* and *Jazz Poetry: Volume Two . . .* are available on Amazon.com. (http://www.amazon. com/Ronald-Joseph-Kule/e/B007OA69AY

His eBook novel *Anyman Dreams of Love Everlasting* is available on Smashwords.com. (https://www.smashwords.com/books/view/308410)

Forthcoming biographies include: *Cassano: Networking Millionaire* with Ray Cassano; *FRAPAR!: Francois Parmentier*, one of France's renowned satirical cartoonists; *Misha Segal: Man of Music* with the award-winning film composer/jazz musician; and *Listen More Sell More*, the second edition of his sales-training book. Forthcoming fiction works include *ThunderCloud*, a young adult trilogy, and *Aleria*, a sci-fi thriller.

Ronald Joseph Kule is the proud father of an NYPD officer and a grandfather. He resides in Clearwater, Florida, with his wife, Sherry Kule, a designer of custom and limited-edition jewelry.

The author may be contacted through KuleBooksLLC@gmail.com.

PHOTO CREDITS

The author and publisher gratefully acknowledge use of photo permissions granted by:

Helga, Torsten, Angelika, and Max Erhardt: 3,5,6,7,9,11,16,30,31, 49,51,52,54,55,56,58,59,64,67,70,80,199,200,263,389.

Nordic Ware: 134-138.

Chef Nunzio Patruno: 102.

Susan Winston: 330.

Faye Litzenberger: 317,338.

Victoria Lang and Tony Baarda: 278-280.

Ian Boxall: 209-211.

Barbra and Falynne Murphy: 233.

Suladda May: 242.

Bunny Erhardt: 74,91,93,100,110,118,107,132,146,154,163,170, 175,177,178-180,214,225,230,260-262,281-282,285,297,301, 306 308,340,342,345,347,366,380,388-389,421.

The Buck Hotel: 363,364.

Page 113 is the cover illustration of an article written by Jim Quinn in *Philadelphia Magazine*.

Bob Croesus: 298.

Chef Paul Drew provided the Sands Hotel *Chaine* dinner *Entremets* chapter menu.

177,229,238 and 258 are promotional images of Chef Tell from Cayman Airways *Horizons* magazine.

227,295, and 303 are found on Google Images.

Visit the Chef Tell biography blog site at: http://cheftellgoodies.com.

Follow the book's success and contribute posts and comments on Facebook at https://www.facebook.com/ChefTellbooks.

420 CHEF TELL

IN THE KITCHEN WITH
CHEF TELL DVD SERIES

Show Titles include:
Alfresco Dining, American Cooking, Appetizers, Cakes and Tortes, Caribbean Cooking, Desserts, Italian Cooking, Cooking with Fish, Light Summer Cooking, Quick Cuisine, Soup, Turkey, and Comfort Foods.

The PBS series *In the Kitchen with Chef Tell* **reveals the tips, techniques, cooking methods, and short cuts that any viewer at home can adapt to save lots of time and energy in the kitchen.**

You can honor this TV pioneer by cooking a recipe, watching any of the episodes of his classic cooking series.

Buy The Chef Tell DVDs http://www.mbctv.com/cheftell/index.html